RUBY'S WORLD

MY JOURNEY WITH THE ZULU

BY KAREN BALDWIN

the apocryphile press
BERKELEY, CA
www.apocryphile.org

apocryphile press
www.apocryphile.org
BERKELEY, CA

APOCRYPHILE PRESS
1700 Shattuck Ave #81
Berkeley, CA 94709

Library of Congress Registration
TXu 1-746-396

Dedicated to
the remarkable children
of KwaZulu-Natal

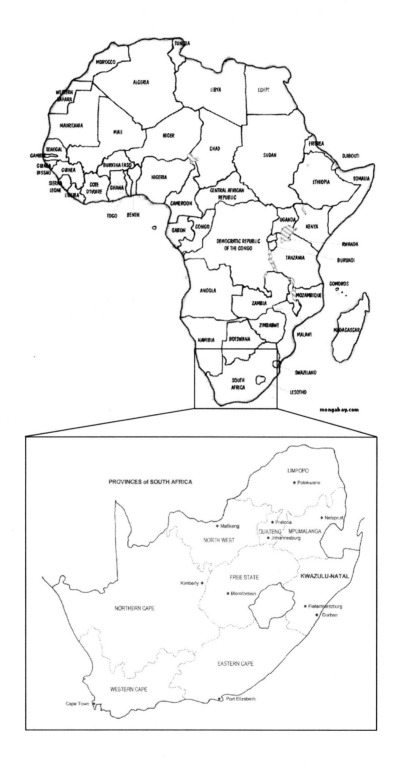

A NOTE FROM THE AUTHOR

This story took place in the foothills of the Drakensburg Mountains in the Province of KwaZulu-Natal, South Africa. Pietermaritzburg and Durban are actual cities in KwaZulu-Natal. I have created fictional names for the rural villages and the school where I taught. Except for my own, all of the characters' names have been changed.

NDLELA FAMILY

- —— related by blood
- --------- related by marriage
- —··—··— other relationship

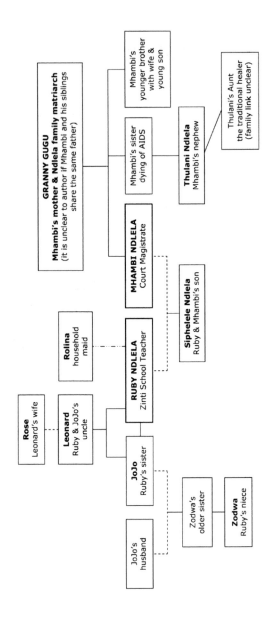

GRANNY GUGU
Mhambi's mother & Ndlela family matriarch
(it is unclear to author if Mhambi and his siblings share the same father)

Mhambi's younger brother with wife & young son

Mhambi's sister dying of AIDS

Thulani Ndlela
Mhambi's nephew

Thulani's Aunt
the traditional healer
(family link unclear)

MHAMBI NDLELA
Court Magistrate

Siphelele Ndlela
Ruby & Mhambi's son

Rolina
household maid

RUBY NDLELA
Zinti School Teacher

Rose
Leonard's wife

Leonard
Ruby & JoJo's uncle

JoJo
Ruby's sister

JoJo's husband

Zodwa's older sister

Zodwa
Ruby's niece

RUBY'S FRIENDS

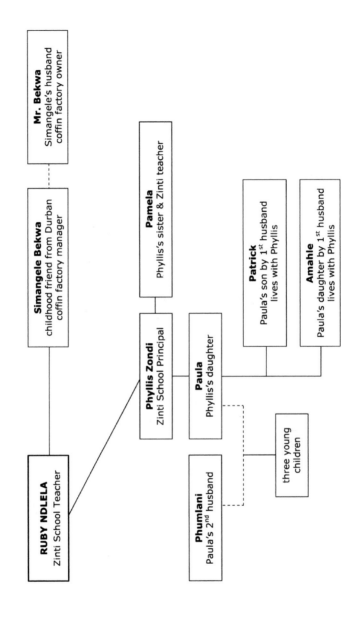

Mr. Bekwa
Simangele's husband
coffin factory owner

Simangele Bekwa
childhood friend from Durban
coffin factory manager

RUBY NDLELA
Zinti School Teacher

Phyllis Zondi
Zinti School Principal

Pamela
Phyllis's sister & Zinti teacher

Paula
Phyllis's daughter

Phumlani
Paula's 2nd husband

three young
children

Patrick
Paula's son by 1st husband
lives with Phyllis

Amahle
Paula's daughter by 1st husband
lives with Phyllis

ZINTI JUNIOR PRIMARY SCHOOL

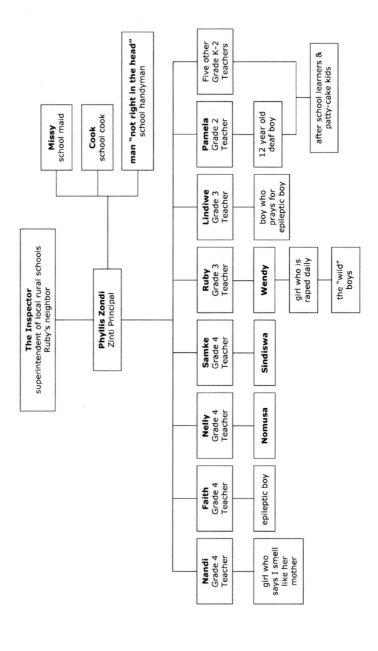

The Inspector
superintendent of local rural schools
Ruby's neighbor

Missy
school maid

Cook
school cook

man "not right in the head"
school handyman

Phyllis Zondi
Zinti Principal

Nandi
Grade 4
Teacher

Faith
Grade 4
Teacher

Nelly
Grade 4
Teacher

Samke
Grade 4
Teacher

Ruby
Grade 3
Teacher

Lindiwe
Grade 3
Teacher

Pamela
Grade 2
Teacher

Five other
Grade K-2
Teachers

girl who
says I smell
like her
mother

epileptic boy

Nomusa

Sindiswa

Wendy

boy who
prays for
epileptic boy

12 year old
deaf boy

girl who is
raped daily

the "wild"
boys

after school learners &
patty-cake kids

ACKNOWLEDGEMENTS

I owe a debt of gratitude to every person who has listened to my stories, encouraged me to trust myself, and supported my desire to write. I am especially grateful for my mentors—Tania Casselle, Phaedra Greenwood and Sean Murphy—who taught me about "butt glue" and coached me through the process of writing this book. I also received invaluable guidance and fortification from my Boundary Crossers writing group—Laura Lynch, Kristin Martinez, Sally Sontheimer and Kelli Williamson.

Many friends and colleagues read portions of the manuscript, made brilliant contributions, and nudged me forward. I offer my sincere thanks to Roy Armstrong, Brinn Colenda, Abbie Conant, Debra Diamond, Beth Goldman, Dorothy Lampl, Suzanne Lampl, Bruce Marshall, Jamie Miceli, Susan Paulus, Jan Smith, Emily Warren, Ed Westley, Sarah Wilder, and my fabulous Saturday morning knitting "committee" at the Turquoise Teapot in Taos.

I send big hugs to my seminary peeps: Reverends Suzanne Nichols, Nancy Schluntz, and Kathy Westley, who answered the phone at all hours, held my heart while I relived painful memories, propped me up through moments of doubt, and taught me how to laugh at myself.

Kathie McClellan, my editor and a gifted sociologist, was a blessing. I'm grateful that she trusted my desire to share this story from the point of view I occupied while on the ground in Africa. Her innate talent for uncovering and explaining subtle human behaviors—both Zulu and American—was invaluable to my process of making peace with this experience.

This journey took place because of the generous donations of funds and supplies from many individuals and businesses in the San Francisco Bay Area. Thank you for believing in me.

My deepest gratitude is offered to Jesus in Amsterdam. Thank you for reminding me what kind of person I want to be.

RUBY'S
WORLD

PREFACE

It's not supposed to end this way—expelled from Ezimolo Village, drenched with rain and nervous sweat, grateful just to be alive. Sitting on my suitcase at dawn, my back against the locked door of a small South African airport, I tremble with the emotions I've suppressed for the past thirty-six hours: rage at being torn away from the Zinti children, betrayal by the ones who invited me, shame that I failed, terror that I would be killed and my remains never found.

As the events of the past forty-five days replay over and over in my mind, I search for clues to what went wrong. How did I slide from being the eagerly-awaited first white teacher in this rural Zulu school—to a reviled outcast? I feel myself tumble into a dark tunnel, unsure if I will ever calm the anger that eats at my heart. Will I ever know what really happened?

FIVE YEARS EARLIER
FRIDAY, DECEMBER 20, 2002

After four days in my local hospital I'm loaded into a critical care ambulance, headed to San Francisco for open heart surgery. As the ambulance pulls away I catch a glimpse of my son on the sidewalk. Kevin tries to smile through his tears. I feel sorry for him. It's easier to be the one who dies.

Why, at age forty-seven, has my heart crapped out? No mystery there. I've lost my passion for life. My relationship is troubled and I'm tired of struggling. Kevin left for college in September. I miss him. A lot. For eighteen years I've devoted myself to being his mother. Now what? I have a successful career, but engineering doesn't satisfy my soul. Ministry has tugged on me forever. I've been a fool to think I could escape it.

Thirty-five minutes into the trip, stalled in bumper-to-bumper traffic on the Bay Bridge, the EKG alarm screeches as my heart slams against my ribcage in irregular beats. My two attendants hurry to silence the alarm. They inflate the blood pressure cuff and wiggle a stethoscope between the EKG wires. The cold metal presses against my chest. Like the hundred other times this week, we wait for the sound of a normal heartbeat to return to the monitor. Nothing. Forever.

They glance across me at each other. Their faces say it all.

The handsome, chatty nurse lays his hand on my shoulder and smiles. "Houston," he says, "we have a problem."

The other nurse pulls tubes and syringes from the overhead cabinets. The paddles have been lying on my legs the entire time.

"What's happening?" I ask.

"Your heart is being stubborn this time. We can only wait a few more seconds before we intervene."

"What will you do?"

"We'll give you an injection to stop your heart. Let it rest for a minute. Then we'll give you another injection to jump-start it. If that doesn't work, we'll use the paddles."

"Do I have another choice?"

"No. Don't worry, Karen. We won't let you die on our watch. We have a perfect record."

They nod at each other.

"Are you ready?" nurse Chatty asks.

Terror pierces me. "Will you do me a favor?"

"Name it."

"Keep your hand on me so I stay connected to life."

"That's easy." He lays his hand on my leg. "Here we go."

The drug enters my vein like molten lava. Within seconds my bones are on fire. Immense weight flattens my chest. I can't move. My entire body feels thick. Dense. I hear voices in the distance. The machine lights overhead fade from vibrant colors to shades of gray.

I close my eyes. Tears burn my face. My life has been hard. I've made mistakes, but none I haven't tried to make right. I'm grateful for my son. He's taught me what love is all about. I hope I've raised him well enough to go on without me.

Maybe I should let it be over. It would be easier to die than face another failed relationship. But I want to see Kevin marry someday. I want to be a grandma. Become the woman I've dreamed about. As I drift into unconsciousness it's time to choose. I can stay. Or I can go. What do you want, Karen? The easy out? Or more life?

DAY 1
THURSDAY, JANUARY 31, 2008

The last sliver of moonlight hangs in an inky black sky outside my airplane window. By the time I arrive in South Africa there will be a new moon, another fresh beginning in the life I now embrace with enthusiasm.

It's been an extraordinary few years, a wild roller coaster of change: engineering new subdivisions is over; interfaith seminary was perfect—bigger than any one religion, inclusive of all; ordination; breast cancer; Kevin's graduation; his engagement to Ginger. The cancer scared me; slowed me down a bit. But only long enough to gather more strength. If God's going to keep letting me live—I'd better do something useful in the world.

The passengers in my row listen to hours of passionate monologue about how helping Zulu kids with their English lessons will improve their lives, make them employable. Can I really make that much difference? For the ten-thousandth time I recite my prayer for this trip: May this work make a difference in the lives of these children, and may it anchor me in my emerging new life.

I ran out of *No. 1 Ladies' Detective Agency* novels halfway across the Atlantic. Only fifty minutes now until the plane lands in Amsterdam where I have time to pee, grab a snack, and exercise my legs before boarding for the eleven-hour flight to Johannesburg. I close my tired, scratchy eyes and run my hand over my head, forgetting there's so little hair to smooth. All but a half-inch is gone; my protection against lice and other creepy bugs.

The past four months have been a whirlwind of preparation: fund raising, inoculations, collecting books and school supplies. There haven't been any extraordinary obstacles, a sure sign I'm on the right path. Even the airlines cooperated, turning a blind eye to ninety-five excess pounds of luggage.

Leslie, my friend who set me up with Zinti, told me about the primitive living conditions in the remote village without running water, plumbing, or a bed. My personal supplies are minimal: a few clothes, rubber Crocs, a flashlight, two rolls of toilet paper, a muslin body sack to discourage crawling creatures as sleeping companions, an Eze-Dri camp towel, two washcloths, high-tech water purification equipment, three blank journals, a snake bite kit, and my luxury item— a new iPod loaded with my favorite music. Hopefully there will be someplace to recharge it.

» » » « « «

My travels have all been in the northern hemisphere. I wonder what it will be like to cross the equator. There should be a red stripe on the ground—like the globes I adore. Maybe the pilot will give a "shout out" to mark the occasion. Will toilet water really swirl in the opposite direction? These juvenile thoughts bounce through my mind.

As we cross the southern shore of the Mediterranean Sea, I feel drawn into the mystery of the African continent. The Sahara Desert stretches to the horizon in every direction. Nothing except pale caramel-colored earth, pock-marked with patches of grayish white. As a fifteen-year-old geography student, I dreamed of crossing the great desert with a nomadic tribe in a caravan of camels. Wrapped in layers of bright, gauzy fabrics, we would set up white canvas tents every evening and recline on sumptuous pillows in the cool shade of an oasis.

The unrelenting monochromatic sand below redefines my concept of isolation. No hint of water or shade. Not a speck of green for over four hours. No place to hide. No relief from the elements. Nothing to mark distance or direction. Any crossing, by camel or vehicle, would necessitate months of planning, a truckload of supplies, and a steadfast partner in survival. My illusions of romance fade.

A shadow approaches on the horizon. In the few minutes

it takes to go from my seat to the bathroom and back, the lightness of the desert gives way to the darkness of the Congo basin. Hints of purple tinge the deep greens as cloud shadows pass over the thick forest. A long, muddy brown snake splits the dense wilderness. It grows wide at the bends as it creeps through the jungle. Narrow fingers of the Congo River slither off into the trees, thinning until they disappear completely.

The jungle canopy hangs over the edge of the river, sheltering the banks from the view of strangers flying overhead. My curiosity loiters there, in the concealed areas, where human life exists. I imagine thin African men, precariously balanced in their narrow dugout canoes, navigating the currents with long poles.

The sun sets over the Congo, leaving behind an oppressive black sky, vacant of moonlight. Not one light is visible from the ground below. A chilling sensation flows through my body, anxiety at being suspended in absolute darkness as I enter a deep examination of myself. I claim this journey as mine alone—one solitary woman, under her own magnifying glass, searching for her path, for meaning and purpose in her life. I feel the first tingles of fear. Stay present in each moment, Karen. Stay with yourself.

On the approach to Johannesburg the cabin crew distributes customs forms. Every question raises concern. Am I bringing goods into the country that are worth more than three-hundred rand? That's only forty dollars! I have an entire suitcase full of brand-new books, each with a $15.95 price tag. I check the "no" box. Is my purpose for being in South Africa business or vacation? Neither feels accurate; there's no box for "volunteer aid relief." I check "other."

Do I have any drugs other than a thirty-day supply of prescription medications *with* a doctor's note? Holy crap! I have a whole medicine cabinet in my backpack; enough for one-hundred days and no note from any doctor. My daily thyroid and heart meds, packed in Ziploc baggies, stuffed in the nooks and crannies, bear no labels. Along with a generous supply of Tylenol and Benadryl, I have meds for common South African diseases: malaria, dysentery, skin infections, and yellow fever. At least *they're* in original containers. Again, I check the "no" box.

How long will I be in South Africa? Eighty-eight days. My visa is good for ninety. Where am I staying in South Africa? The Zinti Junior Primary School in Ezimolo Village, in the foothills of the Drakensburg Mountains—the same location I've registered with the US State Department. It's nice to end on an honest note.

When we disembark, determined to appear confident, I stride through the "green light" section of declarations. The worst that can happen is I plead confusion about the customs form and apologize profusely. My worry is for nothing. No agent is present to inspect my luggage. As far as I can see there's no customs agent on the "red light" side of the glass wall either!

The Tambo International Airport in Johannesburg serves eighty-four destinations in forty-eight countries on six continents—the busiest airport in Sub-Saharan Africa. A cacophony of unfamiliar languages bounces off the concrete walls as I struggle to guide my flatbed luggage cart through the narrow, crowded corridor between customs and the ground transportation hub. It's been thirty-one hours since I left San Francisco. If not for the adrenaline surging through my veins, I'd be passed out from exhaustion. Keep your mind on your next task, I remind myself. One thing at a time.

Anxious for my two-night stay in Johannesburg to recover from travel, adapt to the ten-hour time difference and the sudden change of climate, I've confirmed my reservation at the Airport Game Lodge numerous times. The lodge owner, overtly annoyed the last few times, finally grasped my concern. "I will be at the airport to pick you up," he said. "You needn't worry. I do this all the time."

I don't.

Hundreds of travelers crowd the ground transportation hub. They all seem to know what they're doing. The jumble of languages assaults my senses. Moist summer heat pours in through the open doorways. I struggle to drag the heavy air into my lungs. Luggage carts continually bump against my legs. The payphones along the wall look impossible. My heart pounds as I turn in a circle, one hand always on my luggage cart, eager to spot the lodge driver who has described himself as "a tall white man with a sign that says Airport Game Lodge."

He isn't here.

Panic grips my chest. I stand motionless, frozen in the tornado of activity. If I don't keep moving, I'll drown in overwhelm. I must decide what to do next. A deep, male voice interrupts my thoughts.

"Who are you looking for, Ma'am?" he asks. A gleaming smile punctuates his dark, young face.

I struggle with his thick accent. "Excuse me?"

"Do you need transportation, Ma'am?"

Leslie cautioned me about airport personnel. "If they're official," she said, "they'll have neon yellow vests and name badges on lanyards."

This young man's lanyard is tucked into the chest pocket of his one-piece, navy blue jumpsuit. I assume there's a badge at the end. His filthy vest looks like it may have been yellow at one time. Through a fog of exhaustion and confusion I attempt to decide if he's safe.

"Ma'am," he asks again, "do you need transportation?"

"I'm supposed to meet the driver from the Airport Game Lodge. But I don't see him. Can you tell me where to exchange money so I can use the payphone?"

While I continue to size him up—determine if he's safe or likely to send me down a dark hallway where a friend of his will rob me blind—he pulls a cell phone from his pocket, dials a number, and sticks the phone out toward me.

"I have the lodge driver on the phone for you, Ma'am."

Ashamed that I have assumed the worst of him, heat rises in my face.

He pushes his phone closer to my face. "The Airport

Game Lodge, Ma'am. I have the driver on the phone for you."

"Hello?"

"Ma'am, do you need transportation to the Game Lodge?" the man on the phone asks.

His European accent is a welcome relief. "Yes, I do. I have a reservation."

"Your name, please?"

"Karen Baldwin."

"Yes. I see you on my list. I am parked outside in a white van. I'll meet you there."

I return the phone to the transportation attendant and, to alleviate my guilt, dig in my pocket for two dollars to tip him. I hope he hasn't felt my mistrust. "Thank you for your help," I say. "I don't have any rand yet. Will this be okay?"

"That is not necessary, Ma'am," he says, brushing my arm away. "You must step directly through that doorway to meet your driver." He points toward the inky blackness, pierced by occasional beams of light streaming from the rooftop to the sidewalk.

Outside, a line of pale blue taxis stretches the length of the curb. Airport attendants load passengers and luggage with breakneck speed. Drivers lean incessantly on their horns as if that will speed up the line. Police seem to outnumber travelers. The officers' white-gloved hands slice through the night directing traffic, accompanied by shrill blows on their metal whistles. Chaos reigns.

I feel like a rock in the middle of a rushing stream. From my spot at the edge of the sidewalk, I look up and down the curb one last time. I don't see a white van. Steering my luggage cart away from the crush of activity, I rest my back against the cool concrete wall. Maybe, if I stand still, the lodge driver will find me. That's my new plan.

A red-headed man approaches. I recognize him from my flight. "I see you are looking for transportation," he says. "Where are you staying the night?"

"I'm at the Airport Game Lodge. The driver says there's a van waiting for me, but I don't see it."

"I'm at the same lodge! Maybe they have left already. Let's share a taxi and go together."

Warning bells clang in my mind. "Never get in a taxi!" Leslie said. Of course, if I were to ignore her warnings it would seem prudent to do it with a big Dutchman who looks capable of protecting me. But who would protect me from the Dutchman? My mind races for an alternate solution, not quite ready to abandon all my rules about personal safety.

"I just spoke with our driver," I say. "Not even five minutes ago. He says he's here, waiting for us, and he has a sign. Why don't we look around one more time?"

"Very good," the Dutchman says. "But it is useless for both of us to push these carts around. You stay here with our luggage. I will find our driver." He disappears around the corner.

His plan appeals to me. I'd never agree to leave my bags with a stranger, and I'm too tired to move. A minute later a transportation attendant approaches me from inside the building. "Are you the woman looking for the Game Lodge driver?" he asks.

"Yes."

"Ah. Stay where you are. He is inside looking for you. I will bring him to you."

What good news. Now everyone is helping me reach my destination!

A tall, thin white man in a checked shirt and khaki shorts ambles up to me. His sign, "Airport Game Lodge" scribbled on a piece of white cardboard, dangles in his hand at his side. "Are you Miss Baldwin?" he asks.

"Yes." I smile with relief, happy to finally make my connection. "You must be the lodge driver. It's so good to see you."

"Let's go." He tucks his sign under his arm and grabs one luggage cart with each hand.

"Wait! That cart belongs to a Dutchman who's also staying at your lodge. He's gone off to look for you. Can we wait for him? It should just be a minute."

"Aye, no problem," the driver says. "I've been looking for him as well. You two are my last passengers. The others are already in the van."

The driver and Dutchman maneuver our luggage like toys—over the curb, across the taxi lane, through a dirt lot strewn with rocks—to the rear of a white Volkswagen van that's seen better days. I don't care. I'm within minutes of collapsing, fully outstretched, on a bed.

Including myself, six passengers scrunch into the front and middle seats, our luggage piled in the back. The others, from the Netherlands and Germany, are here on safari vacations. In the morning they head out on flights to Tanzania and Zambia. Their stories of hunting the "big five"—elephant, lion, rhinoceros, water buffalo, and leopard—intrigue me. I'm curious if they're actually hunting these spectacular animals or just taking photographs.

We pull away from the airport into the narrow unlit streets of Johannesburg. The Dutchman says he vacations in Africa every year, that Zambia is *the* place to see the most wild game in one week. He also says that over the past few years, due to the exploding crocodile population, residents of Zambia have begun to build their homes three to four meters above the ground.

"Crocs aren't native to southern Africa," he says. "They were unlawfully introduced by a foreigner and are out of control now. They invade homes and game lodges, especially at this time of year, in the rainy season."

I'm sure he doesn't mean *our* lodge.

We turn onto a dirt road where our driver dodges potholes large enough to swallow the van. The Airport Game Lodge emerges from the darkness, lit by a single halogen lamp mounted on the entrance gatepost. Only five minutes from the chaos of the airport, the sounds of crickets and birds saturate the damp air.

Our driver, Oscar, also the porter and front desk clerk,

moves in quick bursts of energy, stacking our luggage in the gravel clearing. One at a time, he calls the guests into the office to register. After my turn, I follow Oscar along the smooth concrete walkway. He pulls my suitcases to a stop in front of my open sliding glass door. "Have a night of good sleep," he says.

The sheer draperies at the door billow out onto the walkway. It would feel heavenly to sleep in this breeze, but the Dutchman's crocodile story is too fresh. There's also a thick cloud of mosquitoes under my porch light. The small, screened bathroom window will have to do for fresh air tonight.

I dig through my suitcases strewn about on the cool tile floor, searching for the thin nightshirt I packed for humid African nights. I've never been so happy to flop onto a narrow, short bed with a lumpy mattress. Home feels a million miles away. I thank God and all the airlines for my safe arrival, and close my eyes to the lyrics of a million birds.

DAY 2
FRIDAY, FEBRUARY 1, 2008

A loud buzzing noise awakens me in the pre-dawn hours. It's too big for a mosquito, a fly, or even a bee. Adrenaline surges through my body as I remember where I am and that my door was open last night when I arrived. I flip on the nightstand light, stand in the middle of my mattress, and scan the room for a snake.

There aren't many places a snake could hide. I jump up and down on the squeaky mattress, then pause to listen for sounds of life under the bed. Nothing. I step across the narrow space between the two beds and jump on the other mattress. Still nothing. I scramble down from the bed, grab the desk chair and jam it hard against my open suitcase. Then, in what will become my nightly ritual in Africa, I get down on my hands and knees and inspect under the bed. No snakes!

There's no hope of going back to sleep. With two hours until breakfast, I have time to catch up on my journal writing.

> ... it's not good that I'm already this scared. Every spooky story I've ever heard about Africa races through my mind. And I'm still in the big city! If I let myself obsess over this, it will be a very long three months. This intense fear makes me wonder if I've made a huge mistake coming here. Maybe when I get to the village and start working with the kids my fear will subside. Take one step at a time, Karen. Keep breathing ...

By six I'm dressed, ready for breakfast, and step outside to take my first look at South Africa in daylight. Trees and tall grass sway on currents of cool air against the backdrop

25

of a cloudless, electric blue sky. Everything exudes freshness, as though it has just been breathed into existence. I want to lie on the ground and soak up the palpable vibrations of life that emanate from the earth.

As I explore the grounds I'm surprised to discover a two-story brick building behind the lodge, invisible in last night's consuming darkness. Uneven, pale blue letters painted on the bricks spell KITCHEN with an arrow pointing up an open stairway. At the top I'm greeted by a middle-aged black woman dressed in a navy blue smock that hangs to her knees. A bright kerchief, wrapped tightly around her head, frames her long, narrow face.

"Good morning, Ma'am. How are you today?" she asks, staring at the floor. Her slow, measured words have a melodic lilt. English is not her first language.

"I'm well, thanks. And you?"

She ignores my question and stares at my feet. "Will you take your breakfast now?"

Her submissive posture makes me tense as I recall childhood vacations in the Deep South, watching maids slip silently through the back doors of neighborhood homes. I don't know how to behave. I'd like to tell her I'm not one of "them." I smile at her, hoping she'll relax and smile back. She doesn't. Maybe she doesn't *want* to talk to me. These mental gymnastics are excruciating. I want to crawl out of my skin.

"I'd love breakfast," I say. "How does this work?"

"Please make yourself comfortable and I will bring your breakfast." She turns toward the kitchen without ever making eye contact.

The dining room veranda overlooks the lodge grounds, separated from the expansive fields of tall grass by a simple wire fence. The airport control tower is visible in the distance. Planes come and go, but the birds drown out all noise of jet engines and city life. Their melodies play like a symphony, backed by the low resonant croaks of bullfrogs and incessant clicks of crickets and grasshoppers. I take a deep slow breath to absorb the rich, pulsating essence.

Beyond the fence, spotted deer, wild turkeys and ducks mingle in the field with exotic animals. Gazelles with long, graceful legs graze next to thick-bellied bushbuck with stubby antlers. Ostriches hold their tiny, peculiar heads high above their enormous, round bodies. The impalas are my favorite. Their warm brown eyes, alluring long lashes, and elegant curved horns exude magic. In time I will learn that the impala is abundant in KwaZulu-Natal; the most commonly hunted animal. Impala meat is prized. Witch doctors and healers treasure the horns, hooves, and tongues for their medicine. Their bones make sturdy tools. Hides are crafted into shoes, vests, and rugs. Nothing goes to waste.

I return my dirty dishes to the kitchen.

"What time will you take your meal tomorrow, Ma'am?"

"Um, seven, please."

"Very well, Ma'am."

"Have a good day," falls from my mouth by habit. It feels trite.

On the way to my room I bump into Oscar. "Are those animals on preserve land?" I ask.

"No," he smiles. "They're wild. The fence is there to prevent them from wandering into your room."

"Are they really that bold?"

"Yes ma'am! Don't put your arm through the fence near an ostrich. They are aggressive and mean. They guard their eggs ferociously. If they feel threatened they'll take your hand off with one stroke of their beak. But if you're lucky enough to snatch an egg," he laughs, "one ostrich egg is equal to two dozen hen eggs."

In the lounge I'm able to check my email on an old community computer. Friends and family are eager to hear about my travels. I revel in news from home, but the Internet connection is frustrating and slow. I'm repeatedly disconnected and manage to send only one brief, group message. I let everyone know I'm safely on the ground in Africa and promise more details later.

I'm content to spend the morning taking photos of the animals that crowd the fence hoping for an easy meal. They look like pets and I'm tempted to oblige. But common sense prevails. I don't want to lose a hand my first day in Africa!

As the mid-day sun intensifies, I succumb to the need for a nap. Already I love falling asleep to the sound of birds. They will become my faithful companions, comforting me when I'm lonely. When I return home I will ache for the birds' music during the night.

A harsh ring wakes me from a deep sleep. The sweat that drenches my shirt isn't from the heat in my room, but from my interrupted dream.

> *... I stand a short distance from my living quarters watching dark clouds approach. Black tornados swirl in the distance. Nearby, spinning funnels of fire circle around me. Nothing is damaged as they pass by. I'm not hurt ...*

I reach for the phone.

"This is Oscar, Ma'am. Would you like to order your evening meal?"

My greasy dinner, delivered from town, goes down well with a cold beer while I sit on the patio outside my room enjoying the end of my first full day in Africa. As the sun dips behind the acacia trees, the brilliant blue sky fades to splendid shades of vermillion and yellow, capturing the exotic lure of this country. I want this feeling to last forever.

DAY 3

I indulge in a breakfast feast: soft-boiled eggs, British bangers steamed in smooth blends of Indian curry, scones, and rich Earl Grey tea. There will be nothing this lavish in the village. American oldies play on the dining room radio, taking me back to my teen years where music and memory are fused—*On Top of the World* by Karen Carpenter, my high school prom theme; *Killing Me Softly* by Roberta Flack, snuggling with my boyfriend on my parents' sofa after graduation—sweet, long-forgotten memories called back by the music.

My anticipation grows as I repack my bags for the flight to Pietermaritzburg. Tonight I'll be in the village, living a simple life, providing care and affection for children, many of them orphaned by AIDS. My heart swells as I sit on my patio enjoying the impalas.

Zap!

Behind me. The same buzzing noise that woke me during the night. I jump up and spin around. My heart pounds. I scan the ground. Two small birds lie dead on the sidewalk. Tucked under the eave is an electric mosquito-killing machine. Apparently it also kills small, errant birds. I'm sad for the birds, grateful for the reduced mosquito population, relieved that it wasn't a snake. Perhaps my hyper vigilance is unwarranted.

» » » « « «

Oscar drops me off at the airport, refusing my tip for lugging my overweight suitcases all the way into the terminal. "Your transportation is included in your lodging fee," he says. He really means it. What a treat! Once again the airlines let me pass free of extra baggage charges when they hear that my suitcases are full of books.

The departure area of Tambo International has an entirely different feel than the somber transportation hub. Ablaze with neon signs luring travelers into restaurants and gift shops, it's typical, except for the unique wares: long sticks of billabong—South African beef jerky; giraffes, hand-carved from exotic woods; ostrich eggshells the size of small melons, intricately etched with jungle scenes; beaded tribal jewelry. Even baby clothes are decorated with exotic beadwork.

The bustling luggage shrink-wrap business intrigues me. Travelers place their suitcases on a spinning carousel that enshrouds each one in clear plastic until it resembles a mummy. The attendant pulls a sharp knife from his tool belt, pierces the top of each plastic fortress, and pulls the luggage handle through the slit. A sign explains that this is the perfect protection against theft. They must mean protection from airline personnel. No one else will have access to my suitcases. I decide to take my chances.

With no hope of understanding the conversations around me, I enjoy watching people speak. Their mouths form unusual shapes as words roll over their tongues and spill outward in round globules of sound. It's mesmerizing; hard to believe that these intriguing words might mean something as simple as, "Honey, did you turn off the stove?"

Overhead, the electronic departure screen scrolls information in the traditional colors of South Africa: green, red, and yellow. The destinations—Gaborone, Botswana; Lusaka, Zambia; Harare, Zimbabwe—stir my sense of adventure.

» » » « « «

As my twin-engine plane prepares for landing in Pietermaritzburg, I feel foolish for having only two brief email exchanges with the school principal, Phyllis Zondi. The first was to set the approximate time frame for my trip:

three months beginning in early February, allowing the children four weeks to settle into the new school year before my arrival. The second email confirmed my exact arrival date and time. Two single-sentence emails suddenly feel insanely inadequate for a journey of this magnitude.

The plane pulls to a stop fifty feet from the small terminal. My heart pounds as the stairs are pushed into place. I hope Principal Zondi is waiting for me. I hope she recognizes me. I hope I can find her. I hope she is still as eager to have me as I am to be here. Nearly last off the plane, the heat and humidity suck my breath away as I descend the steps. My legs tremble on the short walk across the tarmac.

A welcome blast of chilly air cools my face when I step through the airport doors. I stop to take a deep breath. Then I see them. Two women and two teenagers, twenty feet away, in the center of the lobby. They hold brightly colored, handmade posters that proclaim: GOD BLESS YOU KAREN, WELCOME TO SOUTH AFRICA KAREN, ENJOY YOUR STAY AT ZINTI PRIMARY. Their faces light up as we recognize each other.

We stand a few feet apart, sharing tears of relief. A long moment passes before the woman in the royal blue tank top pulls me into her arms. Her eyes sparkle. She's younger than I am, about my height, with ebony skin. A thick afro frames her face.

"You were so long to get off of the plane," she says. "We were afraid you had changed your mind."

"No! I didn't change my mind. I was afraid you wouldn't be here for me."

She holds my shoulders at arm's length. "You are a silly woman," she says. "We have been waiting for an hour. We did not want to miss your plane."

She releases me and steps back. "I am Ruby. And this is Ma'am, Principal Zondi," she says, pointing to the other woman.

Principal Zondi steps forward and extends her hand. Like Ruby, she is stout, but several inches shorter than me, with milk chocolate skin and thin, loosely-curled gray hair. She wears a modest skirt and a short-sleeved, white knit top. Deep creases fan out from behind her dark, wire-rimmed glasses. I guess her age to be about sixty.

I reach to shake her hand. "Thank you for inviting me here, Principal Zondi."

"You shall call me Phyllis," she says. "We are pleased to have you. The children at Zinti are excited to meet you. You have already met Ruby. This is Patrick and Amahle."

Both teenagers greet me with dazzling smiles and hugs. I let loose a deep sigh of relief. Mine is the only flight to arrive at the airport this afternoon. Within minutes the flight crew rolls our luggage into the building on long, flat carts. As we cross the lobby Ruby pulls me tight against her side. Her hand on my shoulder radiates a deep, warm heat.

"Please identify your bags," Phyllis says. "Patrick will collect them for you."

I point to two oversized brown suitcases. Patrick, rail thin, can't even begin to lift them from the cart. I move to help.

"Ruby will get them," Phyllis says, grabbing my arm.

Ruby reaches for the smaller bag. "Haybo! These are very heavy, Karen. Do you have bricks in here?" Her r's roll over her tongue.

"Just books," I smile. "Lots of books for the kids." I reach for the large suitcase.

"You are too frail to manage such heavy things," Ruby says, pushing my arm aside.

Frail? At five-feet nine-inches, one-hundred-eighty pounds? I've even put on an extra twenty pounds—my insurance against being malnourished. I expect food in the village to be sparse. And I'll be walking to and from school every day. I've planned ahead. I'm proud of that.

Ruby strides for the door, one suitcase in each hand. Her hips sway from side to side. Her flat sandals slap against the concrete floor. The five of us squeeze into her white Corolla with my suitcases stuffed in the trunk. I'm surprised the car can still move. Unaccustomed to their thick Zulu accent, I struggle to understand their questions. Where do you live in America? Do you have children of your own? What does your husband say that you are here alone? What are your favorite foods?

"I live in California, near the ocean. I have one son. He's grown now. Twenty-four. I don't have a husband. And I suppose my favorite food is sushi."

"Sushi?" Phyllis asks. "What is sushi?"

"Sushi is raw fish that's wrapped in sweet rice and seaweed."

The kids turn up their noses, drawing their faces into expressions of disgust.

"Do you not prefer your fish to be cooked?" asks Ruby.

"I like cooked fish, too." Maybe they're asking what they could serve me that would be special. "I like all kinds of food. Rice. Meat. Vegetables. Fruit."

"Uncooked fish?" Phyllis asks. "This is quite strange."

» » »   « « «

We travel through the suburbs of Pietermaritzburg where modest brick houses with manicured lawns line wide streets. An occasional lot stands vacant, overgrown with thick foliage. We could be anywhere in middle America except that each property is surrounded by a tall, steel fence topped with razor wire or sharp spears.

At Ruby's house, the kids jump out of the car to unlock a massive chain that holds an iron gate closed across the driveway. We enter the living room first through a door of vertical steel bars, then a thick wooden door. Inside, Phyllis pulls her cell phone from her bra and begins making calls. Two more teenage boys appear from down the hallway. Ruby issues a flurry of instructions in Zulu. The kids fly into action: one boy disappears out the back door with my luggage; the other boys rearrange the living room furniture; the young girl heads to the kitchen with Ruby.

I feel awkward, uncertain what to do next. From my spot

in the middle of the room, I take stock of the décor. Heavy draperies with a busy blue print are drawn across the front window. The deep maroon carpet darkens the room further. Brown velour furniture, covered with thick clear plastic, lines the wall. White crocheted doilies, embroidered with pink roses, decorate the back of each seat. Several portraits, yellowed with age, hang in a random fashion over the sofa: a boy about ten years old, a middle-aged man in a graduation cap and gown, and Ruby as a much younger woman. There are also two university diplomas. It's clear that this is the wall of honor.

"This seat is for you, Miss Karen," Patrick says. He points to the arm chair and pushes the coffee table up close to my knees. "We are almost ready for your party."

With every window and door shut tight, sweat drenches my body. The ceiling fan stands motionless. Aren't they suffering, too? I scan the walls looking for the fan switch. Maybe I can accidentally lean up against it and get a breeze going. There's no telling how big a river of sweat I'm creating on this plastic seat cover. I mop my face with my sleeve.

"Would you like something cool to drink?" asks one of the boys.

"That would be great. Maybe some ice water?"

"We have orange pop for you."

It's been years. Maybe it's not as gooey sweet as I remember. "Orange pop it is!"

Phyllis answers a knock on the door. Peeling my legs off the plastic chair cover, I stand to greet the visitors.

"Karen, this is …" Phyllis says.

I can't quite catch their names. One at a time, three teachers from Zinti embrace me and thank me for coming to teach at their school. I miss far too much of the conversation, but it keeps right on moving. Ruby and the young girl return from the kitchen carrying trays of orange pop and a chocolate cake.

"Would you like a piece of cake?" Ruby asks.

"Yes, please. Chocolate is my favorite."

A burst of enthusiastic Zulu erupts around me. I imagine they took bets on whether or not chocolate was a good choice. I guzzle my orange soda. It's every bit as sweet as I remember. But it's wet and cold.

Ruby sets a plate with a hefty slice of chocolate cake on my lap. In the heat the frosting has slid down the side of the cake. Everyone watches me take my first bite.

"It's yummy, Ruby. Delicious."

They explode with enthusiasm as they dig into their slices.

"Where do you live in America?" asks one of the teachers.

"In northern California, near San Francisco."

"And what is your weather like?"

"Well, when I left home it was winter. Cold and rainy."

"Ah. You will be very comfortable here."

I can't imagine what she means. This feels like Miami in August.

"Our winter will arrive soon and it is just as you have described," Phyllis says.

"Do you have children?" one of the women asks.

"What does your husband say of you being here?" asks another.

"How do you like our country?"

"What kind of car do you drive?"

"How old are you?"

I feel bombarded by the onslaught of questions. They discuss each of my answers in Zulu. Unusual combinations of n's and g's roll from their mouths, punctuated with an occasional odd "cluck" that emanates from deep in their throats. I recall my interaction with the Barnes & Noble clerk at home. "I'm sorry," she had said, "but we don't have a Zulu-English dictionary. Zulu is a dead language." If she could only hear this!

"Tell me about Zinti," I say. "I'd like to hear about the school and the kids."

Phyllis sits up straight, her shoulders held back with pride. "We have three-hundred and ninety-six learners at

Zinti this term. Our youngest learners, through Grade Two, do not know any English. It is best not to confuse them while they are still learning their mother language. We have two rooms of Grade Three learners, and four rooms of Grade Four learners. Some of our children have moved to the village from city schools and are already proficient in English."

"I teach Grade Three," Ruby says. "I have forty-eight learners in my classroom."

I brought thirty-six plastic recorder flutes, two dozen sets of colored markers, and thirty erasable white mats to save on paper. Unprepared for forty-eight kids in one classroom, I feel instantly deflated. The students will have to work in shifts.

"We have a woman from the village who prepares a hot meal for our children every day," Phyllis says. "And she is very clever. She does not even need a refrigerator. Our children enjoy her meals very much. And she is paid well. Three-hundred rand every month!"

At about seven rand to the dollar, that's only forty dollars. Phyllis makes it sound like an extraordinary income.

"But last week we had a terrible accident," Phyllis continues. Her chin drops to her chest; she shakes her head. The teachers murmur in Zulu.

"What happened?" I jump to the worst imaginable scenario—a child was injured.

"We had very hard rains last week. Our pit toilets flooded. It was a terrible mess."

"That sounds nasty," I agree.

"The boys do not mind. They are accustomed to taking themselves to the hill behind the school. But the girls. It was difficult for them."

"What did you do?"

"There is a man in the village who comes to school every day," Phyllis says. "He is not right in the head, but as long as we pay him straight away, he will do whatever we ask of him."

Not right in the head? And he hangs out at school every day?

"He cleaned the bathrooms with a shovel and buckets of water. You will see. They are now as clean as ever."

I hope I packed enough hand sanitizer.

"You will love our country, Karen," Phyllis says. "There is a legend about the creation of the Zinti valley. It is very beautiful."

"Yes, it is beautiful," Ruby says. "But my farm is even more beautiful. You will see."

The kids and other teachers nod, seemingly content as observers.

"Will I see your farm?" I ask.

"Ruby will take you to her farm during the school holiday," says Phyllis.

"It is in Ntwana," Ruby continues, "far, far away. It is very different from my home here. We have goats and chickens. My relatives take care of the farm while I am away. There is also a boy from Zinti who lives at my farm."

"From Zinti?"

"Yes. He was very young when his parents died and he had no relatives to care for him. He was lonely. One day I asked him if he would like to live with me." Her face lights up. "He said he would like that very much. So that very day I took him from school to my farm. He has lived there ever since. He is twelve years old now. He is very happy there. But you must not tell anyone," Ruby cautions. "They think he ran away. They do not know that I stole him."

I shake my head, stunned. I watch for reactions from the others. Nothing. "I won't tell anyone," I say. My lips are sealed. Who would I tell? Who are "they?" I struggle to comprehend this concept of adoption. Who am I to say if it's right? Maybe it's enough that this boy has someone to look after him and food to eat.

My attention drifts to a Pepto-Bismol pink crocheted doily that covers the dining room sideboard. The doily's scalloped edges curl four inches off the surface. How is that possible with this much humidity? Through the open front door I see teenage boys in the street. They hang on the perimeter fence, peering into the house for a glimpse of me. They must be friends of Ruby's sons. I smile, raise my hand in a gesture of acknowledgment. They smile back. Why don't they just come to the door? Oh, yeah. The locked gate across the driveway. I forgot.

"So where will you start?" asks Phyllis.

"Excuse me? I'm sorry. I didn't hear your question."

"The teachers have been discussing how you can best serve our learners. They want to know if you will also teach mathematics to our Grade Four learners."

"Sure," I laugh. "As long as they aren't ahead of my math skills." I don't remember what Kevin was learning at that age.

"They are having a difficult time adding columns of numbers."

"Sure. I can help with that."

All the teachers smile.

"I can also help with music and art if you like. I brought lots of art supplies. And a friend of mine sent plastic recorders for the kids."

"The children will like that," Ruby says. "You will see. They like to sing and draw."

"Wonderful! I can't wait."

"Boys, please show Miss Karen to her room," Phyllis says. "She is tired and must rest."

This isn't a stopover on the way to the village? "Am I staying here tonight?"

"Yes, of course," Ruby says. She sounds surprised that I don't already know.

"So, I'll move to the village on Monday then? When we go to school?"

"You will stay here with Ruby," Phyllis says. "She has a fine room for you. And she will feed you well."

"Oh. I thought I'd be with a family in the village. That's what Leslie said."

"We have spoken with the Inspector," Phyllis says. "He is pleased that you have come to teach our children. He wishes for you to have excellent accommodations. The Inspector wants you to have the very best experience while you are here. Besides, Karen, the children will tire you if you do not have a break from them at night."

I feel cheated. This isn't what I expected. This is practically like being at home. I want a *real* African adventure. I have dreams of cooking for the kids, walking with them to school in the morning, tucking them into bed at night. I'm not ready to let that dream go. Maybe they'll change their minds in a couple of weeks. It's too soon for me to argue with them. I shake hands with Phyllis and collect hugs from the other teachers as they leave.

"Can I help you clean up, Ruby?"

"No. That is not necessary."

She nods to the boys. They lead me through the sliding glass door at the rear of the living room, onto a patio. A three-foot-high brick wall separates the patio from an immense lawn. And at the far end of the yard—a swimming pool! It's beautiful, surrounded by old-fashioned torch-style lamp posts. I can't quite see the water, but already I dream of a cool dip. We pass a brick barbeque built into the wall next to the steps that lead to the lawn.

"Do you boys help with the grill?" I know how much the men in my family like to cook with fire.

"Ma'am?" They tilt their heads with confusion.

I point to the barbeque. "Do you help cook meals on the grill?"

"Ah." One of the boys raises the cover revealing an overflowing ashtray and several empty beer bottles. "It has never been used as far as I know, Ma'am."

"Please call me Karen. Will you tell me your names again?"

"Yes, Ma'am, I mean, Karen. My name is Thulani. Tool-AH-nee."

"And my name is Siphelele. Seep-eh-LAY-lay."

They smile as I wrestle with the unfamiliar names. "Wow. I hope you'll be patient with me."

"It will get easier, Miss Karen," Thulani says. "Soon you will speak our mother language."

Hah!

We cross the length of the patio and stand in front of a concrete block structure about eight feet square—a pool building. Overhead, pieces of green and yellow corrugated fiberglass lay on wires stretched like clothesline between the block building and the main house. It looks makeshift, but provides welcome shade.

"This is your room," Siphelele says. He opens the door to the block room, sweeps his arm in a grand gesture, and steps back. Hot air rushes out. My backpack sits in the middle of the bed. My suitcases occupy the only available floor space.

"You will be very comfortable here," Thulani says. "Please tell us if you need anything. We will let you know when it is time for dinner."

I am equal parts relieved and appalled. Grateful to have private space, a break from the barrage of questions, a bed up off the ground, time to process everything; yet so humiliated about living in the backyard. I was expecting to share a mud hut with an entire family. I was expecting to roll my inflatable cushion out on a floor made from smoothed cow patties. I was expecting to poop in a hole in the ground. Pump water from a communal well. Cook over an open flame. Why does this room in the backyard feel so wrong?

I push my suitcases against the wall under the window, close the door behind me, squeeze between the bed and the green plastic lawn chair, and hang my face over the sink. My tears mingle with the warm water that has been sitting in the pipes. I take a deep breath. As the water begins to run cool I splash it on my face, waiting for my emotions to subside.

Lying on the bed, my feet propped on my backpack, I examine my room. The window, up high on the wall, has steel bars and sheer yellow curtains. I can't feel the breeze, but I won't have to worry about modesty. I have a full-sized bed with clean sheets and a pillow. The plaster walls are chipped with big holes where things once hung. The tiny closet in the corner has plenty of space for the few clothes I brought. There's also a blanket neatly folded on the top shelf. I can't imagine needing that. A small night table is wedged between the bed and sink. A bare lightbulb with a string hangs over the door.

I'm missing a toilet.

Unpacking takes five minutes. The large suitcase with school supplies fits between the bed and wall, out of the way until Monday. I set the green plastic lawn chair outside my door; one less thing to trip over. My clothes don't even begin to fill the closet. I stash my cameras on the top shelf, journals and toiletries on the night stand.

I lay down again. The room spins around me. Why is this so hard? Everything looks so—so?—American! But it *feels* so different. Deep breath in. Exhale. Breathe, Karen. In. Out. My heart rate eases back to normal. I'm embarrassed by my ignorance. This isn't the Africa I expected.

» » »   « « «

"Miss Karen? Thulani here." He knocks on my door. "My aunt says you should come now for dinner."

Aunt? The boys are cousins? They do weekend sleepovers here, too?

"Okay. I'm coming."

I rinse my eyes again and dry my face on my camp towel that hangs from the curtain rod. On my way to the house, I dash up the steps for a quick peek into the pool. Thick green slime hangs on the side walls. Black sludge covers the bottom. My stomach turns. Why is this beautiful pool so neglected? My fantasy of cooling off under a starry African sky vanishes.

"Have you seen the monkeys yet?" Ruby asks as I enter the kitchen. She stands over the stove, wooden spoon in hand, stirring a pot of rice. Her eyes twinkle with mischief.

I smile. "You're pulling my leg, Ruby. I know you are. There aren't any monkeys here in the city." I'm wising up already. I won't fall for the joke on the white lady from America.

"Yes, you will see." Her grin grows even wider as she raises her eyebrows. "I would not lie to you about these things."

"Uh huh." I roll my eyes. We both laugh. "What can I do to help?"

"There is nothing to do." She fills two plates. "Would you like tea with your meal?"

"Oh, Ruby. I don't think I can drink tea when it's so hot. Maybe just some water."

"No. You must drink tea. It will cool you. You will see."

We eat in the dining room at a beautiful, polished wooden table, on upholstered chairs covered with thick plastic. The fried chicken and cabbage are tasty. Fried anything is tasty.

"What's this?" I take another bite of the white grain. It's dry with a big pat of butter pressed into the middle, sprinkled with curry powder.

"This is putu. Do you like it?"

My nod elicits a smile. "It's tasty. But what is it? It sort of looks like rice."

"It is white corn meal. It is the traditional food of the Zulu people."

Grits! That's what it looks like. Coarse white grits, cooked like polenta.

"You're right about the tea, too. It is refreshing."

"I know what will make your spirit happy," Ruby smiles. "You will be sick in your lungs if you drink with ice when you are so hot."

I point to the pink, ruffled doilies on the sideboard. "Ruby, I'm curious about these. How do you keep them curled in this humidity?"

"They are beautiful, yes?"

"They are." At least my grandmother would have

thought so. Someone spent a lot of time crocheting such tiny stitches. "Did you make them?"

"They were a wedding gift from my mother. After I wash them, I dip them in a bucket of starch. Then I lay them flat and put plastic bottles under the edge until they dry. They will stay curled like that until the next time I wash them."

"That's very clever. I've never seen anything like that before."

The kitchen door opens and shuts. I hear footsteps in the hallway. I turn to see if the boys are joining us for dinner. A tall middle-aged man, wearing olive green dress slacks and a short-sleeved sport shirt, smiles at me. His sunglasses are pushed to the top of his cleanly shaven head. "You must be Miss Karen," he says. "We have been anxiously awaiting your arrival."

I stand and offer my hand. "Thank you. I'm happy to be here."

"I am Mhambi Ndlela. I am Ruby's husband." Despite his Zulu accent, his English is crisp, clean. So easy to understand.

"It's nice to meet you. May I call you Mhambi?"

"Yes, please. And how were your travels from America, Karen?" He looks straight into my eyes when he speaks. It feels like he has all day to wait for my answer.

"My trip was good. I'm amazed how smooth it went."

"And how long does it take to travel from America to our country?"

"Thirty-two hours."

A whistle escapes on his breath. "That is indeed a very long time. And how do you like our fair country so far?"

"It's beautiful, Mhambi. I've never seen such a brilliant blue sky in my entire life. And the vegetation is so lush and green. We have lots of rain at home, but still our trees aren't as green as yours."

He smiles with pride. "This is God's country. I am pleased that you have an opportunity to share it with us."

Ruby slips out to the kitchen and returns carrying a metal

tray with Mhambi's dinner plate and tea. She sets it on the coffee table in the living room, in front of the armchair.

"We are very impressed by your courage, Karen," Mhambi continues. "You are a generous woman to leave your family for three months to come teach our children. We are very grateful for your sacrifice."

"I'm happy to be here. It doesn't really feel like a sacrifice."

"You are too modest. It is a great gift you give our people. We will honor you by speaking English to you in our home."

I hadn't thought of speaking English as an honor, just a practicality. Actually, I hadn't considered it at all. Now that he mentions it, though, I do feel honored. "Thank you."

"In return, will you learn to greet us in our mother language?"

"Absolutely!"

"Very well. Has my wife taught you our greeting yet?"

"No," Ruby says. "Karen has needed to rest this afternoon."

"Then we shall have your first lesson right now."

"Great! Can you wait one second? I want to get a piece of paper to write this down. I'm afraid it won't stick unless I see it in black and white." I race for the back door, across the scorching bricks, grab a journal and pen from my night table and hurry back to the dining room. "Okay, I'm ready now."

Mhambi explains the order of the greeting and how to greet one person versus a group. Ruby spells each word. "S-a-w-u-b-o-n-a. Sah-u-BOE-nah," she says. "This is how to say hello to one person."

By the time we finish I have an outline for the entire greeting:

Sanibonani. Sah-nee-boe-NAH-nee. Hello, plural conjugation.

Unjani? Une-JAW-nee? How are you?

Ngiyaphila. N-gee-yah-PEE-lah. I am well.

Uphila njani? Oo-PEE-la n-JAH-nee? And how are you?

Yebo, ngikhona. YAY-boe n-gee-yah-HOE-nah. Yes, I'm also fine.

Ruby and Mhambi smile, so patient with me as we practice over and over until I can manage some semblance of adequate pronunciation. Thulani passes through the room.

"Sawubona," I say.

"Haybo! Miss Karen," he says, his eyes huge. "You are amazing!"

Mhambi and Ruby smile. "Very good," Mhambi says. "You are a fast learner. You will learn one new word every day. Before you leave us we will speak our mother tongue together."

I feel proud. Hopeful. "I would like that."

» » »   « « «

As I step out the back door headed to my room for the night, Ruby stands in the doorway and wishes me goodnight.

"What should I do if I need to use the bathroom in the middle of the night?" I ask, remembering the backyard camping adventures of my youth. "Will you leave the door unlocked for me?"

Her vacant stare penetrates me, as if I were invisible. She slides a steel mesh gate across the doorway. "You must close your door for the night to keep the monkeys out. I will wake you in time for breakfast."

Her sudden shift from helpful, jovial teacher, to cold, absent stranger, disturbs me. We stand, in silence, on opposite sides of a steel gate. Dumbstruck, I turn and walk toward my room, across bricks that still radiate the day's intense heat. Behind me, the padlock on the gate clicks. What just happened?

» » »   « « «

I can't be the only one who needs a toilet in the middle of the night. What do they expect me to do? I vow abstinence from all things liquid after dinner. Never mind that my doctor advised me to stay well-hydrated as my first line of defense against heat stroke and disease.

My senses feel heightened. Why doesn't Ruby trust me with a key? Do they always lock the house up at night? Even with the barbed fence surrounding the property? Should I be afraid? I close my door and slide the chain into place.

Lying in the darkness, adrenaline works against exhaustion. There are no stars in the patch of sky I can see through my barred window. This feels like prison. Could a snake climb the wall and come in through my window? I inspect under the bed with my flashlight. Nothing. I can't bear the thought of closing my window, sleeping in a sauna. I close my eyes and listen. Animal sounds. Some are familiar and close by: birds, dogs, roosters. Others are further away, unfamiliar. Hyenas? What else howls like that? This is your life in Africa, Karen. You'd better adapt.

Sleep overtakes my busy mind, but I wake at every noise. I lay still, hold my breath, and listen for silence to assure me that I'm still alone. The tenth time I wake, I realize I need to use the bathroom. It can't wait until morning.

My mind races through various possibilities. I don't have a bucket. I might still get to use a hole in the ground. But my skin is so white, I'd glow in the dark. What would the neighbors say? Besides, if the Ndlelas lock up so tight, maybe I should be wary of what looms in the yard. I don't want any creatures to think I'm marking territory they consider their own. My distinction as a human feels lost. I am just another animal.

I dig through my suitcase for a roll of toilet paper, open my door, pull my green plastic lawn chair back inside. I adjust it against the sink, pull my nightshirt up to my armpits and stand on the chair seat. The window is so high no one could see more than my head. As I lower myself against the cool porcelain, it rattles. It's loose! I grab a bar in the window and yank myself up. This is humiliating enough without explaining to Ruby how I knocked the sink off the wall.

Balanced precariously, feet on the chair, hands on the window bars, I relieve myself. I hear water running outside. What is that? I stand on my toes in the chair to peer through the window. My eyes adapt to the darkness, aided by a dim light on the neighbor's shed. A narrow strip of concrete runs between my room and the fence. Below my window a pipe pokes through the wall. That running "water" is my pee landing on the concrete! I run gallons of water down the drain. We don't need evidence of my night's adventure lingering in the heat of the day.

If I wasn't so excited about working with the Zinti children, I'd have to ask myself, "What the hell am I doing?"

DAY 4

There's no need for my travel alarm clock. The sky begins to lighten at four-thirty and the roosters start in earnest. I pull on a pair of shorts and a T-shirt to sit outside in my green plastic lawn chair in the delicious cool air. I made it through my first night! It's hard to believe that yesterday I thought living in the city was cheating.

At five, Ruby opens the iron gate on the back door. She pads across the patio in her bathrobe, her hair slicked against her scalp, heavy with oil. When she looks up and sees me waiting for her, she smiles. "Karen! You are awake already!"

I sense no trace of last night's distance. "Good morning, Ruby. The roosters make a good alarm."

"Did you sleep well?"

"I did." There's no point in complaining. It's a new day. "How 'bout you? Your hair is different this morning."

"Aye, this is my hair. My wig is much to hot to wear every day. Come, Karen. There is time for you to bathe and dress for church before breakfast. Give me your dirty clothes and I will wash them for you."

"Oh, Ruby, you don't have to do that. I can wash my own clothes."

"You must not argue with me. Give them to me and I will wash them now with my own."

I duck into my room and shove my travel clothes into the mesh sack I'd planned to haul to the village well. "Thank you, I appreciate this."

"It is not a problem," she says. "Come bathe now."

Thrilled to have a shower, I collect my toiletries and follow Ruby into the house. The bathroom is sparse: no mirror, no towels, no shower curtain. A bath will be perfect. The drab green tub is wide and deep, but the knobs are missing, leaving only short metal stubs with screw marks. I'm not strong enough to turn them with my fingers. How do they manage this? I survey the room for a tool. I decide to borrow a knob from the sink faucet and return it when I'm finished. Thankfully, they're interchangeable.

Submerged to my neck in warm water, my bath feels as heavenly as the first shower after a week of summer camping. A piece of worn red brick lies on the edge of the tub, along with a well-used bar of green soap—the same soap Ruby used for washing the dishes last night. My one bottle of generic liquid soap for hair, face and body now seems extravagant, as does my three-foot square towel. Refreshed, dressed in a cool cotton skirt and sleeveless blouse, I'm ready for church.

Ruby has a cup of tea waiting for me in the dining room where she irons Mhambi's shirt. The windows have been closed all night, trapping yesterday's heat in the house. Sweat drips from her face. "Do you have clothes that need to be ironed for tomorrow?" she asks.

"No! None of my things need to be ironed." I refuse to iron in this heat, and I won't let her do it for me. Besides, with this humidity, ten minutes later they'd be wrinkled again anyway.

Like last night's chicken, Ruby fries bacon and eggs in an inch of Wesson Oil. Mhambi and the boys, dressed in long-sleeved white shirts, ties, and black dress slacks, collect their plates and disappear back to their rooms. Ruby and I sit together at the dining room table with four empty chairs. I wonder if she eats alone when I'm not here.

"So, what church do you attend?" I ask.

"We are a Catholic family. Our church is not far from here."

"What a coincidence! I grew up Catholic, too. I even went to a Catholic school."

She smiles. "Then you will be comfortable while you are here. Our church is beautiful. You will like our priest. And our music is the best in all of Natal."

A familiar church will be soothing in the midst of every-thing else that feels so foreign. Ruby, the boys, and I stand in the front yard waiting for Mhambi to back his car out of the garage. I imagine the local headlines: Proper Zulu family, Dressed in Sunday Finery, Adopts White Woman from California. It never occurred to me to bring dress clothes.

Mhambi's gold Lexus has plush leather seats, tinted win-dows, and air conditioning! What a relief, especially for Ruby. Her Catholic "uniform" consists of black leather shoes in the style of the Suffragettes, black tights, a long black wool skirt, a long-sleeved white blouse with a tall col-lar, a deep purple wool cape and a black velvet hat. Around her neck hangs a large gold medallion on a red- and white-striped ribbon. It looks like a military medal of honor; some-thing Ruby deserves for dressing like this in the dog days of summer.

"Our uniform identifies the society to which we belong," Ruby said at breakfast. "My society is for married women. You will see. There will be others dressed differently."

Their church sits atop a rise in the road overlooking a lush valley, about ten minutes outside of town. We park in a dusty gravel lot and make our way to the courtyard inside the low rock wall that surrounds the church. It's a beautiful new structure with a tall steeple. The white clapboard siding reminds me of the country church I attended with my grand-parents in Kentucky when I was a little girl.

I feel conspicuous amongst all the Zulu, a bit stupid for assuming the congregation would be mixed. Mhambi and the boys go directly inside. Ruby and I linger in the court-yard to greet the women.

"This is my friend from America, Karen," Ruby intro-duces me.

"Sanibonani," I say, eager to show off my new language skills. Their responses aren't as I've been coached. The women carry on in lively Zulu, cheerfully trying to include me. If only Ruby would translate. Left out, I smile and nod.

Inside, Ruby chooses a bench near the front. I'm surprised

to see that Mhambi is the church organist. Then I remember the tiny electric organ in their home. The choir women sit in the two front pews, between us and Mhambi. The men line the side walls in chairs that face the pews. The gender segregation reminds me of Jewish and Muslim services I attended during seminary. It used to feel like a slight against the women—until I met them. Well-educated and outspoken, the women were respected by their men. I'd like to believe it's the same here.

Beautiful crosses are carved into the façade of the simple wooden altar. A white banner, decorated with blue clouds and white doves cut from felt, hangs behind the altar. Stained glass windows on either side of the banner create rainbows of light on the lacy white altar cloth. Just as Ruby said, groups of ladies' church societies are gathered throughout the church. Some wear red capes and no hats; others wear bright, royal blue aprons over their black skirts and white blouses. Ruby's society is scattered in groups of two or three. They huddle together and pray in soft whispers; I imagine for cooler weather or lighter uniforms.

I lean close to Ruby's ear. "It's okay with me if you go sit with your group of women. I'll be fine by myself."

"That is not necessary," she says. "My group meets in one woman's home on Wednesday evenings. We are married women and our prayers are more private." Despite her reassurance, I will never see Ruby leave home on a Wednesday evening.

She hands me a blue hymnal from the rack on the pew in front of us. "We will practice before Mass begins," she whispers.

"When will that be?"

"At noon."

No wonder the pews are so empty—we still have an hour and a half to wait! I open my hymnal, anxious to see their music. It's all in Zulu. Although the transliterations make it easier to follow, I still don't know what I'm singing.

Thirty minutes before Mass begins, young boys make

their way through the church with a tall ladder. They climb to the ceiling and pull chains that hang from enormous fans. The breeze is a welcome relief.

By the time service begins the church overflows with congregants. The segregation of men and women is clear. Children wiggle through the pews. Everyone stands as Mhambi begins the opening hymn. Nine altar girls and boys process down the center aisle, each carrying an elaborate candelabra with three white candles. I'm impressed to see the girls included; some things have changed since I was their age. They are followed by two adult men. One carries a gilded Bible over his head, the other holds a crucifix. The procession concludes with a tiny Zulu priest, not even five feet tall.

I feel sorry for the young attendants who attempt over and over to light the candles they've placed on the steps in front of the altar. The priest waits patiently, barely visible behind the altar. I wonder if he will ever concede to the unlikelihood of keeping twenty-seven candles lit under the whirring breeze of six-foot fan blades.

"California" stands out in an otherwise completely Zulu welcome by the priest. Every head in the first eight pews turns to look at me. I manage a smile and nod my head as a wave of homesickness sweeps over me. My face burns with this unexpected rush of emotions. I miss my community at Grace North Church in Berkeley. I finger the silver labyrinth hanging at my neck—a gift from my friends to remind me of their support during this journey. Ruby sees my tears and lays her arm on the back of the pew, her hand on my shoulder.

Nearly two hours pass before communion. The heat takes its toll. My legs wobble as I stand in line waiting my turn. Lightheaded, I take deliberate breaths to quell my nausea. As I approach the communion rail I listen carefully to the Zulu response of those before me, hoping to mimic their words. When it's my turn the priest says, "Body of Christ," in perfect English.

My heart warms to the sound of my own language. "Amen."

» » » « « «

"That was an exceptional sermon," Mhambi says on the ride home. They all agree, each translating their favorite part into English for me. Mhambi drops me and Ruby at home. He and the boys have errands to run.

"I have a surprise for you, Karen," Ruby says. "But first you must eat something. You do not look well."

We have tea and bologna sandwiches on white bread. The simplicity—and lack of oil—is a welcome relief.

"So what's the surprise?" I ask, refreshed.

"It is hard for you to be away from your home, yes?"

"It is." My eyes well up again.

"I have spoken with Ma'am, and she believes you will feel better if you speak with your family. We are going to the Internet café!"

"Oh, Ruby!" My heart leaps at the thought of emails from home with fresh coffee and a poppy seed muffin. "Thank you."

» » » « « «

We wind along the Loop Road into downtown Pietermaritzburg. Massive brick estates with expansive rolling lawns line one side of the road. Along the other side single-story tenement houses sit twenty feet off the road. Small children play with balls and sticks in the dirt strip between the sidewalk and ramshackle homes.

As we draw closer to the center of town, small store fronts are squeezed between modern office buildings with blue tinted windows. Traffic clogs Langalibalele Street as passengers slow to make purchases through their car windows from vendors who line the edge of the road with their folding tables. They sell everything from bananas and strings of beads to live chickens held captive under empty milk crates.

Ruby noses into a parking space in front of a row of small shops. "Here we are!"

I stand at the curb, ankle-deep in trash, and look up and down the street. I don't see a café, but there's a Kentucky Fried Chicken at the end of the block. She opens the door right in front of us. The narrow shop I have somehow mistaken for a laundromat is actually the "Internet café." Just inside the door, two red cafeteria-style chairs are wedged between the front window and a high wooden counter. Behind the counter, three folding tables line each side wall. Each table is divided into separate work stations by cardboard boxes that have been cut open. Each station holds a computer monitor and keyboard, connected to a CPU under the table. A single twelve-inch fan battles the heat produced by twenty computers operating in a room without ventilation. My hopes of coffee and a muffin die.

"Ruby, do you have errands to do?" I ask. "We can meet up later so you don't have to wait for me."

"I will wait here for you, Karen. It is best this way."

At the counter I purchase a twenty-minute voucher for seven rand. I'd like to stay a whole hour, but twenty minutes at a time is the maximum—in case anyone is waiting. Ruby sits in one of the red chairs as I squeeze between the two rows of Internet users to find my assigned computer.

Dozens of emails await me. I cry as I read the news from home.

> *... the weather is foggy and rainy ... Kevin enjoys his new teaching position ... American Idol finale drew more voters than the last presidential election ...*

I imagine my family's and friends' voices speaking to me.

> *... we think about you every day ... hope everything is going well ... what animals have you seen ... what is the food like ... do you like your host family ...*

I savor the feeling of being loved before composing one lengthy letter to catch everyone up on my life in Africa. I plug in my pre-made group of addresses and hit "send." Delivery of my message fails and I'm kicked out of my email account. I try again—this time with a shorter message. It fails. I don't understand. I tested this group of email addresses before I left home; it was fine. My time is running out. I shorten my message to two sentences and send to the group again. It fails. I want to scream.

Ruby sits on the edge of her chair wiping sweat from her face with her handkerchief. The timer on my computer blinks a three-minute warning. I'd like Ruby to leave me here for the entire afternoon. I try one more time, two sentences to one address—my son. This time it goes through. The timer blinks my thirty-second warning. At least Kevin knows I'm safe. I feel isolated, choking on all the words trapped inside me.

» » » « « «

My concrete block room in Ruby's backyard now feels like a refuge from the overwhelming strangeness. It's been many years since I've slept to avoid feeling lonely.

I'm wakened by a knock on my door. "Karen?" Ruby asks. "Are you okay?"

I open my door and motion for her to sit next to me on the bed. "I'm fine."

"You have slept a long time. Dinner is ready now. I am worried that you sleep too much. Do all white people sleep as you do?"

It seems odd that napping should be consider a white person's affliction. "No. I'm still sleeping off the jet lag." A convenient excuse. I prefer to keep my personal struggles to myself. I explain the ten-hour time difference between California and South Africa. Her face registers confusion. Ruby has never been on an airplane; has never traveled outside of KwaZulu-Natal.

My second dinner with the family. Well, sort of. Although everyone's home, the boys eat in Siphelele's room, and Mhambi settles himself in the living room for his evening soccer match on television. Ruby says he rarely eats dinner before nine. She'll fix his meal later. She and I sit at the dining room table. My beef and cabbage swim in oil. The putu soothes my stomach. We talk in hushed voices, careful not to interfere with the television.

I have a million questions for Ruby: Do you have a hobby? Do you ever go out with your girlfriends? Will I meet them? Are there *really* monkeys and zebras living in the forest across the road? Why don't you all eat together at the table?

I swallow them all. I don't want to appear intrusive or rude. It's far too soon to know how my questions will be received. This is an opportunity to improve my patience, I tell myself, already stretched beyond my usual limit for holding my tongue.

Ruby says we'll leave for school early in the morning; I can bathe at five-thirty, before Siphelele gets up. Eager to meet the kids and dive into my work, I excuse myself for the night, mindful to use the toilet before I go to my room.

DAY 5

When I hear the steel gate slide open I hurry into the house for my bath. It's smoother this morning—I have the knob routine nailed. Afterward, alone in the kitchen, I prepare tea for the family. Through the window I watch a thin Zulu woman in a blue T-shirt and flowery skirt at the bottom of the driveway. She pulls a key from her bra and opens the padlock on the gate chain.

"Sawubona," I say, as she comes in through the kitchen door.

She looks at me with yellowed eyes and mumbles a few words I don't understand. Every other tooth is missing. She pulls something from the kitchen cabinet and walks past me into the living room.

Ruby's face lights up when she joins me in the kitchen and sees that tea is ready.

"Good morning, Ruby. I hope you don't mind that I poked around in your cabinets to find everything."

She gives me a squeeze. "No, Karen. You look comfortable in my kitchen. Like you belong here."

"A woman just came in. She's in the other room."

"This is Rolina," Ruby says, "my maid. Come and I will introduce you."

Rolina stands in the dining room in her bra and half-slip. She lays her folded skirt and shirt on a chair before pulling a threadbare pinafore apron over her head. She ties it in back at her waist. Ruby speaks to her in Zulu. I hear my name. Rolina glances at me with a squint and nods her head. I assume we've been introduced.

"It's nice to meet you," I say.

Rolina nods again, ignoring my outstretched hand. She and Ruby carry on in Zulu. Rolina spits her words in short bursts and waves her arms in swift, choppy movements. It's an interesting game for me—trying to understand what's being said by facial expressions and tone alone. This woman sounds angry and ends her half of the conversation with her hands closed in fists, resting on her hips.

Ruby and I return to the kitchen to make breakfast. While I fry eggs, she watches the toast with a cautious eye. The pop-up feature on the toaster is broken, and Mhambi likes his toast a particular shade of brown.

"I must go and dress myself before I eat," Ruby says. "I will be right back." She heads down the hall, teacup in hand.

"You must be excited, Karen." Mhambi's voice startles me from behind. I turn to see him collect his breakfast plate. He wears a starched white shirt with a striped tie and has an identification badge hanging on a lanyard around his neck. "Today you will meet the children you have come to teach."

"Good morning, Mhambi. I *am* excited. This is what I've been waiting for."

"I know they are also eager to meet you, Karen," he says with a broad smile. "Ruby will make certain that you are treated well."

"I'm sure she will." I pause while he sips his tea. "So where do you work, Mhambi?"

"Ah. I am a magistrate in a town not far from here."

"Magistrate? I'm not sure what that means."

"How shall I explain? I have a courtroom. I listen to the complaints of the people and make decisions that are fair according to our laws."

"A judge. I understand now." It's easy to imagine Mhambi commanding respect in a courtroom.

"Yes. We shall talk more at dinner this evening," he says. "I have many questions for you about your country. But now I must study. There are many cases that I must review every day."

He takes his breakfast and tea to a small alcove attached to the living room that serves as his home office. No bigger than a walk-in closet, it contains a desk, chair, filing cabinet, and stacks of papers piled on the floor. The window between it and the living room, combined with the overhead fluorescent light, create the feel of a fish tank.

Siphelele and Thulani, dressed for school in gray slacks, white shirts, and blazers, greet me in English.

"Oh, Thulani. I didn't know you'd still be here. Let me make you some tea, too."

"Excuse me, Miss Karen," he says. "What do you mean 'still be here'?"

"I assumed you went home last night."

He cocks his head to the side. "I live here!" He sounds hurt.

"I'm sorry, Thulani. I didn't mean to hurt your feelings. Didn't you say Ruby is your aunt?"

"Ah. I see now where you are confused," he says, smiling once again. "Ruby's husband, my uncle, is my mother's brother. I have lived here with my aunt and uncle for a very long time."

I'd like to ask why he doesn't live with his own family, but he and Siphelele have already taken their breakfasts to their room. Besides, it feels nosey on my part. It's really none of my business.

With yesterday's heat still trapped in the house, Ruby and I drip sweat onto the table as we once again eat alone. I wonder if this is normal, or if everyone's just giving us lots of space to talk. After breakfast, I stack our plates in the sink with the others' dishes. Filling the sink with hot water, I look around for the washcloth and bar of green soap. Ruby lays her hand on my arm to stop me.

"You do not need to wash the dishes," she says. "My maid will do them after we have left for school. When you have clothes that need to be laundered, bring them to the kitchen in the morning and she will wash them for you."

"Oh, Ruby. She doesn't need to do my laundry. I can do that."

"You must allow her to take care of you," Ruby says.

"But Ruby, that doesn't feel right. I came to help, not to make work for you."

"I am doing my duty," she says, irritated. "It is my responsibility to employ someone of a lower class than myself. Rolina does the same. She hires a man to tend her garden. She will also make your bed for you. This is the way we do it." She turns and walks away.

I feel small for arguing with her, but still uncomfortable with the idea of having a maid. This is so different than what I expected. Reaganomics' "trickle-down theory" crosses my mind. Maybe this is exactly what it would look like if it played out as planned: everyone gives to those who have less, until everyone is covered. After a little consideration, I actually admire this social practice. But I still feel guilty. Everyone at home who supported this journey expects that I'm living in rugged conditions. I'd be embarrassed to admit I have a maid. Thank goodness my clothes are all clean and I've already made my bed this morning.

The entire family gathers in the living room, ready for their day. Mhambi stands at the front door with his black leather briefcase in hand, waiting to take the boys to school on his way to work. Rolina sweeps the living room carpet with a broom made of loosely bound straw. Clouds of dust float through the air, illuminated by the sunlight streaming through the back door. My questions are piling up. I wonder if I'm the only one who's uncomfortable with her working half-naked in front of the guys. Why is it okay? Is it because of her position as maid? Is it simply a practicality because of the heat? Does Rolina not know English? Does she not like me? If none of this bothers them, why should it bother me?

» » » « « «

At six forty-five we leave Ruby's for my first day at Zinti. It's been less than a week, but feels like an eternity since I left home. Finally I get to meet the kids. That's why I'm here. Kids always respond to attention and nurturing. They just want to know they're important. There aren't very many things in my life I'm sure of, but I know I can give them love.

Ruby negotiates wild traffic through Oribi Village, a suburb on the southern fringe of Pietermaritzburg. I'm not used to being on the opposite side of the road yet and close my eyes as we enter each traffic circle. I squeal when Ruby slams on her brakes. She shakes her fist out the window at the driver who has cut her off.

"I am sorry, Karen. I did not mean to scare you. The coombie drivers are crazy. They do not know how to drive."

"It's not your fault, Ruby. You're right. He looks totally out of control."

Coombies—Zulu for taxi vans—with radios blaring at chest rattling decibels, swerve in and out of traffic, avoiding oncoming cars by inches. The drivers lean on their horns incessantly while the passengers sit expressionless, straight-backed, enduring their treacherous ride.

"My husband decides the fate of these coombie drivers every day," Ruby says. "Nearly every traffic accident in Natal involves a coombie. I tell him he should put them all in jail and never let them drive again."

We turn the corner along a cloverleaf guardrail and pull into a gas station on Alan Paton Drive. Ruby parks alongside the building, away from the pumps. Within seconds a sleek, dark gray Nissan sedan pulls in next to us. Principal Zondi winds down her window and pops the trunk latch from inside her car.

"Sawubona," she says with a broad smile. "How are you today, Karen?"

"Sawubona! I'm well, thanks. Excited."

Ruby and I transfer my large suitcase from her trunk to Phyllis's. It's loaded with school supplies: erasable white mats, dry erase markers, books, and English manuals for teachers through Grade Four. My backpack holds my personal necessities: a bottle of purified water, a roll of toilet paper, and a bologna sandwich and apple for lunch. I'm prepared for my first day of teaching.

"Have you slept well?" Phyllis asks as we pull away from the gas station. "Is Ruby taking good care of you?"

"She's taking very good care of me. And I'm sleeping great. I love listening to the birds at night." Although I can't see them, their music is soothing; so many different qualities of sound ranging from tiny sweet melodies to wild, raucous caw-caws.

"We are teaching her to speak our mother language," Ruby says proudly. "She must practice her greeting with you."

"Sawubona," I say, eager to show off what I've learned so far. "Unjani?"

"Yebo," says Phyllis. "Ngiyaphila. Uphila njani?" She speaks much faster than Ruby and Mhambi have practiced with me. I'm confused, not sure where to go from here.

"Yebo, ngikhona," Ruby coaches.

"Yebo, ngikhona," I say, trying to mimic the lilt of air that rolls over her tongue. Ruby glances at me in the rearview mirror. Her smile tells me my pronunciation is good.

"You did that very well, Karen," Phyllis says. "Soon you will be speaking our mother language as well as we hope to speak English."

We all laugh. I appreciate their good humor as I butcher their beautiful words. We practice once more—just in time to pick up another Zinti teacher. Pamela runs up the hill from her little yellow house to where we wait at the curb. She reaches the car, breathless. She looks like a college student in her pumps and summer skirt with a white sweater tied around her neck. Phyllis introduces Pamela as her sister. They do look alike, the same chocolate-colored skin and graying hair. Pamela radiates an easy smile as she slides into the back seat with me.

"Sawubona," Pamela says.

Ruby and Phyllis listen intently, correcting my pronunciation as I stumble through the greeting one more time.

» » »   « « «

The morning mist hangs low to the ground; the air is still cool. We head west, through an industrial area, on Selby Msimang Road toward the foothills of the Drakensburg Mountains. Brick buildings with grimy windows stand side-by-side; their tall concrete stacks billow black smoke into the air. Massive chain-link fences, laced with rolls of razor wire, surround the parking lots. Shanty homes, built with layered pieces of corrugated metal painted in varying shades of blue and pink, line the road. Vendors, under blue tarps, occupy each street corner selling brooms, bananas, and chickens. My attention lingers on a billboard: BE A MODERN WOMAN. OPEN YOUR ACCOUNT AT THE FIRST NATIONAL BANK OF SOUTH AFRICA.

A complex of red brick buildings stands on a hill to the south. Trees and shrubs with colorful red and yellow flowers decorate the grounds. But the effect is lost to the harsh fencing and razor wire that surround the property. The sign reads EDENDALE HOSPITAL. It looks more like a prison.

Hundreds of pedestrians crowd the street, making their way to work and school. Everyone seems identified by their dress: blue long-sleeved coveralls for the factory workers; yellow pinafore aprons for the female hospital workers; matching yellow shirts and khaki pants for their male counterparts; red canvas aprons for the vendors who stand in the middle of the road selling newspapers; khaki shorts and shirts for the school boys; simple cotton dresses for the girls. Even the professionals' conspicuous street clothes feel like uniforms.

At the last stoplight on the edge of town, a Muslim woman with several young children in tow crosses the street in front of us. Dressed in olive green abayas and hijabs, they head toward a simple stucco structure on the north side of the road, recognizable only by its royal blue color and a discreet star and crescent painted on the door—an Islamic school. My silent question of how Muslims are regarded in this region of the world is answered quickly.

"Muslims!" Ruby says. "We have no use for them." In the rearview mirror I see her snarled face as she flicks her finger under her chin at them.

"They have their own schools," Phyllis tells me, "because they are not welcome in ours. It is best that they stay to themselves."

My stomach tightens as I rush to sort through what this might mean for me. No one's asked about my profession yet. Now I'm not sure it's a good idea to say anything. If I tell them I'm a minister, they'll want to know what denomination. I'll have to say Interfaith. They'll want to know what that means. Sooner or later we'll come around to the fact that I acknowledge all the world's religions as beautiful—and valid. I hope this conversation never happens.

Feeling vulnerable, as if they can read my thoughts, I turn my face to the window. A black and white cow exhales steamy breath, through enormous nostrils, right into my face.

"Cow in the road!" I shout, fumbling for the button to raise my window. Long blades of grass hang from the sides of her mouth and the black hair on her head stands straight up. She chews the grass, unaffected by my scream. The women burst into giggles.

"Do you not have cows in your country?" Pamela asks.

"We have cows, just not in the road."

The light turns green and town gives way to countryside. Our road narrows to two lanes winding uphill. Lush tall grass sways in the breeze on the hillside. Pygmy palm trees dot the higher regions of the slopes. As the sun crests over the hill, the mist evaporates from sight, lingering as dense humidity, thick enough to slice. The valley below radiates a green glow against the deep blue sky. The carnelian-red dirt at the edge of the road begs to be rubbed between my fingers to see the rich color stain my skin.

Goats wander along the edge of the roadside, straining against the weight of cinder blocks tethered to their necks by long ropes. Tiny, round mud homes—*rondavels*—sit on flat areas that have been carved into the hillside. Some rondavels are as close as ten feet from the edge of the road. Others are much further up the hill. They offer an entirely new perspective on "carving out a life." Pieces of overlapping gray sheet metal serve as roofs, weighted down with old car tires. A few rondavels have small glass windows; most manage with only a rough wooden door. From time to time we pass groups of children walking to school; each school identified by the girls wearing different colored dresses.

Forty minutes outside of town we turn off the paved road onto a rocky dirt path. A small corrugated metal shed, painted Coca-Cola red and lettered with white Zulu words, sits in the field at the corner. Ice cold Coke sounds appealing. Phyllis is quick to tell me that the building belongs to the phone company. It's where the villagers purchase minutes for their cell phones.

A few hundred yards up the road, a small trailer-style building sits in the middle of a paved parking lot surrounded by chain-link fence and razor wire. Phyllis pulls through the opening in the fence.

"This is our school district headquarters," she says. "I have promised the Inspector that he will meet you first thing this morning."

I wish she would tell me these things ahead of time.

The building looks new. A young woman sits behind a modest desk just inside the door.

"Good morning, Ma'am," she says as we walk right past her.

I follow Phyllis to a small office at the end of the hallway. She knocks on the wall next to an open door. Inside, a rotund bald man with olive colored skin, wearing a white short-sleeved shirt and a tie, hunches over papers spread across a long desk. A beautifully framed diploma hangs on the wall behind him. Bookcases line the other walls.

"Good morning, Inspector," Phyllis says. "I would like to introduce our teacher from America, the woman I have spoken about who will be with us for several months."

He looks up, staring at me from behind wire-rimmed glasses. His expression says he's not impressed. I'll have to do more than just show up to make him happy.

"Good morning," I say, extending my hand. "It's nice to meet you."

"We are pleased that you are here." He shakes my hand. Doesn't stand. "It is our hope that you will have a pleasant stay in our country."

"I'm sure I will. Thank you for having me."

"Have a nice day, Inspector," Phyllis says. He returns to his papers. The entire visit lasts all of twenty seconds.

Our tires kick up clouds of red dust as we bump along the rocky road toward Zinti. Before long we encounter children walking along the road, through the grass on the hillside, all headed in the same direction we're traveling. The boys have the same khaki uniforms I've seen since leaving town; the girls wear simple salmon-colored dresses with short sleeves and round collars. Recognizing Principal Zondi's car, they wave with wild enthusiasm and run alongside the car.

"They are very excited to meet you today," Phyllis says. "We have told them of your kind offer to assist with their English lessons. Most of them have never had the privilege of being taught by a white teacher. They are curious about you."

"Why is that?" I ask. "Why aren't there any white teachers here?"

"They are able to secure positions at the schools in Pietermaritzburg where they are paid well. They have no need to come to our rural schools."

For a split second I'm shocked that the government isn't more concerned with spreading capable teachers evenly throughout the districts. This passes quickly, though, as I review a mental list of school districts in the San Francisco Bay Area. There, the most qualified teachers also often land in the predominantly white schools. America has its own education inequities.

"In Pietermaritzburg the children take their lessons from teachers who speak English as their mother language," Ruby says. "This is why we are so fortunate to have you at Zinti."

"You must always speak to the children in English," Phyllis says. "You may practice your Zulu with the teachers, but you must speak English with the children."

That won't be hard; I know a grand total of ten Zulu words. That won't take me far in the classroom.

"We are doing our best to teach them English," Phyllis continues, "but English is our third language. We struggle with it ourselves. It is very hard to teach our children a language that is still so new for us. The children are lucky to have you. And they are very excited to meet you."

"What is your other language, besides Zulu?" I ask.

"Zulu is our mother language," Phyllis says. "Before our government determined that English will be our official language, we spoke Afrikaans."

I knew that! How could I be so stupid?

"Our children do not know Afrikaans," Ruby says, breaking the awkward silence. "It is a language that is dead to our people now."

Conversation dwindles as we approach the horde of children up ahead. They line a steep driveway that leads from the road to a cluster of brick buildings stepped up the hillside. The large wooden billboard, painted in bright yellow and blue, fuels my sense of purpose:

WELCOME TO
ZINTI JUNIOR PRIMARY SCHOOL
THE SCHOOL THAT STRIVES TO PROVIDE
QUALITY EDUCATION AND
TO PRODUCE MARKETABLE LEARNERS
WHO CAN COMPETE LOCALLY
AND INTERNATIONALLY
EDUCATION IS LIBERATION

Hundreds of adorable kids with beautiful smiles wave as Phyllis inches her way up the driveway, parting them with the bumper of her car. Motherly emotions flood my heart. *This* is why I'm here. If I have my way I'll hug and hold each one of them. I'll listen to all their stories, kiss away their skinned knees, rock every hurt feeling until it melts into laughter. If I have my way, I'll leave a smile on each heart.

Their shouts are muffled by the raised windows. As Phyllis parks in the concrete area at the top of the drive, tiny faces peer through cupped hands pressed against the tinted windows. We can't possibly open our doors with the crush of little bodies against the car. If they were adults, this might be scary. But they are just excited children.

"They are very happy to see you," Pamela says. A huge smile spreads across her face when I turn toward her and she sees my tears.

"Haybo!" Ruby whispers.

Phyllis and Ruby wind their windows down a few inches and speak to the kids in Zulu. Their instructions go unheeded until they raise their voices to a sharp tone. The children back away from the car, their hands on their cheeks, mouths open in wonderment. I feel like a rock star stepping out of a limousine.

"Mees Karreen! Mees Karreen!" scream hundreds of little voices. Their thick Zulu pronunciation makes it all the sweeter.

"Good morning," I say.

"Good morning, Mees Karreen," they shout in unison.

"It is so good to see you." Overwhelmed by their welcome, I'm short on words to express my joy.

A tall woman wearing black rubber boots and a bucket hat pulled low over her forehead approaches the car. The white paste smeared over her face does nothing to hide her sour expression. The kids don't even seem to notice her gruff manner as she sweeps them aside with her hands and legs. She opens the trunk of the car and sets my suitcase and backpack, along with Phyllis's bags, on the ground.

A swarm of boys surrounds the bags, diving headfirst toward my suitcase. They shove each other with their elbows, fighting to drag it away. When they realize it's far too heavy, they grab my backpack instead. Two boys engage in a tug-of-war, each with a firm grip on one strap.

"Stop! Stop!" I shout. This bag needs to last another three months. I can't let them rip it apart on the first day.

"You must not stop them," Phyllis says. "They want to carry your bag to the classroom for you."

"Oh, they don't need to do that. I can carry my own bag." My camera's in there. I don't want it bouncing off the ground.

"But you must allow them to carry it. This is how they show their respect for you." Phyllis speaks to them in Zulu. The boys look pleased. They each take hold of one strap and march up the hill, apparently satisfied to share the task. They tip their chins toward the sky, bragging as they speak to their friends who run alongside.

Phyllis says a few words to the woman in the boots and bucket hat before she disappears around the corner of the building with my suitcase—and a string of kids—trailing behind. She reminds me of the Pied Piper. I want to shout instructions for how to use the wheels, but it's too late. I hope everything in my bags is intact the next time I see them.

The other teachers, all women, gather around the car. Rather than look directly at me, they steal glances. I smile. Ruby speaks with them in Zulu. I feel awkward, like the new kid on the first day of school. Will I make friends? My gangly adolescent hope of fitting in is uncomfortable—even at age fifty-two.

Phyllis and Ruby send the remaining kids up the hill with a wave of their hands. The teachers file into the school office to initial the daily log book. Phyllis shows me my line: Miss Karen Baldwin, Grade Four Teacher. I sign my initials and arrival time, 8:05, with great pride. I've finally made it to my destination!

» » » « « «

We follow the kids up the dirt path and crumbling brick steps to the upper level of the school, along a grassy foot-path, to the assembly room at the end of the long, red brick building. The size of two classrooms, the concrete floor is polished to a sheen. A mangled heap of chairs, desks, and tables—at least eight feet deep—occupies the rear of the room. Fluorescent fixtures, sans lightbulbs, hang from the beams in the open ceiling. A comfortable breeze floats easily through the open, broken windows.

The children line up in rows, youngest at the front of the room, oldest at the rear. One row of kindergarten girls, one row of kindergarten boys. On and on until every class is present. The teachers stand along the wall next to the kids in their class.

It feels so natural to be here, like I have known them for-ever. I smile as I look up and down the rows of faces. All but a few smile back before they shyly look away. Their uni-forms run the gamut from nearly new to threadbare. Some of the girls' dresses are faded, nearly colorless. Most of the kids wear a small backpack over their shoulders. Mutant Ninja Turtles and Spider-Man are popular with the boys; the girls seem to favor Dora the Explorer. The backpacks look empty and worn, as though they've been run over by a truck.

Principal Zondi calls the morning assembly to order. "Good morning, learners," she says.

"Good morning, teachers," the kids shout in unison.

Memories of my own elementary school years at St. Winifred's in Pittsburgh come rushing back. Are there still schools in the US where students greet their teachers this way?

Phyllis introduces me, partly in English, mostly in Zulu. I hear "America" a few times and wonder what it is that she says about my country. At her prompt, three-hundred nine-ty-six kids say, "Good morning, Mees Karreen."

Emotion chokes my words. All I can do is smile and nod.

Phyllis delivers the daily announcements, followed by

Pamela leading music. She taps a piece of steel rebar against the front wall to keep time. The kids' voices are strong. They clap their hands over their heads, turn in a circle one way, then the other way, stomping their feet in unison. They close with the South African national anthem.

At the end of their songs, the kids bow their heads, close their eyes, clasp their hands, and scrunch their little faces in prayer; in beautiful rolling words that melt together. The only word I recognize is "Jesus."

Finally, Phyllis distributes rewards to one girl and one boy who exhibited excellent behavior the previous week. Their prize—a fresh banana from the town market. They beam with pride. The boy bows and the girl curtsies as they collect their treats. They eat their bananas as they return to their places in line.

When assembly is over the kids leave single-file through the rear door, trying to maintain silence. Once outside, mayhem reigns as they yelp and chase each other up and down the hill all the way to their classrooms.

The teachers file out behind them. Phyllis motions for me to wait behind. "We will go together to the library," she says. "The teachers want to meet with you to discuss how best to schedule your time with their learners."

The library? I follow the dirt steps carved into the hillside, worn smooth by the traffic of a thousand daily footsteps. At the bottom of the hill we head toward the building on the right, past the office.

Phyllis uncoils the keychain from around her wrist, unlocks the steel mesh door first, then the heavy wooden door. As she spreads her papers on a long wooden table at the far end of the room, I take stock of the library: a large, white deep-freezer, with its power cord curled on top, sits against the wall near the door; piles of brown cardboard boxes, labeled as supplies from the South Africa Rural School District, sit next to the freezer; stacks of terracotta floor tiles, still bound in their original strapping cords, lie in the center of the room.

Fifteen computer desks, paired with black chairs on wheels, line three of the walls. Fluorescent light fixtures, sparsely populated with bulbs, hang from the false ceiling. Rows of windows on opposite walls, each covered with welded steel mesh, provide plenty of light. An empty bookcase sits under one window. And there, in the middle of the room next to the tiles, sits my suitcase. I can't wait to unload the books onto that lonely looking bookshelf.

Six teachers, including Ruby, file into the room behind us. We pull computer chairs up to the table rather than use the small, wood-backed student chairs that are scattered around the room. The teachers smile hesitantly at me, waiting to be addressed by Phyllis, who introduces them as the Grade Three and Grade Four teachers. Each one spreads a class schedule on the table. Ruby slides me a notepad and pen. I'm ready for my teaching assignments.

Samke, Faith, Nelly and Nandi teach Grade Four. One at a time, in slow, broken English, they explain their students' struggles. They need help with vocabulary and verb tenses. In math the kids need to learn to add columns of numbers, with carry-overs. I feel confident that I can help with everything they've requested. After all, I did help my son, the university math major, through elementary school math and English.

Ruby and Lindiwe teach Grade Three. Their students haven't had any formal exposure to English prior to this year. They'd like me to teach their kids in groups of twelve to focus on word recognition, pronunciation, and simple sentence structure. Flashcards would be perfect for them, if only I had some. I can improvise though. This will be fun.

It's decided that in the mornings I'll rotate between the Grade Four classrooms, teaching in thirty-minute sessions: English on Mondays and Tuesdays, math on Wednesdays and Thursdays. Friday mornings I'll take ten kids from each class—those who need extra help—to the library for more individual tutoring.

After lunch, I'll teach Grade Three in small groups at the

library. We'll have two one-hour sessions of twelve kids each. It will take Monday through Thursday for all ninety-six Grade Three students to have one turn with me. On Friday afternoons I'll spend one hour in each Grade Three room teaching art and music.

It's a full schedule: eight-thirty to ten-thirty, break for lunch, then eleven-fifteen to one-fifteen. From one-fifteen to two-fifteen I'll have free time in the library to prepare lessons for the following day. They seem happy with the plan. I'm thrilled.

Phyllis sounds the siren in her office at ten-thirty, signaling lunch break. Having removed their shoes before entering the classrooms, the children—each carrying an aluminum plate—race across the hillside in their stocking feet to line up in front of Cook's table on the upper tier. She ladles white rice and beans onto each plate. The kids scoop the food with their fingers, blow on it to cool it, and with heads tilted backward like tiny birds in a nest, they drop the morsels into their open mouths.

Phyllis sends one of the older boys to retrieve my backpack from wherever it ended up. In what will become our daily routine, she, Ruby, Pamela and myself eat lunch around the library table while the rest of the teachers remain in their classrooms. I devour my bologna sandwich. It tastes just as yummy as it did forty-five years ago. Ruby eats leftovers from last night's dinner. The others share a bag of white bread and a stick of margarine. I should have offered to share.

Missy, the woman in the bucket hat and apron, arrives with a kettle of hot water and a tray of tea supplies. The women wait, I assume to allow me to go first. I reach for a cup. Without a word, Missy smacks my hand, points to herself, and pulls the tray closer to her seat. She points to herself again as she puts a tea bag in each cup; again as she pours the hot water; and yet again as she adds sugar.

"Missy is our maid," Phyllis says. "It is her job to fix our tea."

"I'm sorry, Missy. Thank you for making my tea," I say, rewarded with her beautiful smile. She may not speak English, but we seem to understand each other.

When my tea has cooled enough, Missy fixes her gaze on me as I take my first sip. She waits patiently for my reaction. The rich, deep red Rooibos tea is delicious, but I need more sugar. I reach for the sugar bowl. Missy smacks me hard, then stirs another spoonful of sugar into my cup. It turns out I'm a slow learner.

"I'm sorry, Missy," I smile apologetically. "I forgot. Thank you."

She smiles and pushes my cup across the table to me. It will become our daily ritual that Missy points to herself and makes me watch while she puts two spoons of sugar in my cup, reminding me that she knows how I like my tea.

At noon, well past the scheduled lunch break, Phyllis sounds the siren again. Ruby, Pamela and the kids meander back to their classrooms. I follow Ruby.

"Karen," Phyllis says, "you should begin your lessons tomorrow, when you are fresh."

But I'm finally here! I don't want to wait. "Isn't there something you'd like me to do? Maybe I can spend the rest of the day organizing the books I brought."

"We shall discuss how to paint the library," Phyllis says. "It would be good for the children to have a bright room for their reading."

She's right. The walls are deep maroon on the bottom, a bland cream color on top. Dirty, too. "You know," I say. "I could paint a mural around the room. A blue sky toward the top of the wall, with grass and trees at the bottom. The kids could add birds or butterflies as part of their art lessons. It would give them a sense of ownership; a proud feeling when they come to read."

"We do not have the finances for such expensive projects," Phyllis says.

It can't cost too much more than what she already plans, maybe a few small cans of different paint colors. But I don't want to push. "When you decide on a color I'll do the painting for you," I offer. "I can do it in the afternoons when I'm finished with the Grade Three classes."

"And how would you reach up so high to paint near the ceiling?"

"I'm tall. I can stand on the table and reach easily."

"We shall see," Phyllis says.

» » »   « « «

At one-fifteen the siren in Phyllis's office blares, signaling the end of the day for the youngest kids. They spill from their classrooms, an hour before grades three and four, and find me in the library shelving the books I brought. They look sparse on the bookcase. I wish there were more. I spread them over several shelves, sorted by reading level.

The kids watch from the open door. I smile and invite them in. They don't understand my words, but a wave of my arm does the trick. They push and shove to be first through the doorway. Slipping out of their little black shoes, they run across the polished concrete floor, sliding the last few feet on their socks. They stop a few feet away, their arms around each other, heads tilted down. Their eyes watch every move I make.

"Hi there!" I say. "You can come closer."

Their blank faces tell me my words don't register. I pat my hands on my lap and wave my arms again. They are slow to respond. The girls are the first to take the last few steps toward me. One little girl stands next to me and smiles at the others, as though she's just won a game of Red Light-Green Light. I pick her up and set her on my lap. She leans her head against my chest and looks up at me. Her deep brown eyes and tooth-gapped smile melt my heart.

The others are bolder now. They move closer until I'm surrounded by twenty-five kids squirming around my chair for position. Slowly some reach through the throng to touch me.

"You are all so beautiful," I say, knowing they don't understand. But it needs to be said before I can think of anything else.

"Let's say our numbers together. One."

They look at each other, then at me.

"One," I say, pointing to them.

"One," about half of them say.

"One," I say again, pointing all the way around the circle of mesmerized faces.

"One," they all say.

I smile. "Very good."

"Very good," they scream in unison.

We understand each other now. They repeat my numbers from one to twenty. I look up to see Phyllis and Pamela peek through the door. Our eyes meet and we smile at each other. They turn to whisper in each other's ears. Pamela runs her finger under her eye to wipe a tear.

"One," I say, starting again.

» » » « « «

The upper grades are released at two-fifteen, and the library swarms with kids. Most of them are satisfied just to stand and look at me. I'm happy to do the same, allowing the reality of where I am and what I'm doing to soak into my bones. Time with them is like being in heaven.

Ruby joins Phyllis and Pamela at the door. They allow the kids to linger for ten minutes before they shoo them off for the day.

"You will see Miss Karen tomorrow," Ruby says. Then she speaks in Zulu, presumably repeating herself for the little ones.

I wave at them as they back out the door. "Bye. See you tomorrow," I say.

"See you today," the older ones say.

"See you tomorrow, Miss Karen," Phyllis corrects them.

"See you tomorrow, Mees Karreen."

Everything—even peeing in the sink—feels worth it now. I float through the ride home. Ruby makes a detour into downtown Pietermaritzburg to pick up Siphelele from the coombie depot. We park in front of the same Kentucky Fried Chicken I saw yesterday, across from the city park where hundreds of vendors spread their wares on blankets on the ground. Smoke rises from pits where men roast meat. Coombies race to the curb in front of the park, unload passengers, take on new ones, and dart again into traffic. Lane markings appear to mean nothing. Screeching brakes fill the air.

The park looks like too much to explore today. Besides, Ruby's in a hurry, impatient with Siphelele for being late. She calls him a half-dozen times on her cell phone while we wait. Ruby sees a man she knows and jumps out of the car to chat. I'd like to race up the street to the Internet café to tell everyone at home about the adorable Zinti kids, but there's a line out the door. It will have to wait. I'm grateful for my curtailed urgency about emails. It's not so much now about hearing from home as it is about sharing what's here.

» » »   « « «

At dinner I devise a subtle system for easing my stomach distress caused by all the grease. I slip my spoon handle under the edge of my plate. The grease pools on one side of my plate while I eat from the other. Ruby doesn't seem to notice.

When we're finished with the dishes, Ruby disappears down the hall while I join Mhambi in the living room. Soccer isn't really my thing, but at least I understand how the game works.

"So, who's playing?" I ask.

"Ah," Mhambi says. "This is a match between Uganda and Kenya. Kenya is sure to win, but it is an excellent match." He turns the volume down a bit, lights up another cigarette. "So, Karen, how was your first day at Zinti?"

"It was amazing. I'm already in love with these kids."

"Ruby says that the children are very fond of you. They are eager to learn from you."

"I hope I can teach them well. Today I just did numbers with the little ones. They were good about practicing their pronunciation."

"And what surprised you most about Zinti?"

"That the kids pray at school. At home, public schools are forbidden to incorporate prayer."

"Yes, we are a Christian country. We encourage our children to be humble, to ask for assistance from God in their school lessons. This is not restricted to the public schools. It is this way in all our schools."

It seems unnecessary to open the question of religious discrimination. That was answered this morning. There are differences I just need to accept.

"Karen," Mhambi say, "I have a question for you."

"Sure hope I can answer."

"I am curious. I have read much about this in our newspapers. Do you believe that O.J. Simpson got away with murder?"

I blink. Stunned. Why this? At least it's easy to answer. "Yes, I do."

Mhambi leans back in his chair and throws his arms in the air. He takes a deep drag on the cigarette hanging from his mouth before he leans forward, resting his elbows on his knees. His head hangs between his hands. Is he disappointed with me or my answer? When he finally raises his head, he looks as though he's lost his last friend.

"How can this be?" he asks, his voice low. "How can this happen in the most powerful country in the world? How can the strongest judicial system in the world let someone go unpunished for such a brutal murder?" He looks at me with pleading eyes, begging an answer.

I take a deep breath to buy time. I'd like to answer without being flippant. "Mhambi, our legal system is far from perfect. People get away with murder all the time."

"How does that happen?" he demands.

"Well, in our system people are innocent until proven to be guilty. And they can only be convicted by a jury of their peers. O.J. Simpson's jury decided he was innocent."

"Yes. This much I understand. But there was convincing, incriminating evidence against him. Could the judge not see that he was guilty?"

"I'm sure the judge knew lots of stuff that the jury was never allowed to hear. That happens all the time. Maybe the judge did know that he was guilty."

"And he did nothing about it?"

"It's the jury that makes the decision."

"And if the jury makes an incorrect decision, the judge does nothing?"

"That's right. If a jury convicts someone of a crime and the judge has conclusive evidence that the person is innocent, the judge can reverse the jury's decision. But the judge does not have the power to reverse an innocent decision."

"So he gets away with murder?"

"Yes."

Mhambi shakes his head, his belief in the American judicial system shattered.

"The judge, the prosecutor, the defendant's lawyer; they all do their best to choose a jury that will be fair," I say. "But sometimes they're not. Sometimes the jury has their own agenda."

"And the prosecutor cannot demand a different jury?"

"No. That only happens when the jury can't agree on a decision. Then the prosecutor can ask for a new trial. If they have a new trial, there's a new jury."

"I am disappointed. I was certain you would tell me something different than what you have said."

"I'm sorry, Mhambi. It's hard to watch our system fail. It's a decent system. But it's not perfect."

"I see this now," he sighs. He leans back in his chair, his face drawn with irritation. "Here in my country, we frequently use your American system of justice as an example for how we should run our own."

I pause to decide how I'm going to break the news that America isn't a flawless country.

"Thank you for your honesty, Karen. I appreciate that you have shared the imperfections of your country with me."

"You're welcome. I think our imperfections are hard to hide."

"You have given me much to think about."

"I'm going to my room now, Mhambi. I have a full day of teaching tomorrow. I'm excited and want to have plenty of rest. Please tell Ruby good-night for me."

"Yes, I will. Have a pleasant evening."

Alone in the living room, watching soccer with a blank stare, Mhambi's vulnerability feels raw. My heart aches for him; for his shattered, proud ideals.

DAY 6
TUESDAY, FEBRUARY 5, 2008

Thirty-five Grade Four kids jump from their seats when I walk through the door. Wooden chairs with metal legs clang against each other. Although the room is large, their tables sit clumped together in the center arranged in pairs with two students on each side. They poke and shove each other to make room to stand between the chairs and tables.

"Good morning," I say, happy to see that my backpack has arrived safely. It sits at the front of the room under the chalkboard where Samke's written my name.

"Good morning, Mees Karreen," they say in unison.

"How are you today?"

They pass quizzical, nervous looks between themselves.

"You can sit down," I say, motioning with my hands. Another round of clanking chairs. "I'm very happy to be here with you. Today we're going to learn about nouns and verbs. Take out your notebooks."

The pink chalk, damp from the humidity, slides across the chalkboard. It takes several tries to draw two columns labeled "nouns" and "verbs." When I turn back to the kids, their backpacks still hang on their chairs. They stare at me with wide eyes.

"Take out your notebooks to write." I wave my arms through the air as if I'm sending them off on an errand.

"Yes, Mees Karreen," they say in unison, glancing anxiously at each other as I wait. One girl in the back raises her hand.

"Yes?" I ask.

She stands at her desk. "Miss Karen, may I tell the others what you have said?" Her English is perfect.

"Yes, please."

"Thank you, Miss Karen."

She gives directions in Zulu to the rest of the class before she sits. They scurry to pull paper, pencils and rulers from their backpacks. I feel stumped already by our language barrier.

"Who can tell me the difference between a noun and a verb?" An outrageous question, but I don't know what else to say at the moment.

"Yes, Mees Karreen," they respond in unison.

I raise one hand in the air as an example of how I'd like them to respond. I point with my other hand, waving it slowly from one side of the classroom to the other. "What is a verb?" I ask.

The girl in the back of the room shoots her hand into the air.

"Yes," I say, pointing to her. She's quickly becoming my favorite.

She stands at her desk and waits.

"What is your name?" I ask.

"Sindiswa."

"Thank you," I say, knowing I can't repeat it. Maybe the language will grow on me. I'll ask the teachers to have the kids write their names out for me, put them in front of themselves on the desk so I can learn names as I go. "So, tell me, what is a verb?"

"Run," she says.

"That's right. Run is a verb."

She beams as she sits down. I hoped to hear the definition of "verb," but this is a good place to start. "Who knows another verb?"

A boy in front shoves his hand into the air. I point to him; he stands. "Throw." He sits down.

"Very good!" I'm uncomfortable with all this standing to address me. They're squeezed together so tightly, every "stand and sit" generates another round of poking. It takes forever for them to settle back down again. I hate to frown on their custom for showing respect, but this eats up precious teaching time. I turn to write these two words in the "verb" column while I decide where to go from here. At the end of our thirty minutes together we have five verbs and three nouns.

I move down the row of Grade Four classrooms repeating this exercise, grateful that every class has at least one child who understands English and is willing to help me out. Faith is the only teacher who remains in the classroom while I teach. She's so gentle with her kids, nudging them into action when we get stuck. At the end of class she gives me a big hug.

"Thank you," she says in a soft voice. "Our children will learn well from you."

I hope so.

» » » « « «

At ten-thirty, it's already been a long morning. Relieved to be off my feet for lunch, I smile as I watch Missy add an extra spoonful of sugar to my tea. I slide my feet under the table, up onto the chair across from me. Flushed from the heat and the effort to communicate, I guzzle the contents of my water bottle and finish my bologna sandwich before the other teachers arrive.

DAY 7

"Sawubona," Pamela greets me as she slides into the car this morning.

"Yebo."

"Unjani?" she asks.

"Ngiyaphila. Uphila njani?"

"Yebo, ngikhona," she says.

Thank goodness the greeting never varies! I still struggle to remember the words in the right order, but my pronunciation improves daily. Or so they tell me.

When we arrive at school, activities at the water spigot are in full swing. Four kids from each class wait their turn to fill two five-gallon buckets for each classroom—one for washing hands, faces and lunch plates; the other for dipping a communal cup for drinking.

Cook also waits for her turn at the spigot. She giggles with delight when I greet her in her own language. Her smile is brilliant white against her blue-black skin; her eyes hidden in the shade of her wide-brimmed straw hat. Phyllis assures me her laugh is not because of my poor pronunciation, only that she has never heard a white person speak her mother language.

I greet Missy as she pulls my backpack from the trunk of the car. My Zulu salutation flows easily now after several rounds of practice. She mistakenly believes that, because I can greet her, I actually speak Zulu. She carries on talking to me, her arms moving in animated gestures. She pauses, her eyebrows arched in a quizzical expression. I believe she's asked a question and is waiting for my reply. I look at Phyllis for an explanation.

"Missy wants you to come to her house. She wants to fix a mealie-meal dish for you," Phyllis says.

"Yebo, yebo," I say, looking back at Missy. Her eyes dance with a smile.

Phyllis speaks to Missy in Zulu, in a stern tone. Missy's face clouds over. She stomps her foot on the concrete, pursing her lips as she responds. She looks like a child demanding her own way.

"Missy wants you to spend the night at her home in the village," Ruby says, as Phyllis and Missy carry on with their disagreement. "Ma'am will not allow it. She is scolding Missy, telling her that she must not say this again."

Phyllis finishes with an angry burst and points toward the office. Missy sulks off with her head hung in shame.

I'm on Missy's side. I don't see what would be wrong with me spending a night in the village. I'm sure I could handle one night. Missy's offer feels generous, warm, and friendly. We do fine together even without a common language. And I'd love to have at least one experience in the village other than being at school. Visiting Missy's home would be a treat.

"I have told her that you will not be staying in the village during the night," Phyllis says. "Perhaps one day after school we will go together to her home for a meal."

"I'd like that," I say, as I admit to myself that it probably won't happen. Intuition tells me that Phyllis has promised a compromise that she has no intention of keeping. Graciously, I accept being told that I'm not allowed to do something; not my typical attitude. But I trust they have their reasons.

» » »   « « «

At morning assembly I stand with my back against the cool bricks to ward off the muggy heat. Phyllis gives the daily announcements in Zulu. Ruby, in her striped jersey shirt and black skirt, stands on the other side of the window, perspiration beading on her face. I look to her, hoping she will translate for me, but she doesn't look my way.

As one of the boys in Grade Two prays, his chin nearly touches his chest. The front of his khaki shirt is wet and greasy from the collar to mid-chest. My eyes move up to examine his face; perhaps he is crying. But no, his chin oozes puss. What hasn't dripped onto his shirt has dried to a hard yellow crust on his face. How long has this infection gone untreated?

When prayers are over and he's waiting for his row to file out, I step up to him and place my hand on his head, gently tipping it backward for a closer look. It's hard to see through the yellow crust, and I'm afraid to touch his face. I have two washcloths in my luggage and resolve to sacrifice one. Clean water and the anti-bacterial ointment I brought is better than nothing.

» » »   « « «

Phyllis, Ruby and Pamela engage in their usual Zulu conversation on the way home from school; whatever it is that teachers need to resolve at the end of a school day. I'd feel hurt about not being included, but I'm wrapped up in my own review of the day. I see how much needs to be done. What can I actually accomplish?

At home if we say our teeth "need attention," it probably means they aren't perfectly aligned and Hollywood white, or we're overdue for our semi-annual visit to the dentist. Here, teeth needing attention means half the child's teeth are missing and his gums are rotting before your eyes. These kids have beautiful smiles, but a full set of teeth is rare.

At home if a child needs new school clothes, it most likely means they've grown tired of the same old clothes or they're beginning to look worn. In a really serious case it might mean there's a hole in one knee or the pants are too short. Here, needing new school clothes means a girl has worn the same dress since kindergarten. The hem has been let down several times and she's grown so much that it can no longer be zipped up the back. She either wears a T-shirt underneath or goes naked from the waist up in back.

Needing new shoes doesn't mean they're scuffed, the wrong color or style, or even too tight. It means the backs were cut out of the shoes last year to make room for growing feet, and now the child's heels hang over the back so far that socks are threadbare from walking a mile to school.

Phyllis interrupts my thoughts. "The teachers have been talking about you," she says from the front seat.

That can't be good. Maybe they aren't happy with the way I handle their classes.

"They speak of your bravery," she says. "You have come from far away and put shame on white people from our own country who will not teach at our rural schools."

"Why is that so?" I ask, relieved that I haven't stepped on anyone's toes. "Why are they so unwilling to come teach here?"

"Because they are afraid. You are *not* afraid. You show us that it is possible for a white person to be brave. And a woman!"

"I'm sorry they won't come out here," I say. On the other hand, "we fear what we don't understand" crosses my mind. Have they even bothered to come out and see how much is needed here? Maybe if they'd come out and spend some time, their fears would fade. These women have been nothing less than welcoming and grateful. The white teachers wouldn't have to *live* in the village. None of Zinti's teachers even live here. I have plenty of fear, but it's not about *being* here. My fear is about being inadequate, not doing enough.

"It would be better for our children to learn English from the white teachers," Phyllis says. "It is difficult for Zinti's teachers because English is not their mother language. They struggle to teach English without knowing it well for themselves."

Of course they do. Surely this problem could be solved without importing teachers from overseas.

We pull up to Ruby's car at the gas station and transfer our purses and bags from one car to the other. "See you tomorrow," we all say. It doesn't seem important to do goodbyes in Zulu.

» » » « « «

"How do you like Zinti?" Ruby asks on the drive home. "The children are very excited for you to be their teacher. Do you have any questions about our school?"

"I have lots of questions," I say. "But most of them aren't really about the school. They're more personal."

"What are your questions, Karen?"

"What is the white paste on Missy's face?" I have more substantial questions, but this one feels safe.

"This is ash. Missy makes paste from the ashes of her cooking fire. It protects her face from the sun."

Oh. Natural sunscreen.

"Do you have more questions?" Ruby asks.

"Well, why do some of the women wear scarves around their heads, and some don't?"

"Women who are married must cover their heads when they are in public," she says. "The women who are unmarried may leave their heads uncovered."

"Why don't you cover your head?"

"Because my husband has given me permission to leave it uncovered. I do not come from the traditional way as he does, and he understands that it is hard for me."

I suppose that's generous of him.

"When we go to Ntwana at the school break, I will cover my head. You will see."

"Why is that?" I ask. "Why there, and not here?"

"Because in the city it is not always expected that women follow the traditional way. But in Ntwana I must show respect for my husband and his family. In Ntwana women must also cover their arms and their legs above their knees. You will see. There are many ways we must show our respect."

"Will I need to cover my arms and legs, too?" It won't be a problem. Most of my clothes are modest, but I do have a few sleeveless blouses.

"No," Ruby giggles. "You are a visitor. No one will expect you to follow the traditional ways."

"Do you mind, Ruby? I mean, since you weren't raised with traditional customs, do you mind doing this for Mhambi?"

"I do not do it just for my husband!" she says, her voice sharp and edgy. "It is for the family. When I married a traditional man I knew it would be this way. I must show my respect. I have been married for twenty-six years. I am used to it now."

She fell in love and made choices—the compromises of living in partnership, joining families and cultures. It feels sexist to me, but maybe she really doesn't mind. I wonder if the men make similar personal sacrifices to show respect for their wives' families.

Ruby's already told me she's forty-nine years old, three years younger than me. She married at twenty-three after graduating from college. She and Mhambi were married ten years before Siphelele was born. And they're Catholic! I was nineteen when I married the first time; my son was born nine years into that marriage. And I was raised Catholic.

A continual stream of comparisons and contradictions flows through my mind. How is it possible that a Zulu woman, thirty years ago, had an opportunity to go to college before marriage, while I, a middle-class white American woman, by necessity have worked since the age of twelve? I marvel at the parallels between my life and Ruby's, between my parents' marriage of the 1950's and Ruby and Mhambi's marriage nearly sixty years later.

Despite my best intentions to come to Africa with an open mind, I truly expected that our life stories would not overlap—at all. It seemed a given that the average American life would be superior to the average Zulu life. But what's average? Abundance and opportunity? There are plenty of people in the States who live in abject poverty. My perceptions have become clouded in only a few days. No one at home will believe me when I tell them of the similarities between us and the Zulus.

"Do you have other questions?" Ruby asks.

More than you can imagine. "I notice that many of the children have scars on their faces. They seem so similar; it can't be an accident." It looks like they all fell on the same sharp rock, repeatedly, until their faces are now covered with long, eye-shaped, vertical scars, several shades lighter than the rest of their skin.

"This is a question you should ask my husband. He is a traditional man and he will explain this to you."

Her response feels odd, but I'm already on overload and willing to let it rest for now.

» » »   « « «

In my room at Ruby's, I'm happy to lay on my bed with my feet up. They're killing me. It's been years since I've had to stand so long, on concrete no less. What I need most, though, is to rest my mind.

"Miss Karen?" Siphelele knocks on my door.

I sit up quickly. "Come in."

"For you, Miss Karen. From the ice-cream truck." He offers me a chocolate-covered ice cream on a stick. The wrapper already removed, ice cream drips into his cupped hand below. As he extends the stick toward me, he lays his free hand, gooey drips and all, on his outstretched forearm.

"Thank you, Siphelele. That looks yummy!" I eat from the bottom up, catching every last drop of cool sweetness. "What do I owe you?"

"This is my favor," he says, "from my allowance. It is very hot today and my mother says you are very tired after teaching all day. You are not accustomed to our heat."

"You're so kind, Siphelele. Did you get one for yourself?"

"Yes, Ma'am," he smiles. "I have already eaten mine."

"So, how was school today?"

"Good. Our basketball team won. We practice very hard and today we won our match."

"Congratulations. What position do you play?" I have two uncles who went to college on basketball scholarships. Family events I haven't thought about in years flood my memory.

Siphelele looks surprised. "I play point guard. I made eight points today."

"I would love to see you play while I'm here."

"I would like that very much," he beams.

"What else do you like to do, besides basketball?"

"Ah. When I have allowance for the coombie, I go to the movies with my friends. The American movies are best."

"Yeah? And what's your favorite subject at school?" I feel like such a mom.

"I am preparing to study architecture when I go to university," he says. "So now I have mathematics and drawing. They are my favorite studies."

This is the first conversation I've had with Siphelele. I'm struck by his impeccable English. What a difference it makes that he goes to school in Pietermaritzburg.

"It sounds like you have good plans for your life, Siphelele."

"My parents say that I must prepare myself to be a good citizen. I must make a contribution to my country."

I like that, a different twist on the conversation Kevin and his friends had when they were choosing majors at college. "Can I ask you a different kind of question, Siphelele?"

He nods.

"I notice how you held your hand like this when you handed me the ice cream." I show him my arm outstretched with my other palm resting on my forearm. "The boys at Zinti do the same thing when they hand me something. Why do you do it like that?"

"This is our custom, Miss Karen. This is the proper way to give a gift."

It's such an unnatural position, there must be a reason. I

feel pushy, but I need to know. "How did that custom come about?"

"If I hand you a gift like this then you will know that I intend you no harm."

"Excuse me?"

"When I place my empty hand over my arm you can see that I am not holding a weapon. My gift is genuine. I do not intend to harm you when you take it from me."

"Oh." I imagine the look on my face says much more.

"And there is a proper way to receive a gift," Siphelele says.

"Will you show me?"

"Yes, of course. When you receive a gift you hold both hands out like this." He holds his elbows tight against his sides, his hands cupped together, palms up. "This way you are showing that you will not grab; you will not harm *me* when I give you something."

"Oh," I say again. I wonder how many generations it's been since this practice was really necessary. "Thanks for showing me, Siphelele. I don't want to offend anyone."

He laughs. "No one would mistrust you, Miss Karen. But they will appreciate that you have learned our way, that you respect our tradition. My mother says when you have finished your ice cream you should come into the house. She is waiting for you to take Granny GuGu to the store."

"I'll be there as soon as I wash my hands." Our trip to the store is a surprise, but I'm eager to meet one more family member.

» » »   « « «

Ruby paces the kitchen, impatiently. "We must leave now so I will be home in time to fix my husband's evening meal." She heads down the hall for her purse. When she returns, an elderly woman—maybe a hundred years old—walks ahead of her. Four feet tall, and every inch as wide, she slowly shifts her weight from one foot to the other. Ruby appears frustrated with the elderly woman's pace, poking her shoulder to hurry her along. The elderly woman mumbles her disapproval in Zulu.

I follow them to the car, confused. Is this Granny GuGu? Where did she come from? We didn't bring her home with us and I *know* she didn't walk from the local coombie stop. She pushes away Ruby's offer of help and settles herself in the back seat. One lone tooth sits on her lower gum. Her thin silver hair piled on top of her head is held in place with bobby pins. A small, black leather pouch hangs around her neck on a narrow strap. She grips it in her gnarled fingers, pounding it repeatedly against her chest as she mutters at Ruby. When she stops to cough, I'm alarmed. The deep raspy sound of fluid in her lungs is unmistakable. As a hospital chaplain I've heard it a million times: the death rattle.

"My husband's mother insists on going herself to cash her government check," Ruby says. Her tone belies her resentment. "She does not trust me to do it for her. I must take her all the way across town to the only store that will cash such a check. It would be much easier and faster to go alone and do it for her. But even though it is difficult for her to leave the house, she insists on going herself. My husband says I must do this for her if it makes her happy."

"Where does she live?" I ask.

"We care for her," Ruby says. "My husband is the eldest son. When his father died it became his responsibility to care for his mother. After we were married and came to live in town, she moved with us. She has lived with us since before Siphelele was born."

I've been here five days and this is the first I know of Granny GuGu? Where is her room? There are only two small bedrooms off the hallway, one for each of the boys. Ruby and Mhambi's bedroom is at the end of the hall. Granted, I haven't ventured past the bathroom yet. Maybe there's another room I don't know about. I doubt it, though; the house isn't that big. Maybe the boys share one room, and Granny lives in the other. I scramble to rearrange my understanding of who lives in the house. But I've never seen Granny in the living room. She never sits at the table to eat with me and Ruby. I know the boys eat in their rooms, maybe she does, too. The doors in the hallway are always closed. I can't believe she lives in the house and I've never seen her.

We pull into the empty parking lot of a warehouse-style grocery store. Ruby parks as far from the door as possible and heads for the store without so much as a glance toward Granny. I offer Granny my arm as leverage to lift her enormous weight out of the car. Every step across the lot is an effort. GuGu talks to me in Zulu the entire way, stopping every few feet to cough.

» » »   « « «

Ruby frantically prepares dinner. I offer help and don't understand why she consistently refuses, especially when she's so rushed. Mhambi, usually home by six, rarely eats before nine. But Ruby still worries about having it ready before he gets home, then about keeping it warm until he announces he's hungry.

When the boys fill their dinner plates, I see that Thulani has two plates. I didn't notice this until tonight. This must be how Granny GuGu gets her meals. Once again Ruby and I eat alone at the dining room table. She seems happy to let me help with the dishes after dinner. Then, like every night so far, she disappears down the hall to iron while I sit to watch soccer with Mhambi.

"Ruby tells me that you would like to learn more about our customs," he says. "She says you have many questions."

I never see Ruby and Mhambi speak to each other, but apparently they do. "I do have questions," I say, and tell him about the scars on the children's faces. "Ruby says that you can explain this for me."

Mhambi beams with pride as he shares. "This is the identity mark of the Zulu tribe. When a baby is born into a family, a ritual is performed to bleed the evil spirits from the child so that it may have a pure life."

My stomach begins to knot. I fear what is coming next.

"When the child is three months old the men in the family are required to cut the child's face, very deep, all the way until the inside of the child is exposed. This way the unclean spirits will evacuate the child with the blood."

Silently, I will him to stop before I throw up. I don't need to know more.

Unaware of my repulsion, Mhambi continues. "The witch doctor determines how many cuts are necessary. There are most often ten or twenty. Then the openings must be allowed to heal in a natural way." He makes it sound like a most natural thing to do to babies.

My mouth hangs open. I can't tell him how disgusting and barbaric it sounds. As a guest in their culture, I'm committed to being an observer, not a critic. But this is beyond anything I imagined.

"Each family has a distinguishable pattern for this ritual," Mhambi says. "The Ndlela family does theirs like this." He moves his finger in a vertical motion across the scars on his own face, first across his forehead, then his cheeks. His scars are so old now they meld into the folds of his skin. I hadn't seen them as being similar to the kids' at school until now. His skin is so black they look more like remnants of severe adolescent acne. Siphelele and Thulani have the same marks on their faces. I've ignorantly assumed that acne is a genetic trait.

"Some families cut the child's arms or chest or legs." Mhambi pauses. "This tradition also serves another purpose."

"Really?" I can't imagine. I don't want to imagine.

"Yes," he says, eager to share more. "Every Ndlela is identifiable by their markings. In the old days this was important when there were battles. You would not want to harm someone from your own family."

You don't want to harm each other in battle, but it's okay

to mutilate your children at birth? I feel the color drain from my face. I'm dizzy. Nauseous. My silence feels uncomfortable. It also seems unavoidable. I struggle to speak. "Thank you for explaining it to me. I appreciate that you're so willing to answer my questions."

Aside from sounding barbaric, this tradition also sounds dangerous. How do they make the cuts? With clean surgical implements? And anesthesia? My stomach turns. Surely this custom has outlived its purpose. You don't hear about Zulu wars in the news. And evil spirits? Babies are so pure and innocent. Original sin flashes though my mind. I rush to remove the comparison from my thoughts.

"Ruby tells me that you will be going with her to Durban on Friday," Mhambi says.

"Oh? This is news to me," I say, stumbling to change gears. "What's happening in Durban?"

"There is a meeting for rural teachers. Every school will send a representative and Ma'am has asked Ruby to take you."

"I look forward to it."

"This is quite an opportunity," Mhambi says. "You will see more of our country. Durban is a fine city. When your meeting is over Ruby will take you to the outdoor market and the beach. You will find many treasures at the market. Beautiful gifts to take home to your family. And you will enjoy our beach. The water is warm and clear."

"That sounds wonderful." My body relaxes a bit. It seems odd that Ruby didn't mention this to me, but it's something fun to look forward to at the end of the week.

After as short a time as I can possibly call polite, I excuse myself and head to the backyard for bed. "Please tell Ruby good-night for me."

"I will," Mhambi says, with his usual warm smile. "Have a pleasant evening."

I was exhausted before this conversation. Now I feel something I can't even name. Every time I begin to fall asleep, I see pictures of helpless babies pinned to a table, screaming in pain and terror as their fathers, uncles, and grandfathers—the same men who are supposed to love them and protect them—splay them open, over and over. With what? A razor blade? A knife?

My heart pounds as these questions roll through me. Afraid to go to sleep and face the nightmares, I lie awake wondering where the mothers are when this happens. How can they allow their babies to be tortured like this? Do they actually *agree* to it? How can a mother's heart be so shut down that she can stand by and watch her husband do this to her baby? How can she ever love him again? How can she look at her child's face for a whole lifetime and not relive the agony of this ritual?

DAY 8

THURSDAY, FEBRUARY 7, 2008

Exhausted and still crying, my back aches. All night I dreamed of screaming babies with wide eyes that plead for mercy. I splash cold water on my face to quell my nausea.

"You do not look well," Ruby says when I see her in the kitchen after my bath. "Every day you appear to be more tired, as though you never sleep. Are you sick?"

I struggle to suppress my tears. "I didn't sleep well last night. I'll be okay though."

Ruby reaches for me and I collapse into her arms. "You must not work so hard at school," she says. "You must take a break between classes. Ma'am has also noticed that the children are tiresome for you. She thinks it is best if you do not take the Grade Three students after lunch. You must take that time to rest."

"Oh, Ruby," I sob on her shoulder. "I don't want to teach less. I like being with the kids."

"But look at you." She holds me at arm's length. "You are already so tired. Even my husband says that you work too hard."

"I'm not working too much. Being away from home is just harder than I expected." I imagined the suffering I'd witness would be due to poverty and illness, not intentionally inflicted. I thought I was prepared. It feels impossible to tell her that I'm already overwhelmed by the life she lives every day; that I have such harsh judgments. I'm afraid I'll never fit in here. I'm afraid of more surprises. "Besides, Ruby, I'm not teaching any more than the rest of you. If I teach fewer classes, that would be lazy on my part. I don't want to do that. I'll be okay. I just need a little more time to adjust."

"No one believes you are lazy! You must not be so hard on yourself. I will talk to Ma'am about it. You go and sit at the table and I will bring your breakfast."

She hugs me before I head for the dining room. Now I feel guilty about her waiting on me while I harbor judgments about her, her husband, her whole culture.

» » » « « «

Phyllis has a principals' meeting at district headquarters in Pietermaritzburg today. It's nice to be alone with Ruby for the drive to school. Her car radio doesn't work; relief for my senses.

"My husband says he spoke to you last night about the scars on the children's faces."

Oh, my God, I can't talk about this again. "He did."

"And? What do you think of our custom?"

This feels risky. I choose my words carefully. "This is something that doesn't happen in our country. I can't even imagine what it must be like for you, as a mother. It would be very hard for me to watch my baby suffer like that."

"It was very difficult for me, too! I would rather have it happen to me than to my son. I was furious with my husband that he insisted on this tradition." Ruby's emotions are still raw. Tears slide from her face into her lap.

Relief washes over me as I realize we're going to have a conversation about this, mother-to-mother. "What was it like for you?" I ask.

"I did not think that my husband was capable of such cruelty. When he said it was time to take Siphelele to Ntwana for the ritual, I begged and begged for him to change his mind. He would not hear my pleas. I was angry. More angry than I have ever been in my life. I trusted him before that day." She pauses to grab a breath. "When it was time for the ritual, the men held my arms at the edge of the circle. They would not let me stop my husband. I screamed and screamed for him to stop. I screamed that Siphelele is only a baby, he has no evil in him. I begged for my husband to have mercy on our child. He would not hear me. There were many times I cried while I held my son to my breast after this happened.

I wanted to tend to his wounds. But I did not. If I did not allow them to heal without my help, the men would just do it again. I could not let that happen. I was so angry I did not speak to my husband for a very long time."

The thought of my son being tortured this way grips my gut. "I can't even imagine, Ruby. I think I might kill my husband if he did that to my son. How did you manage to forgive Mhambi?"

"I have never forgiven my husband! He does not deserve to be forgiven. But, he is a traditional man. What can you do?"

I'm dumbfounded by her last remark. This must be a defense mechanism against something so vile. Of course you're going to take your baby and run away. Maybe she didn't have a chance to run. Maybe this is why they didn't have a second child. I'd like to believe Ruby rebelled in the only way she could—by refusing to bear another baby.

"Do baby girls go through this ritual, too? Or is it just the boys?"

"It is all of the children. Sometimes I believe it is harder for the girls to live this way."

"How so?"

"Because the girls must learn to accept themselves as beautiful, even though their faces are scarred. It is hard for them. Many of them suffer from depression when they become older. Modern women are beautiful because they have beautiful skin. Our girls see pictures of them in magazines. They want to be like them. None of the African women on television or in magazines have scars on their faces. The girls who have these marks on their arms and chest where they cannot be seen are fortunate."

Hopes and dreams are everywhere. All little girls want to feel pretty. American teenagers struggle with weight and image. These girls struggle with their scars. At least there are ways to deal with weight. It must be hell for these girls to be stuck between the old traditions and the new values.

» » » « « «

Phyllis puts an end to me working with the Grade Three kids after lunch. Maybe it will only be temporary. I spend the afternoon wandering through the office, fascinated by the contradictions between what I've experienced so far and the posted schools rules:

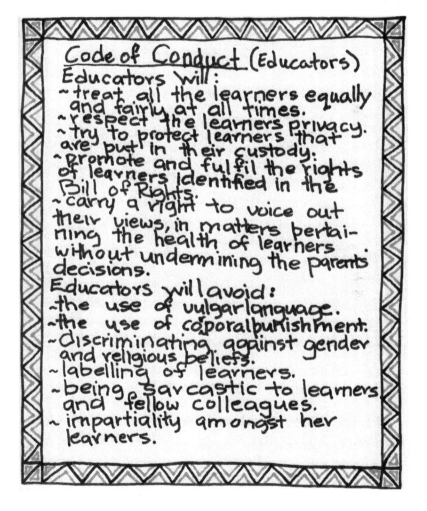

Code of Conduct (Educators)
Educators will:
~ treat all the learners equally and fairly at all times.
~ respect the learners privacy.
~ try to protect learners that are put in their custody.
~ promote and fulfil the rights of learners identified in the Bill of Rights.
~ carry a right to voice out their views, in matters pertaining the health of learners without undermining the parents decisions.
Educators will avoid:
~ the use of vulgar language.
~ the use of corporal punishment.
~ discriminating against gender and religious beliefs.
~ labelling of learners.
~ being sarcastic to learners and fellow colleagues.
~ impartiality amongst her learners.

Code of Conduct (Learners)

* Learners should practise respect (Learner to learner and learner to educator).
* Learners should be self-disciplined, at all times.
* No vulgar language.
* No dangerous weapons.
* No use of drugs.
* No late coming.
* No leaving of school premises without permission.
* No absenteeism.
* No sexual harrassment.
* No cultural discrimination.
* No religious discrimination.
* No sex discrimination.

» » »   « « «

Ruby surprises me with a trip to the Internet café on the way home. "Ma'am says you will feel better if you hear from your family."

"Thank you, Ruby. That's probably true."

"Ma'am says we should do this every week."

I'd prefer every day. But sitting in that red plastic chair for thirty minutes every week probably feels like plenty to Ruby.

Logging on is a challenge. The news from home feels odd.

> ... *great Super Bowl game, the underdog*
> *NY Giants won ... I'll never teach again at a*
> *poor school where the parents won't partici-*
> *pate ... I'm up to 72 miles of jogging for the*
> *year ... we look forward to your pictures ...*

That world feels beyond my reach. I can't quite remember what it's like to be there. I send a brief message to let everyone know I'm okay.

DAY 9
FRIDAY, FEBRUARY 8, 2008

Ruby stands at the stove, frying eggs. Unlike her usual clothes—skirts and T-shirts—today she's resplendent in traditional dress: white leather sandals, a white cotton skirt that falls just above her ankles, a deep red short-sleeved shirt, and a black vest trimmed with rows of colorful ribbon. A wide hand-beaded belt in pink, blue, and green diamond patterns circles her waist. Cylindrical beaded ropes adorn her neck and wrists; stunning against her ebony skin. She wears the same wig as the day she picked me up at the airport.

"You look beautiful, Ruby!"

She backs away from the stove and turns a slow circle in the center of the kitchen. "Thank you, Karen. My husband likes to see me dressed as a traditional woman. He has given me permission to leave my head uncovered today."

"Can I take your picture?" I ask, swallowing my discomfort with her excitement over having Mhambi's *permission*.

Her smile broadens. She strikes a pose in the open doorway to the yard, standing tall, her shoulders back with one hand propped on the door frame. The other hangs gracefully at her side. She's gorgeous—the epitome of an African woman.

Jealousy stabs my heart; my typical response in the presence of foreign cultures where heritage feels deep and meaningful. I envy Ruby's ability to claim her culture with something as simple as clothing. As long as I can remember I've ached to belong to something bigger than my immediate family.

It's been easier since I made a pilgrimage to Scotland in search of my heritage. There, my body responded to the weather, food, and music in ways that surprised and delighted me. For the first time in my life I felt anchored, proud of my lineage. My ancestors have two tartans: green and yellow for work, blue and red for festivals. I love wearing them to Scottish gatherings. They take me back to sitting on stone walls in the sheep-herding region of Scotland. But they still don't identify me as an American woman.

How do we Americans identify ourselves? Blue jeans and T-shirts? Navy blue business suits and pumps? Pearls? A Betty Crocker apron? Do we even *want* to be identified as Americans? Our clothes say a lot about our economic status but not much else.

» » » « « «

The two-hour ride to Durban takes us through lush farmland and an occasional small village. As we draw closer to the coast, villages give way to suburban towns and the four-lane road becomes a wide highway with frequent tollbooths. Our trip is uneventful except for the overturned onion truck where I learn a valuable lesson about South African economics: there is no waste. One man cannot guard every onion rolling across the pavement into fields alongside the highway. We can't be more than ten minutes behind the accident and already news of free onions has spread. By the time a tow truck arrives to upright the onion truck, every pantry within walking distance of the road will overflow with fresh, sweet yellow onions, an extravagant addition to putu and cabbage.

As we exit the freeway in Durban on a ramp high above the city streets, I catch a glimpse of the harbor, the busiest port in Sub-Saharan Africa. Enormous mechanical loaders loom over the docks, reminding me of the Port of Oakland in California. Cargo ships leaving Durban stop in Madagascar, Kenya, and Somalia before crossing the Arabian Sea to India. My imagination conjures up romantic images of rich spices and exotic cargo traded over ancient routes.

My childhood included vacations on the white sand beaches of the Gulf of Mexico and the Atlantic shore. As an adult I've enjoyed the Pacific Ocean from the warm waters of Hawaii and Mexico to the frigid Gulf of Alaska. Now I have a chance to experience the Indian Ocean. Water holds such emotional power; I'm eager to wade where the runoff from the African jungle mingles with the Ganges River. Will I feel the history of Africa and the deep traditions of India? I imagine myself standing knee-deep in this magical ocean, soaking in all that the water has to share.

We continue down the curving off-ramp and dump into the filth of the hotel district service alley. Against the rear walls of the hotels, plastic garbage bags lie heaped, ripped open by animals—or hungry street people. Their contents spill over the curb, under the wheels of traffic, and swirl in the steamy air that spews from sidewalk vents. There's no pedestrian traffic this early in the day, but the stench of urine and piles of human feces are unmistakable. My stomach turns.

One block down the narrow alley, we enter the Royal Hotel parking garage. Ruby is nervous, uncertain of her ability to negotiate the tight turns of the spiral ramp. We park on the fourth floor, the designated level for conference attendees, and cross the footbridge over the alley. She's as excited about being in a high-rise hotel as I am about my visit to the beach and outdoor market after the conference.

We enter the hotel through ornately carved wooden doors and pause for a few seconds to let our eyes adjust to the dim light. Thickly upholstered furniture, arranged in intimate seating groups, lines the hotel hallway. The dark wood, similar in color to Ruby's skin, is polished to a high sheen. It glows in the soft yellow light that penetrates the stained-glass windows. We locate our conference room: a plain room with beige walls, folding tables, cafeteria-style chairs, and a podium in front. The curtains are drawn, leaving only the light from the overhead fluorescent fixtures.

We're the last to arrive. The other teachers—thirty-five women and two men, all Zulu—are gathered at the front of the room. They wear typical city clothes: khaki trousers, shirts, and ties for the men; conservative skirts and blouses for the women. Every other day Ruby would blend right in. Today though, being the only woman dressed in traditional attire, she's lavished with compliments.

Without any introductions from Ruby, I'm already known as "the white woman from America who teaches at Zinti." It takes only a few minutes before the teachers surround me, each determined to stand closer than the others. The crush of warm bodies unnerves me. Their concept of personal space and my comfort zone are two entirely different things. Unlike America, where I'm taller than most women, here my height is average and I can't breathe over their heads. Their damp skin and warm breath threaten to suffocate me. I feel faint. I need fresh air. Only my fear of being rude prevents me from pushing my way out of the crowd.

With deep resonant voices, they fire questions at me in heavily accented English. Where are you from? How do you like South Africa? What does your husband say about you being here? Do you like our food? Has Ruby fed you putu? How long will you be here? Is Ruby taking good care of you? They're easy questions; nothing I haven't already answered, but I struggle to hear them over the side conversations they have going with each other in Zulu. Their questions come so quickly I need to ignore one woman to answer another. Patience doesn't seem to be their strong suit; they poke me with their fingers to elicit faster responses.

The emcee calls the conference to order. I'm relieved to retreat to a seat at the back of the room where Ruby joins me. She feels like my life-line.

"They are all very excited to see you," she whispers in my ear. "You are the first white person to teach in our rural schools. They are very eager to speak with you."

She seems pleased that it's going so well. Confusion reigns in my mind. I have no idea what to say. I'm happy to be here, startled by my apparent celebrity status, and uncomfortable with their style of interaction. My intention to be an observer at this conference feels naive.

The Director of Rural Education speaks briefly to everyone in Zulu before switching to English. He introduces me as an "honored guest from America" and announces that I'll be speaking later in the program about how American schools promote literacy and writing skills for their learners.

Surprise, Karen! At least I have a little warning to come up with something reasonable to say. I dig through memories of Kevin's elementary school days—twenty years ago—dredging up recollections of his homework assignments and the back-to-school night academic plans laid out by his teachers. I scribble notes on a pad of beautiful hotel stationery.

Our first speaker, director of the South African School Library Department, presents strategies for improving literacy by putting books in the kids' hands and encouraging each school to implement a lending library. School sanctioned trips to local city libraries highlight his plan. The teachers nod their heads in agreement. It sounds great. It also reeks of the same bureaucratic nonsense I hear so often at home. He's said nothing about funding these projects. One week at Zinti has already provided enough ammunition to shoot holes in his proposal: there are no school buses; parents don't own cars; the school can't even afford consistent electricity, much less books. I want to scream. At least Zinti will have the two-hundred or so books I brought, even if some of them are used.

He finishes his presentation and opens the floor for Q&A. No one asks the obvious. Maybe *I* should. But it feels too much like stirring the pot and would definitely spoil my plan to keep a low profile. The teachers applaud politely before they jump from their seats and rush toward me. I stand behind my table for a little extra breathing room.

This time their questions are more tricky: Why did you choose Zinti? Are the children at Zinti good English speakers? How do you structure your English lessons? What is the most important lesson when teaching English? I look for Ruby to come to my rescue. She stands at the edge of the group, clucking away in Zulu with friends she rarely sees. Apparently she thinks I'm okay on my own.

"Zinti is an accident of fate," I say. I want to explain, but no one listens to my answers. They should know that I'm not a professional teacher—just a woman who helped her own child through school, who enjoys working with kids, who has a simple desire to do something useful.

"Verb tenses are important. Sentence structure is also key." I haven't spent much energy thinking about their lessons this way. The children's English is so poor, simple repetition is valuable. "I make them repeat their sentences using proper grammar and pronunciation."

When the session is called back to order, I drop into my chair, my heart pounding as I begin to absorb the enormity of what they want from me. I'll never live up to their expectations. Post-Apartheid, parents have been promised education, freedom, financial success and equality for their children. And English, they seem to believe, is the key to it all. If the kids master English, doors will burst open and their world will expand to meet the American and European standard of living.

Their perspective feels accurate to some degree—English may be the preferred language of commerce around the world. Their perspective lacks a few key elements, though. Apartheid has officially ended, but racial inequities are far from over. Less than half the kids at Zinti will graduate from high school. Zinti, better situated than many of the rural schools, is still forty minutes from the nearest possible opportunity for employment. Very few rural families own cars. If they're able to scrape together coombie fare, they must walk three miles to the main road to catch the coombie. Aside from their school uniforms, most of the kids have one set of clothes and one pair of rubber flip-flops. If they do make it to town, they'll find the available jobs have already been filled by white workers or Zulus who have been fortunate enough to be raised in the city school system. Unemployment in South Africa stands at sixty percent.

Progress with English is slow for the rural kids. They don't even have a chance to practice at home because most of their parents speak only Zulu. These teachers have an awful lot of hope riding on me. I feel inextricably deflated. I miss most of the next presentation wondering how I have become so discouraged in less than a week. How did I ever believe I could make a difference? Still, that's why I'm here: to teach English; to provide an opportunity that might change a child's destiny.

When we break for lunch a hotel employee leads the entire group to the dining room on the tenth floor. From there I catch another glimpse of the Indian Ocean. Palm trees, their fronds waving in the breeze, line the boardwalk. Gentle waves lap against the white sand. I'd prefer to take a walk alone on the beach rather than deal with the current argument over who will sit next to me at lunch. Women cram nine chairs around a table intended for six. I feel myself slump into a stupor, albeit with a smile forced across my face. This is not fun.

Our buffet includes chopped lettuce swimming in oil and vinegar, beef-and-chicken stew covered with a layer of orange grease, potato salad slathered in mayonnaise, marsh-mallows and pineapple chunks molded in red Jell-O. And for dessert: chocolate cake with thick butter cream frosting. After a few bites, my stomach feels like I've spent the morning in a small boat rolling on stormy seas.

"Do you think it is fair that the children at Zinti have you and our children do not?" asks one woman.

"I think *all* the kids deserve to be well educated. It would be ..."

"Why did you choose Zinti? Do they pay you?"

"No! No one is paying me to be here. I'm ..."

"Good. Then you can come to my school, too!" one teacher says. This idea catches on quickly with the others.

"I don't know if that's possible," I say. "I promised my three months to Zinti, then I need to go home."

"Three months! That is enough time for you to visit many

schools. You should not be the one who determines where you teach. We should make that decision."

Their conversation with each other, all in Zulu now, grows heated.

"But I'm staying with Ruby," I say. "I don't even have my own transportation."

"That is not your concern," someone says. "You tell us where Ruby lives. We will pick you up and drive you to our schools."

"You should teach at every school to be fair to our children," another says.

"You will like our school even more than Zinti," someone else says. "We are in the most beautiful region of Natal, and we will feed you well."

This can't be happening. I look for Ruby to come to my rescue. She's seated with others at a table near the window. As the representative from the only rural school in KwaZulu-Natal to have a white teacher, she's enjoying her own celebrity circus.

There's no point in answering any of their questions; I can't give them what they want. The noise fades away as I pull into myself. I watch them like a silent movie, waving their arms in conversation as food dribbles from their mouths. They eat as though it's been days since they've seen food. They suck the last drop of juice off the chicken bones. Grease spreads over their mouths and chins, runs down their fingers, drips onto the white linen table cloth. Plates of dessert are piled high in the center of the table, insurance that they have plenty before the buffet closes.

"You do not eat much. You look very weak. You must eat to keep your strength," one woman says as she pokes my ribs. "When you come to my village we will feed you better than Ruby does."

"Ruby feeds me fine. I'm just not hungry." My voice sounds frail.

"May I have your cake?" she asks.

"Sure."

» » »   « « «

It's an overwhelming effort to stand and address the conference this afternoon. The front of the room feels too far
away; I choose to speak from my table. As they turn to listen I decide to shorten the speech I've mentally prepared. I
focus on creative writing.

"Children must be encouraged to use their imaginations,"
I say. "Have them write about whatever interests them. They
can write about their families, their villages. Or they can
even make something up. They should have time every day
to write at least one page. The more they write, the better
they'll get. And the better they get, the more they'll want to
write."

I pause to think of something else I can add. I've seen the
teachers at Zinti wield their red pens like weapons.

"Don't be too hasty about correcting their spelling and
punctuation. At least not at first. You don't want to discourage them. Praise them for being creative. Once they're excited about writing, then you can begin to correct their work.
Children who like to write also like to read."

The applause I receive is unwarranted. My face burns as
I slink into my chair. As the emcee prepares to release everyone for another break, I slip through the door at the rear of
the room. I race down the hallway to the ladies' room, into
an empty stall. I hear them looking for me in the hallway. I
lock the door behind me, sit on the toilet lid, prop my feet
against the back of the door, my skirt wrapped up around
my legs so no one can see me if they peek under the door.

I breathe in silent, metered inhalations as I attempt to
calm my nerves and sort through my thoughts. Who *deserves*
me is exactly the opposite of how I feel about being here.
This is crazy. I don't deserve this kind of attention. Just
because I care? They should at least wait until I accomplish
something. This was supposed to be simple—I come, I help,
I go home. I've been caught short. Too late to turn back.

That wouldn't be my preference anyway. I hate quitting. I'm adaptable. I can make this work. Surely I can.

On the ride home Ruby says nothing about our abandoned trip to the market and beach. She's worried about preparing Mhambi's dinner on time. The maid will take care of Granny GuGu and the boys.

"You know, Ruby, they all want me to teach at their schools. They say they'll come and pick me up at your house. Take me around to visit each school."

The grin on her face hints this is just as she intended. "I will see to this," she says.

» » »   « « «

Mhambi eats his fried chicken and cabbage in front of the television. The boys and Granny GuGu are in their rooms, as always. Invisible. Ruby and I eat at the table. The rooibos tea soothes my tummy. The spoon under the edge of my plate works beautifully. No one talks.

Ruby retreats to the back of the house to iron. Rolina has ironed everyone else's clothes. It seems Mhambi can only wear clothes that Ruby irons.

I join Mhambi in the living room. He turns down the volume on the television for our ritual of nightly conversation over soccer. "So, Karen," he asks, "how was your trip to Durban?"

"It's a beautiful drive. I enjoyed seeing more of your country."

"And the conference?"

"The conference was odd. I didn't expect the type of reaction I received."

"In what way did it not meet your expectations?" He sounds concerned.

"I'm afraid that everyone expects too much of me. They each want a piece of me, as if I'm doing something fabulous. And really I haven't done much of anything yet. I'm not even sure I can accomplish what I came to do."

"You are quite wrong, Karen," he says. "Think of it this way. You are a white woman from America who has come to help our children without asking anything in return. Your presence alone is enough to change the life of every person you meet here. You are giving the gift of reconciliation, the gift of hope. You must allow our people to show you their gratitude."

It didn't feel like gratitude. And reconciliation is more than I signed up for.

DAY 10
SATURDAY, FEBRUARY 9, 2008

The house is so quiet this morning, I stop in the living room to listen for sounds of life. Granny's lilting voice floats down the hall from the bathroom, along with the sound of gently splashing water in the tub. I tippy-toe into the kitchen to make tea, stopping short when I see Ruby. Bent over the kitchen sink, her elbows propped on the counter like someone in the midst of vomiting, she keeps her face down, tilted away from me as I approach.

"Ruby, are you okay?" I lay my hand on her shoulder.

As she turns toward me, I see a coat hanger in her hand, opened into a straight piece of wire. She's been crying.

"Ruby, what's wrong?"

She turns away without a word and plunges the wire up and down in the stagnant, dirty water in the sink. "The water will not leave my sink," she says. "I do not know what is wrong."

"It looks like the drain is clogged."

She looks at me as if my words make no sense. "I must have clean dishes to prepare my husband's mid-day meal. Soon the clothes washer will empty. I have put a pail under the pipe to catch the soapy water."

My mind races through the scenario she's described. The washing machine empties via a pipe that pokes through the front wall of the house. I've seen the gray water splash onto the lawn. Washing dishes in dirty laundry water feels even worse than the kids at Zinti rinsing their lunch plates in cold water from the well spigot.

"Can I take a look?" I ask, as she continues to stab at the drain.

Inspecting the plumbing takes little effort—the cabinet under the sink has no doors. The coat hanger has poked a hole in the rotting rubber pipe. Water seeps into the cabinet, runs along the edge of the curling, yellowed shelf paper, and spills out onto the floor in front of Ruby's feet. I imagine her standing in a puddle of water electrocuting herself while she monitors the toaster.

"Stop! Ruby, wait. Hold the wire still. Look down here."

She stoops to look at the pipes. "Now I have a new problem. There is water coming out into my cabinet." She begins to cry.

"It's okay, Ruby." I push a sauce pan under the leak. "See, it's all connected. Here's the end of your coat hanger. It poked a hole through the pipe."

She reaches to pull the wire from the drain.

"No, no. Leave it there," I say. "If we pull it out, the water will leak faster. Let's leave it where it is while we decide what to do."

Ruby resumes her stance at the counter, her head in her hands. Perspiration drips from her forehead into the dirty water. I take a closer look at the plumbing: a hodge-podge of worn rubber pipes wrapped with layers of yellowed and cracked scotch tape, spongy to the touch, nearly rotted away. The kitchen's already somewhat of a disaster. Only two of the four stove burners work. Knives and silverware are thrown together in one drawer that no longer slides. Yesterday, the door between the kitchen and hallway fell off the hinges. Now it's propped against the stove, held in place by two concrete blocks wrapped in newspaper.

"When will Mhambi be home?" I ask. "Maybe we can do the dishes in the bathtub until he has a chance to fix the pipes."

The look on Ruby's face says, "you have no idea what you're talking about."

"What? We can't use the bathtub?"

"It is my responsibility to keep the house in proper condition," she says. "My husband will just say, 'Figure it out, woman.' He will not accept an excuse for his meal being late."

I try to conceal my disgust with a smile. "Maybe I can fix

it," I say, motivated by desire to eat from clean dishes. My eager response runs ahead of my experience. I've *never* made plumbing repairs! But it doesn't look *that* complicated. "Is there a store in town that sells pipe?"

"There is the shop owned by the Pakistani man. He sells all the things that are necessary to keep a home in good working order."

"Well, let's go."

"How will you know what to ask for?"

"Hmm." I pause for a moment. Good thing she asks. "I can take pictures of the pipes and take my camera along to show him what it looks like now. Then he can sell me the right pieces." The photos will also help me remember what it looks like after I've taken it all apart.

» » » « « «

Near the hardware store, streets are full of trash, storefronts are narrow, thick steel bars cover every window, and the paint on the dilapidated wooden doors has faded to mere hints of red and blue. Groups of men, dressed in oil-stained khaki pants and threadbare T-shirts, smoke cigarettes while they linger at the curb. Ruby and I are the only women in sight.

She jumps out of the car and strikes up a loud conversation with the men. You'd never guess she was crying over her sink thirty minutes ago. If I didn't know better, I'd swear she's flirting with them. The only conversation I catch is Ruby's question to one of the men about his many wives. He smiles, revealing a few brown teeth, and offers to take her as his next wife.

The door to the hardware shop hangs on loose hinges, held open by a well-placed hump in the pavement. I step through the narrow entrance, leaving Ruby in the street, laughing with the men. Inside, light filters through one filthy window at the rear of the shop. As my eyes adjust to the dimness, I realize I'm standing in a customer service area that is barely four feet wide, eight feet long, and caged from floor to ceiling by a cyclone fence. Small openings in the fence allow shop workers and customers to exchange money. Merchandise too large to fit through the small openings can be delivered to customers through a padlocked gate at the rear of the service area.

Behind the fence is a narrow wooden counter. Behind the counter, rows of tall metal shelves overflow with rusty coffee cans filled with screws, rulers, and hand tools. On the floor, piles of pipes, in all shapes and sizes, spill out into the aisles. Cobwebs hang between the dusty shelves, giving the impression that the shop was abandoned years ago and only today the shop keeper threw his doors open again for business. I feel discouraged. It will take hours—if it's even possible at all—to find the parts we need.

The shop owner, Mr. Bhojani, an immigrant from southern Pakistan, greets me with a friendly smile. "Some day I will visit your fine country," he says. "My brother and his family live in New Jersey." Despite his heavy accent, his English is precise. He insists that I must see all of South Africa while I'm here, especially the coast near Cape Town.

"One moment," he says, holding his finger up to indicate that I should wait, "I have something for you." He disappears behind the shelves. When he returns, he unfolds a pocket map of South Africa on the counter and points out the regions he finds most beautiful. "You will like our country. I know you will." He refolds the map and slides it to me through the opening. "Now, what can I do for you?"

I hold my camera up to the fence to show him the plumbing configuration I want to build.

"Ah, no problem, Ma'am," he smiles. "I will be right back."

In record time he gathers rubber pipes and metal fasteners that resemble my photos and spreads them out on the counter in front of me. I'm impressed.

"Do you have tools?" he asks.

I step out of the shop to grab Ruby. She finishes her conversation with her head thrown back in a full belly laugh.

"What tools will I need?" I ask Mr. Bhojani.

"You will need a sharp knife to cut the hoses to the proper size, and a screwdriver to fasten the metal bands around the pipes."

"I have sharp knives in my kitchen," Ruby says. "And I have two screwdrivers."

"Perhaps you would like to purchase a utility knife," he offers. "It is more suited for this type of work and we would not want to ruin Ma'am's fine cooking knives."

"That sounds good," I say. "I'll take a utility blade. Anything else?"

"Once you have cut the pipes to the proper length, you will need rubber cement to glue them in place."

I love that he coaches me through the process without making me feel stupid. I glance at Ruby. "Glue?"

She shakes her head.

"I guess I'll need glue, too."

Mr. Bhojani totals my bill. Two-hundred rand for new kitchen plumbing, only twenty-six dollars, seems reasonable, even cheap compared to plumbers' wages. Definitely a fair price to pay for Ruby's peace of mind and eating from clean dishes.

He hands me the bag through the gate. "Remember to cut the pipe a little bit at a time. This way you will not cut it too short and need to return for more pipe. Slip the wire bands over the pipe before you glue the ends together. And don't glue any pipe until you have cut all the pieces to their proper size. It is best if you assemble it all and make certain it works as you need before you glue anything."

"Thank you so much," I say, grateful for the crash course in Plumbing 101. "Your instructions are very helpful."

On the street, Ruby makes one last flirtatious display before we head home. Her silence in the car affords me the opportunity to wallow in my confusion. If it's a wife's responsibility to make home repairs, why were we the only women at the hardware store? Why do the men linger around outside? Is it a good place to pick up women? The good traditional women who are busy taking care of their homes? If what Ruby says is true, that most of the men have more than one wife, how does that happen without the women having more than one husband? Is the ratio of women to men that overwhelming? If it is, why? I have so many questions, so little confidence in which questions are acceptable.

"Thank you for purchasing the pipes for my sink," Ruby says as we approach her street. "It is most generous of you. I have only two-hundred rand left until I receive my next pay and I still need to buy food for my family."

"You're welcome. It's the least I can do. I appreciate your hospitality."

Ruby washes our breakfast dishes in the bathtub and pre- pares lunch for Mhambi while I dive into my project. The pipes are covered with a thick layer of sludge that's oozed through the rotting rubber. The disposable latex gloves I brought along, intended to protect against poop germs while caring for the kids in the village, come in handy. Using a pan, I scoop most of the water from the sink and dump it on the grass out front before I slide it under the drain to catch the rest of the water while I disassemble the old plumbing. Removing the old pipes is harder than I expected. I resort to cutting them out, one at a time, rinsing each piece at the spig- ot out front before I set them aside. Following Mr. Bhojani's instructions, I cut the new pipes an inch at a time, measuring them against the old pieces. The new configuration doesn't match the photos exactly, but it works.

Two hours into my project, Mhambi and the boys arrive home. They watch from the doorway: Mhambi with a dead- pan expression, his arms folded across his chest; Thulani and Siphelele with their mouths agape.

"Haybo! Miss Karen," Thulani says. "What are you doing? Can I take a photo of you?"

"I'm fixing the pipes so they won't clog or leak. You can

take my picture if you want. My camera is right there on the counter."

"Karen, you are a very talented woman," Mhambi says. "Ruby is fortunate to have your assistance."

I look up from the floor and smile for Thulani's photo. None of them offer to help. The boys take their plates of bologna sandwiches to their room. Heat rises in my face as I hear the television flip on in the living room. The African national soccer championship has already begun. Ruby rushes to the living room with Mhambi's sandwiches and tea on his favorite tray. I swallow my resentment and ask Ruby for her screwdrivers. She returns from the garage, empty handed.

"Karen, I cannot find them," she says, a look of despair on her face. "They are not where I expected." She digs through the kitchen drawer and hands me a small butter knife. "Here. You may use this instead."

"Are you sure you want me to use this, Ruby? It might get bent. Ruined. Maybe we should go back to the hardware store."

"The shop is open only until mid-day. We cannot go back now. They will not open again until Monday. It is okay to use the knife, I have done it myself. You must not worry. I have many more if this one is damaged."

After four hours, and only one cut on my finger, Ruby and I stand next to each other and watch the water run down the drain. Plumbing, it turns out, isn't that tricky. I'm proud of my success. I'm also happy to see the smile on Ruby's face.

"Thank you." She wraps her arm around my shoulder and gives me a tight squeeze. "I am very happy that my sink works well again. Thank you very much, Karen."

We eat our sandwiches and tea at the counter, enjoying the delicious breeze through the top half of the Dutch door. Zulu family roles seem well defined now. Mhambi's role is to go to work, demand meals, watch soccer, play the organ, and come and go as he pleases without explaining his whereabouts or when he might be home. Ruby's role is to go to work, do the shopping, keep the house and her car in running order, fix meals, wash dishes, iron Mhambi's clothes, clean Mhambi's briefcase, and care for Mhambi's mother. Siphelele and Thulani's roles are to be invisible until Mhambi needs someone to find the TV remote, wash his car, or polish his shoes.

I squirm with discomfort, remembering my family in the early sixties. I expected gender inequities here, but I didn't anticipate that they would hit so close to home. It's probably still the case for many American families. I've just become so complacent in my own life that I've forgotten the struggles that women still face. First hand experience of discrimination makes it all fresh again. I can't change it; that's not my purpose here. But I can work at being more aware and sympathetic.

Ruby hugs me again as I head for my room. She slips a can of "Doom!" bug spray into my hands, my reward for making her life easier. Tonight I'll sleep without smacking mosquitoes.

DAY 11

I beg off going to church today. No one questions my difficulty coping with the extreme heat. Ruby promises me a trip to the Internet café this afternoon; I promise her an American spaghetti dinner tonight. Spar Grocery only carries Ragu brand sauce, but even that doesn't squelch my desire for familiar food.

The family locks the chain around the gate as they leave. Trapped on the property, I wave good-bye, thrilled to have several hours to myself. I pull my green plastic lawn chair out under the shade of the fiberglass awning to enjoy my tea and toast. Overhead, dozens of large gray birds, reminiscent of the pterodactyls in Kevin's childhood dinosaur books, fly in well-formed circles, creating a murky halo over the property. Their raucous "caw-caws" demand attention.

For the first time since my arrival, I feel calm enough to focus on a book. Elizabeth Gilbert's travels in *Eat, Pray, Love* feel like an enchanted fantasy. Have I invented romance for her situation that I just can't see in my own? I take to my journal to sort through the myriad of contradictions that jumble my mind. Away from home for only ten days, I already feel unmoored from all things "normal."

» » » « « «

I'm wakened from my nap by a wild pounding on my door. "Karen! Come quick. Karen. Do you hear me? Come quick. You must see this!"

I fly out of bed and open my door. Thulani's eyes dance with a boyish grin. "Miss Karen, you will not believe what I will show you. Come with me."

I slip into my Crocs and hurry after him across the patio, through the house, to the kitchen door, where Ruby stands, hands on her hips, a dishtowel slung over her shoulder. "Aye, Karen," she laughs. "You see. I told you there are monkeys."

I peek over her shoulder. Dozens of monkeys have invaded the front yard. About eighteen inches tall, with long tails, white beards, and deep amber eyes ringed with a black mask, some swing from the house gutter to the carport awning, to the cross beams on the fence while others sit perched on the mailbox, the brick wall, even Ruby's car.

"Oh, my gosh, it's amazing. Look at all of them!" I squeal.

"Where is your camera?" Thulani asks. "I will bring it for you to take pictures."

"On the shelf in my closet," I say, without turning around. I don't want to miss even one minute of their antics.

"You must not let them come very close to you," Ruby says. "They carry nasty disease. They will steal food from your room if you leave it in their sight." She pauses. "All that remains now is for you to see the zebras in the forest over there." She nods toward the jungle-covered vacant lot across the street. "You will see."

She might still be teasing about *some* things.

» » » « « «

Thulani and Siphelele heap their plates with second helpings of my spaghetti—ground beef sautéed with onions and garlic, smothered with a jar of Ragu sauce. Ruby turns her face inside-out as she forks little bites into her mouth, trying not to let it touch her lips.

"I do not know, Karen," she says. "I thought I would like American food. But this is something I am sure I do not want to eat again."

"I'm sorry, Ruby. How about next time I'll make something different?"

"Yes. Something different would be better."

I follow Ruby to the kitchen with her half-eaten meal. "Now I must make my husband's meal," she says.

"Mhambi doesn't like my spaghetti either?" My cooking's not *that* bad.

"It is not that. My husband is a traditional man. He eats only food that I prepare."

» » »   « « «

I sit alone with Mhambi in the living room watching him eat putu and fried cabbage. I thought I was doing Ruby a favor by fixing dinner. Not only does she hate my meal, but she has to cook for Mhambi anyway.

"Karen," Mhambi says. "May I ask you something rather personal?"

"Sure." It can't be more personal than me asking why they cut their kids' faces.

"Are you a healer?"

Of all the things he could have asked, why this? I feel cornered. It feels like a question with a definite right and wrong answer. I stall for time. "What do you mean by healer?"

"There are people who use their extraordinary power to inflict harm on others. And there are people who have special power to bring good to others. These are the healers."

His definition eases my concern. "I believe I am a healer. I try hard not to hurt anyone."

"Yes!" He leans back in his chair, pumps his fist in the air. "I have told my wife that you are not like other white people. You have a special ability to bring healing to those around you. It is an honor to have you in our home."

Mhambi touches something deep in my heart that wants to grow. But I sense an edge to the pedestal he has placed me on.

DAY 12

Commotion at the rear of the room interrupts morning assembly. An eerie hush falls over the room as the Grade Four students move out of line and form a circle. They stare at the floor in the center of the circle. Phyllis, without a word, walks along the windows to the back of the room. Ruby and I fall in behind her.

The ring of students parts, revealing a boy lying on the floor—his back arched, legs drawn to his chest in the fetal position, arms flailing against the concrete floor. He's in the midst of a gran mal seizure. As his chin twists up over his shoulder, his eyes roll backward in their sockets.

It's been over twelve years since my son's last seizure. Still, the mom in me takes over. Instinct drops me to my knees beside this boy. I pull his head into my lap to cushion the blows of his spasms. Behind me, a collective inhalation sucks the remaining noise from the room. Compelled by the stored memories of my experience with Kevin, I gather the boy's arms close to his chest and hold them tight with one arm while I stroke his head with my other hand.

"You'll be okay," I whisper in his ear. "You're safe. It'll be over soon. I'm here. You're safe." Over and over I repeat the familiar reassurances. My tears drip onto his shirt as I rock back and forth on my knees. It's as though I'm holding Kevin once again, waiting out his torturous seizure. Kevin told me once that the scariest part of his seizure was when he tried to talk to me and I didn't answer. "I screamed and screamed for you," he said. "Why did you ignore me?" Whatever he heard in his mind, never made it to my ears.

As this boy's seizure subsides, I lean over, kiss his forehead. His body falls limp in my arms. I recall my fear the first time Kevin slept for twenty hours following a seizure. "Having a one minute seizure," his doctor told me, "takes the same amount of physical energy as running a marathon."

Phyllis dismisses the students from assembly. They leave in whispers. Some, eager to be as far away as possible, race to their classrooms. Others linger outside the door.

"He will be okay now," Phyllis says. "This happens quite frequently. The spirits take hold of him, but they do not stay long."

"He had a seizure," I say, my voice flat.

The boy's eyelids flutter.

"He has epilepsy."

"What do you mean by that?" Phyllis asks.

I look up for the first time. Phyllis, Ruby and two other teachers stand at a distance. "It's a brain condition," I say. "Too much electrical energy in the brain. This is what happens when it builds up beyond the brain's ability to contain it."

"I do not know about that," Phyllis dismisses my explanation. "He will be fine. But see, he has wet himself. This is an embarrassment for the other children. We must not fuss over him."

"He needs to sleep now," I say. "Can we send for his mother or father to come pick him up and take him home?"

"That is not necessary. We must take him out into the daylight where his pants will dry."

Phyllis nods at two of the oldest boys and instructs them in Zulu. They drag the epileptic boy by his arms, out of my lap, across the floor, outside onto the concrete walkway where they position him against the brick wall. Limp, like a rag doll, he lies with his mouth open. One of the boys kneels beside him, makes the sign of the cross, closes his eyes, and begins to pray.

I raise my eyebrows at Phyllis.

"The boy is praying for the evil spirits to release his friend. He does this every time." She taps the praying boy on the shoulder, nodding for him to be on his way. Phyllis moves along the walkway, ushering the last of the kids ahead of her. "Come Karen, we must resume our lessons."

"Wait. We can't just leave him here." Leave him to sleep on concrete? No. What if he rolls off the narrow walk, falls two feet to the dirt and cracks his head on the brick steps in the process? No!

"He will come to class when he is ready," Phyllis says.

"Can't we at least take him someplace where he's more safe? Like maybe down to the library? Give him something soft to sleep on?"

"Very well. We must not waste any more time. We shall do as you ask." Phyllis calls down the hill to the man from the village who is "not right in the head" to carry the boy to the library. "You must go teach your lessons now, Karen."

I drag my feet along the dirt path. From the top of the hill I watch the man carry the limp boy into the library where Phyllis flattens an empty cardboard box on the floor. The man lays the boy on the box as Phyllis wads an old jacket into a bundle and sticks it under his head. I step into my classroom, satisfied that this is at least an improvement over a concrete ledge.

Of all the things I tried to anticipate for this journey, revisiting Kevin's epileptic years wasn't included. I'm exhausted.

» » »   « « «

Phyllis sounds the lunch siren. I hurry down the hill, eager to check on the epileptic boy. He's gone. There's no trace of the cardboard or make-shift pillow. From my seat at the lunch table I scan the hillside through the windows hoping to catch a glimpse of him, although it's hard to imagine he has his energy back already. Maybe they've sent him home after all. No one says a word about this morning's trauma.

Phyllis lingers in the lunch room after Ruby and Pamela return to their classrooms. This hour of the day, waiting for the younger children to come spend time with me after their classes are dismissed, always drags.

"I see that you have displayed the new books for our learners," Phyllis says.

I nod. "I've arranged them more or less by reading level. The easiest are on the top shelf. The most difficult are on the bottom."

"Perhaps we should begin to send the children to the library to choose a book to read."

"That would be great. Maybe I can help them read out loud."

Phyllis's chin drops to her chest. Her downtrodden look deflates my enthusiasm about the new books. "What we really need," she says with a labored sigh, "is for our learners to be computer literate. If they expect to find jobs in the city they must know how to operate a computer."

She jogs my memory about some research I did before leaving home. "You know, Phyllis, there's an organization called One Laptop per Child. They're amazing. They provide indestructible laptops for underprivileged kids around the world. Maybe we could work with them to get computers for Zinti."

"We do not need their computers! We already have our own."

I jerk my head back, eyes wide. "You do?"

"Zinti is one of the fortunate schools. We have fifteen brand new computers!"

How did I miss this? "Where are they?"

"Come with me. You will see."

She marches from the room, her chin jutted forward, shoulders back, head high. In the office she pulls the bungee key strap from around her wrist, unlocks the corner closet, revealing a six-by-six storage space. Inside, stacked to the ceiling, are cardboard boxes still wrapped with their original strapping tape. Each one reads: DELL – THE POWER TO DO MORE.

"Holy cow! You do have computers. Lots of them."

"We have fifteen brand new computers. We are very proud of them."

Rightfully so. I hesitate before probing further. "Did you just get them recently?"

"No. We received them last year. Along with the computer desks and rolling chairs in the library. We would have received them earlier, but we were not prepared. Before we could accept them we needed first to provide adequate protection."

"What do you mean?"

"If anyone in the village learned that we had computers, and they were not properly protected, they would be gone overnight. Sold on the black market. Zinti spent a great deal of money on security for them. We had iron bars welded to the windows of the library. We replaced the old wooden door with a steel door with strong locks. And we put razor wire in the ceiling."

"In the ceiling? Whoa!"

"There is no use in securing the windows and door if they can still gain entrance through the roof."

Good point, albeit not one I would have thought of on my own. Now that she mentions it, this storage room is bricked over and has a steel door.

"So now that you're all prepared, maybe I can help set them up." I would love to do something productive between lunch and the little kid time.

Phyllis shakes her head. "We still have a problem. There are only two electric receptacles in the library. As you have seen, we do not always have adequate funds to maintain our electricity."

"Phyllis, I have friends in the computer industry. They would hate to know that you have all these beautiful computers and still lack the ability to use them. I know they'd help." It would be nothing for my IT friends to ship a box of industrial extension cords and surge protectors. And fifty dollars a month for the electric bill? That's nothing. They spend that much on one bottle of wine. I already have the email composed in my mind. "Before I left home, they all said, 'Let us know what we can do to help.' If I send a list of what we need, I bet it would be here next week. What do you think? In the meantime, I can set up the computers."

She pauses. She doesn't look nearly as thrilled as I expected. "Yes. That would be very kind. But we still have a problem. We do not have the necessary software to run the computers."

That's easy. "My friends have access to all kinds of software. I could probably get them to include some fun programs to teach the kids reading and math." They'd be all over that in a heartbeat. I nearly bounce with enthusiasm. This could be a great project.

Phyllis looks sullen. She puffs another weighty sigh.

I don't understand. I'm offering to solve her dilemma. In a week. Her school could rock. She takes a deep breath and sighs yet again as she steps out of the closet. "It is not as simple as you suggest," she says. "Many of our teachers do not know themselves how to operate a computer. It would be impossible for them to teach the children." She locks the closet door and drops into the chair behind her desk.

I sit across from her with my elbows propped on her desk, chin between my hands. I try to smile. "You know Phyllis, you might be surprised how quickly kids learn to use computers. It's like a game to them. They can learn anything they're excited about. And I can give computer lessons to the teachers. I can teach them computer basics and show them how to run the math and reading programs. It wouldn't be that hard. I bet by the end of April they'll be pros."

She looks at me as if I should know better. "And what would we do if the computers did not work probably?"

I sigh with exasperation. Her million excuses for why this can't happen frustrate me. She said herself that the kids need computer training. My friends are presidents and CEOs of IT firms. Yes, it would be self-serving, but they would love to be heroes to four-hundred kids in Africa. Why can't Phyllis jump at this opportunity?

"I can make sure they're working well before I leave. And if something happens to one of them, I'm sure we can sort it out one way or the other. I really do know some incredible people who'd love to help your students."

"We shall see," she concludes, adjusting her glasses on her nose. "I must finish my work now."

» » »   « « «

In stunned disbelief, I stare at the empty computer desks in the library while I wait for the little kids. Clearly this is not an issue of money. I'm missing something.

The kids slide across the slick floor in their stocking feet and clamber to see who can be first in my lap. They are the highlight of my day.

"Nose," I say, laying my index finger on the tip of my nose.

They look at each other with confused expressions. I touch the nose of the girl who stands in front of me. "Nose," I say again.

"Nose," they scream in unison as their fingers fly to their smiling faces.

» » »   « « «

From my bed I watch billowy, white clouds form in the patch of cerulean blue sky visible through my window. Feet propped on my backpack to lessen the swelling in my ankles, the sheer yellow drapes sway on the afternoon breeze. Bird and monkey chatter fills the air. My concrete room serves as respite from a world I don't comprehend.

Every day Phyllis hauls a beautiful laptop to school to pump out reports that the district office requires. Siphelele and Thulani have an old-model computer in their bedroom. They type their school reports and download them to a portable drive to print at the Internet café. Leslie said the Zinti teachers begged for books, yet they sit untouched on the library shelves. The curious dichotomy, between what they say they need and what they actually do when it's available, swirls through my mind.

Church hymns from Mhambi's electric organ float across the patio to my room, my signal that it's time to go see if Ruby wants help with dinner. She never does, but it feels rude not to offer.

"How was your day, Mhambi?" I ask, squeezing past the organ just inside the sliding door.

"It was very busy, as it always is. There is never a day that I am without a courtroom filled with vagrants of all kind."

"Your music is nice. Different from what I'm used to. What is it?"

"This is the year of the priest. Next Sunday we will have a special celebration to honor Father Mnganga. This is his favorite hymn. Do you play the organ, Karen?"

"No. I play piano."

Mhambi jumps up, offering me the bench. "You must play for me."

Heat rushes to my face. "I can't. I didn't bring any music."

"You must not be modest, Karen." He pulls the bench out for me. "If your music is different as you say, you must show me."

I sit, embarrassed; my hands in my lap. I should have kept my mouth shut. I have a grand total of two songs memorized—almost.

"Mhambi, I can't. Really. I can't play without music in front of me."

"You can read the music? Haybo!"

"That's the only way I know how to play. I'm not as talented as you."

"You are being too modest, Karen. You must play something for me."

Humiliated, I stumble through one piece.

"May I try now?" Without hesitation, Mhambi repeats my song as though he has known it all along.

"That's amazing," I say. "You have a real gift."

"Please play another song for me," he says.

"I can't. That's all I have memorized. I'm completely dependent on reading music."

"You are fortunate," he says. "Because you can read the music, you can learn any song, even one that you have never heard before."

He makes it sound more grand than it feels. I've always been jealous of people who can hear something once and play it by ear with such ease.

Mhambi folds his arms across his chest. "You must teach me to read the music, Karen."

"I'd be happy to." I've taught dozens of people over the years. It will give us something to do besides watching soccer. "Do you have staff paper?"

"Staff paper?"

"You know, the paper that music is written on."

"No. I have no such thing." He waits, expecting me to make another suggestion.

"I don't know how to teach without staff paper. There must be a store in town that sells music supplies."

"Yes. I will ask my wife. She will know where to find it. We shall begin my lessons tomorrow."

DAY 13

"Karen! You do not look well," Ruby says, frying the morning eggs.

"I have a sore throat. I'm dizzy, too. I don't think I can go to school today." Guilt overcomes me as I utter my complaints. She deals with this life every day and still manages to go to school.

"You must rest. I will tell my maid to prepare your lunch today."

"No, she doesn't have to do that."

"Do not argue with me. Rolina will care for you. I will tell the children at Zinti that you will return tomorrow."

Little inconveniences are taking a toll. Scratching my mosquito bites leaves my skin raw, susceptible to infection. The anti-itch cream melts off my skin. I skimp on fluids to avoid the pit toilets at Zinti. But it's the build up of emotional irritations that really affect me: foggy car windows in the morning because Phyllis and Ruby refuse to open a window or use the defroster; a child who's lost his pen and sits idle in the classroom while boxes of school supplies sit stacked in the library, just waiting to be opened; watching Thulani ride to school in the bed of Mhambi's pickup truck, in the rain, while Siphelele rides in the cab.

Just witnessing life here is a struggle. I'm in the middle of everything, not really a part of anything. I wonder if I'll ever fit in. Am I even supposed to fit in? I'm an outsider, after all. I'll never *really* belong, even in three months.

My plan for the day? Drink as much water as I can manage. The cleanse can't hurt. I even have a flush toilet all day. On my way to the bathroom I pass Granny's open bedroom door—my first peek into her room. She sits on the floor, eyes closed, her hands limp in her lap. Her chin rests on her ample bosom.

135

"Granny GuGu. Are you okay?"

She looks up at me. Her face, layered with deep wrinkles, breaks into a broad smile, revealing her one tooth. "Thank you!" she says, as saliva rolls over her bottom lip.

"You're welcome." It takes a second to realize that her answer wasn't really appropriate for my question. "Unjani? How are you?" I ask again.

Granny launches into an animated monologue, in Zulu, waving her arms about, ending with a question mark on her face.

"Yebo, yes." This feels like a safe answer. Whatever she said, I wouldn't want to tell her she's wrong.

She throws her arms in the air, resuming her Zulu tale with enthusiasm. I love her smile. She ends with, "Thank you! Thank you!"

"Yebo," I say, eliciting one more smile.

Ruby says Granny doesn't know a word of English. She's wrong. Granny knows two words.

» » » « « «

"So, Karen, I am ready for my first music lesson," Mhambi announces after he's changed out of his work clothes.

"Great. Were you able to find staff paper?"

"No. My wife has never heard of such a thing in the shops in town."

He sits at the organ, waiting for me to carry on. I understand Ruby's refusal to run all over town looking for paper. She does plenty already for this man who expects to always have his way. I side with Ruby. "I can't teach music without staff paper, Mhambi."

"I am disappointed. I was certain you would improvise. Tomorrow I will find the paper."

» » » « « «

Committed to less grease in my diet, I volunteer to make dinner again: cucumber and tomato salad, baked white fish coated with saltine cracker crumbs, and mashed potatoes. The boys will eat anything.

After dinner, the entire family gathers in front of the television. Well, everyone except Granny GuGu. I sit on the sofa next to Thulani, Mhambi in his armchair, Siphelele and Ruby on the loveseat. Enthralled by the black and white Zulu show, no one says a word.

The action revolves around a simple mud house at the edge of a clearing in a forest. A primitive mud oven sits in the clearing, not far from a fire pit ringed with bowling ball-sized rocks. A young boy and girl, maybe eight- and six-year-olds, play barefoot in the dirt with long sticks. The boy, bare-chested, wears ragged pants that are far too large, cinched at his waist with a piece of rope. The girl wears a simple cotton dress. A middle-aged woman comes from inside the house to the open doorway. The children rush to her, crying, screaming. They point at the ground in front of the woman's feet, then push her backwards, into the house. The camera moves inside the house and shows the woman sitting on the edge of a bed in a stark, open room. The children kneel at her feet, their hands clenched in prayer, wailing.

I nudge Thulani with my elbow. He tilts his head toward me without taking his eyes off the television.

"What's happening?" I whisper in his ear.

"Haybo!" he whispers back. "The village witch doctor has put a curse on this woman. She cannot leave her house."

"Really? Why not?"

"Her husband is dead. She has brought shame against him. He has spoken to the witch doctor from the other side to punish her."

The woman rises from her bed, holds her head high, determined to leave her home. The children, lying on the ground, hang on the hem of her skirt. She pulls herself free of them, crosses the doorsill and falls to the ground in agony.

The camera zooms in on her feet. Her toes rest in a scattering of white powder at the threshold.

"Haybo!" Ruby screams, her mouth agape as she wipes her tears with her apron. "The ancestors are supposed to *protect* the living from the witch doctors. This is not right!"

"See there!" Thulani whispers. "See that white powder on the ground? The witch doctor has sprinkled his medicine across the doorway so that every time she leaves her home she will be in great pain. Even crippled from walking!"

I also sit with my mouth agape, for a different reason. Vague memories of television shows from my youth stir in my mind. Shows that were racist, uncultured, derogatory. Without turning my head away from the television, I scan the family's faces. Each of them, even Mhambi, appear entranced. I cannot wrap my mind around why they buy this.

The two children drag the woman back into her home. She lays on the floor, her legs crumpled under her body, her face twisted with pain.

"Now what?" I whisper to Thulani.

"She will die. She has refused to obey. She will die."

"And the kids?"

"There is nothing to be done. They cannot help her."

The show ends with the woman sprawled on the floor. The two children sit nearby, clutching each other, in tears.

I feel as if I've just watched a bizarre episode of *All My Children*—bad acting and all. I scramble through a mental examination of soap opera plots. Do they address current cultural issues? They try. Do they resemble real life? Sometimes. Do they contain elements of truth? Sure. Does that mean there are elements of truth in this show? I hope not. Can't be. Who, in this day and age, believes in witch doctors?

Mhambi reaches for the remote and clicks off the television. The entire family exhales a collective, cathartic sigh, as though they have just witnessed something earth shattering.

Without speaking, in a near state of reverence, Ruby retreats to the back of the house to do her evening ironing. The boys head to their room.

"So, Karen," Mhambi asks, "how do you like our program?"

I can't share what I *really* think. "It's kind of like an American soap opera." I pause to think of something positive to say. "I wish they had subtitles so I could understand what's happening." Not that I think that would make it any easier to believe.

"It is a very popular show. I apologize that we are too involved in the story and forget to interpret for you."

We sit together in silence while I struggle to comprehend the irony of this intelligent man holding equal space in his heart—and mind—for global politics and the unfortunate death of a woman at the hands of a witch doctor's curse.

"Karen," Mhambi says, "I believe it is important that you visit our traditional healers while you are here. They will have a great deal to teach you. I believe you will find it most interesting."

I nod. "I'd like that."

He smiles, pleased. "I have spoken with Ruby. She knows of a traditional healer in Pietermaritzburg. I have told her that she must take you to visit this healer very soon. When you visit Ntwana for the school holiday you will meet Thulani's aunt. She is also a traditional healer. You remind me of her in many ways."

I smile, flattered and nervous, wary of Mhambi's fascination with me as a healer.

DAY 14

"Karen? Can I come in?"

The sky is just beginning to lighten. Ruby doesn't usually come to my room in the morning. Adrenaline clears my lingering grogginess.

"Sure, Ruby, just a second." I jump out of bed and pull my pink nightshirt down from my armpits where it's settled during a night of tossing and turning in the heat. I unlock the door to my room as quietly as possible. Why am I afraid Ruby will be offended if she realizes I lock my door at night? She isn't concerned about *my* feelings about being locked out overnight.

Still in her white cotton nightgown, she looks scared.

"What's wrong, Ruby? Come sit down." I pat my hand on the edge of the bed. She leans her head against my shoulder, weaving a lace handkerchief through her fingers. My anxiety builds as I wait to hear her news. "Ruby, tell me what's wrong."

"It is my mother-in-law. Something is not right in her head. She says that there are people in her room. I do not see them, Karen, even though she is speaking to them. I am afraid the spirits have taken hold of her."

At least it's something I can handle. "Oh, Ruby," I sigh. "I'm so sorry."

She lifts her head and spins toward me with wide eyes. "You have heard of such a thing?"

Granny GuGu's raspy cough, the death rattle, comes near the end. I want to be honest with Ruby. I also want to be careful.

"I've seen this before, Ruby. At the hospital. Sometimes when people are approaching death they see a relative or a friend, someone they love who's already passed on. They talk to these deceased people as though they're standing in the room. They often say how these people have come back to keep them company on their journey to the other side."

Ruby's mouth falls open. Her eyes flit back and forth. I sense that my explanation strikes a familiar chord, but perhaps she didn't expect me to be so straight forward. She untangles her handkerchief from her fingers and wipes the sweat from her forehead. "What you say is true, Karen. The hadidas have circled."

"The what?"

"The hadidas. The gray birds that have circled over my home for many days now. You must have seen them. They are very large, and very loud. When they circle, someone will die very soon." She pauses. "I have wondered if my husband's mother is the one who will die. But I did not expect the spirits to take hold of her like this. I cannot tell my husband. He will be very angry that I have allowed her to become so sick."

"Ruby, GuGu is a very old woman. I doubt that this is your fault. Why would Mhambi blame you?"

She side-steps my question. "What should I do? I cannot allow my husband see his mother this way."

I feel confused by Ruby's reaction. She isn't an ignorant woman. She's had two spinal surgeries to fuse vertebrae in her neck—too many years of carrying heavy water buckets on her head, from the creek to the house in Ntwana, before she and Mhambi moved here, to their "brick house." She has ulcers, too. And a purse full of pills from her doctor. There's a disconnect I don't understand. Does she feel guilty for mistreating Granny in some way? Ruby can't prevent Granny's death. She certainly can't hide it from Mhambi. In fact, she should probably be having this conversation with him instead of me.

"Do you think I should take my mother-in-law to the hospital?" she asks. "Perhaps the doctor will give her medicine that will stop her nonsense."

"That sounds like a good idea, Ruby. What can I do to help?"

"You have helped already. There is nothing more for you to do. Thulani will dress GuGu. I will call my maid to come straight away. We will leave as soon as Rolina arrives. She will stay with my mother-in-law at the hospital while we are at the conference today. I will instruct her what to tell the doctor."

"That sounds like a good plan. Are you sure I can't help? Can I make breakfast?"

"We will eat at the conference. I must go and make my husband's tea now."

She pads across the bricks with her bare feet. Uncertain how fast Rolina can get here, I skip my bath, sponging at my sink instead. Besides, it seems best to stay out of the house. I don't want to be caught in the middle of whatever's going on between Ruby and Mhambi.

I slip across the patio, through the carport on the far side of the house, and wait for Ruby in the driveway. Thulani ushers Granny GuGu to the car. Ruby and Rolina follow. Engrossed in a heated conversation, they barely notice me as I slide into the back seat next to GuGu.

Mhambi's red truck still sits in the carport. Surely he's noticed the unusual activity this morning—only the second time Granny's left the house since I arrived. I've never seen him talk to his mother. Is he ignoring this whole event? Or does he already know what's happening? His interest in traditional healers makes me wonder why we're taking his mother to the hospital. But I won't ask. Not yet, anyway.

» » »   « « «

A narrow walkway connects the parking lot with the front entrance of the public hospital. Walled with cyclone fence on both sides and an arch of razor wire over the top, it looks like an escape-proof cage. Coombies unload hoards of employees in the parking lot at the entrance to the odd tunnel. Why here? Why not the front door? I don't understand anything anymore. I offer to wait in the car. Ruby insists I come inside to see their fine medical establishment.

We join the hospital workers in the wire tunnel. Dressed in white aprons, navy blue pants, and pale yellow shirts, their long faces project a sense of doom. It's no wonder. This walk through barbed wire feels like the walk to the death chambers.

Inside, chairs line the hospital corridors—old wooden chairs, cheap plastic chairs, ragged upholstered chairs, metal patio chairs—every chair occupied by a patient hacking sputum into blue plastic buckets scattered around. This is the public hospital. Anyone can receive free treatment here. All you need to do is show up and have infinite patience.

We walk the maze of dim hallways, Rolina on one side of Granny GuGu, me on the other. Ruby forges ahead in search of the right department. We pass an occasional office door, top half open, bottom half closed. The offices, lit with bright overhead fluorescent fixtures, look like openings into the bowels of the hospital. Nurses, recognizable by the striped epaulettes on the shoulders of their crisp white uniforms, instruct us to follow the green stripe painted on the floor. We leave Granny GuGu and Rolina settled in the Green Ward hallway with instructions for Rolina to call Ruby once Granny has seen the doctor.

» » »   « « «

In the heart of town, we enter the tiny lobby of the Pietermaritzburg Royal Hotel. It resembles the Royal Hotel in Durban in name only. Surrounded by an odd assortment of cafeteria chairs, a single loveseat—its upholstery dirty, faded and frayed at the seams—defines the atmosphere: a rundown hotel desperate to maintain its once upscale reputation. Brown folding tables and chairs pack the adjoining conference room, leaving just enough space to squeeze between the rows.

The seventy-five conference attendees are mostly women.

Loud women. We're only a few minutes late and already they've formed a conga line, snaking through the aisles. With heads tilted back they wave their arms, stacked with colorful bangles, through the air as they sing in their mother language. Where is my camera when I need it? I've been to plenty of conferences in the States—and none of them began like this!

I'd love to jump in, dance to unload some of the morning's tension, but no one makes an effort to include me. Ruby drops into a seat at a table near the door, pulls her phone from her bra, and immerses herself in conversation. I feel awkward, the only white woman in a sea of black faces. Jealous, too. Wishing I could fit in, I sit next to Ruby.

Our emcee for the day, Stanley, the only other white person in the room, calls the conference to order. The teachers continue their raucous call and response song. Either they don't hear him, or they can't be bothered. Eventually the noise dies down, with only an occasional shout from one woman to another clear across the room.

Stanley lays out the agenda for the two-day conference. A young Zulu woman translates for him. Today's presentation is by an organization from Durban that specializes in HIV/AIDS education and prevention. The focus of the two-day event is to train one teacher from each rural school in KwaZulu-Natal to function as the HIV/AIDS counselor for their school. Not exactly what Phyllis and Ruby told me. They did mention that Ruby would be trained as a counselor. They left out the HIV/AIDS piece.

News in the States identifies the AIDS epidemic as Africa's most critical issue. In an odd way, I'm excited to learn more about it firsthand. In the late 1980's as a volunteer for the Contra Costa County AIDS Taskforce in northern California, we created training panels to educate nurses and other healthcare providers about HIV transmission, sat with AIDS patients in hospitals, cleaned house for patients who were too weak to do it themselves, bought groceries for patients who'd spent their last dime on medication, encouraged families to stay involved in patients' lives, attended way too many funerals. I've been tested twice myself. I know the agony of waiting for test results. I remember the stigma that came along with an HIV diagnosis. It was a painful era.

Just before Stanley dismisses us for the morning break, hotel employees deliver trays of finger sandwiches and fruit to tables at the rear of our room. I'm relieved. We never did eat breakfast. Stanley motions that he'd like to speak with me. Still in my chair, I miss the stampede to the food table.

Stanley crouches on the floor next to my chair, shouting over the noise in the room, "I hear that you're visiting from America."

I nod, unsure who told him, or when.

"I will apologize in advance," he says, the hair of his mustache brushing against my ear. "It is unfortunate that you have chosen to attend this particular conference. Most of our presentation will be in Zulu."

"No apology necessary," I shout. My attendance was decided for me.

"It's unusual that we have an opportunity to hear from someone from America. We would be honored if you would say a few words this afternoon."

"I don't speak Zulu."

"No problem. Most of these teachers speak English. We use Zulu because we feel it's a better approach. Culturally. We hope they'll be more receptive if they hear the material in their own language."

"Are you sure they're going to want to hear from a white woman from America?" I shout.

"I am sure they'll want to hear about your country's defeat of AIDS. America's success is uncommon. Especially here in Africa."

"I'm not sure the US has actually defeated AIDS. Just managed to control it better."

"But even that is a success. Our organization focuses on prevention. As you probably know, that's ninety percent of the struggle. Perhaps you can speak to the need for prevention. And testing. We have a difficult time convincing our citizens to seek testing and early treatment."

"You're right. The drugs are so effective these days, AIDS is no longer a death sentence if you begin treatment early." As soon as I close my mouth, I remember how expensive the drugs are. Shame fills my face with heat. Maybe AIDS *is* still a death sentence here. I grab Stanley's arm. "I'm sorry. I feel awful. How presumptuous of me to assume that the people here can afford the drugs."

"The drugs are free!" Stanley shouts. "The problem is getting them to *take* the drugs."

Yet another thing I don't understand. But, I'm tired of shouting and eager to eat before we start again. "How long do you want me to talk?"

"Five minutes. No more than ten." We shake hands.

I hurry to the back of the room, wiggle my way through the crowd, and nearly lose my appetite when I finally make it to the food tables. The egg salad sandwiches, cut into cute triangles, are decimated. White paper doilies that once lined the trays lie ripped on the floor. The women grab fistfuls of sandwiches, stuff them into their mouths, and reach for chunks of fresh pineapple and cantaloupe with their bare hands. Egg salad dribbles down the front of their dresses as they talk and laugh while they eat. The linen table cloth is drenched with deep red tea from the silver urn. The sugar, clumped together in the bowl from splatters of tea, sits next to the overturned milk pitcher. I choose a few undamaged sandwiches and an apple. Stepping over bits of food ground into the carpet, I return to my seat to prepare my speech for this afternoon.

» » »   « « «

The conference is barely underway again when Ruby's phone rings. I give her credit. Most of the women talk on their phones at their seats. Ruby steps outside. A few minutes later she pokes her head through the door and motions for me to gather my things and meet her outside.

"That was JoJo, my sister, who called," Ruby says. "Her daughter, Zodwa, is sick at school. JoJo rides in a carpool to her job at the factory and cannot leave in the middle of the day. I must pick Zodwa up and take her home. You can stay here, or come with me. It will not take long."

I don't speak until after lunch. Missing a few Zulu presentations is fine. "I'll go with you."

Zodwa's school, an old stone building surrounded by tall, ivy covered walls and lush gardens, looks like a 19th century castle. Ruby pulls up to the curb and leaves the car running. It must be serious—she's left me, and her purse, behind. Within minutes she struts back across the lawn. Zodwa, several paces behind, doubled over, can barely walk. Her face clenches with each spasm of pain.

I jump out of the car to open the rear door. Zodwa drops her backpack on the floor and slumps her tiny body across the seat. She grips her belly with her arms, writhing in pain. The flu? Cramps? As we pull away from the curb, I reach over the seat to feel her forehead. She's burning up, damp with perspiration.

"Auntie, I must throw up. Please stop the car."

Ruby drives on. "When did this start?" she asks.

"This morning," Zodwa moans, her voice weak.

"What did you eat last night? Are any of your friends also sick?"

No answer.

"Did you have physical education this morning? What have you eaten today?"

"Nothing, Auntie. I did not feel like eating this morning."

Ruby drives in a circle, around the block. Her questions feel harsh. "Did you take any pills from your mother's purse? Did your friends give you remedies?"

She thinks Zodwa's using drugs? I look in back again. I've never seen an overdose, but Zodwa looks awful. One arm hangs limp over the edge of the seat. Her face contorts with pain. Her breath is shallow; her eyes closed.

Ruby turns to me. She looks scared. "What should I do?"

No hesitation on my part. "She needs a doctor."

"Zodwa, do you have your medical card with you?" Ruby asks.

Nothing from the back seat.

"Zodwa!" Ruby shouts.

"Yes, Auntie." Zodwa's voice is barely audible. "It is in my bag."

"Take it out. We will go to the clinic."

Ten minutes outside of town, we pull into a gravel driveway and park alongside a row of banana trees. In an otherwise vacant lot, a quaint, pink stucco house sits on a grassy hillside in the shade of a sprawling acacia.

"Karen, you must take Zodwa inside," Ruby says. "I need to call my sister."

Zodwa hands me her health card as I drag her from the back seat. Her school uniform is disheveled; her white blouse half-tucked into her unzipped skirt. Her ponytail drips sweat. She can't stand up straight. She's in much worse shape than I realized.

I stick the card between my teeth and slide one arm around Zodwa's back, the other across her chest for balance. She hangs over my arm as we climb the rocky path up to the clinic. Her breath is shallow and fast by the time we reach the front door.

The living room, filled with women and children of all ages in various states of discontent, serves as a waiting room. In the far corner, a sixty-something slender white woman sits behind a small desk. She wears a gray shirtwaist dress and a matching cap. I recognize the epaulettes on her shoulders. She takes one look at Zodwa and rushes to meet us.

"I am Sister Sarah," she says. "Come with me."

"Thank you," I say, relieved that she understands the urgency.

At the back of the house she shuffles us into a small room and helps Zodwa onto the exam table. She turns toward me, irritated. "How is it that a white woman from America brings this pregnant Zulu girl to the clinic to have her abortion?"

My mouth falls open. "What?"

Sister Sarah turns back to Zodwa and flies into action. Rolling Zodwa onto her back, she pulls the girl's skirt down to her thighs and rips open her blouse—revealing Zodwa's pregnant belly.

I feel stupid and scared. Surely Ruby knew this. Her questions in the car make sense now. Where is Ruby anyway?

"How far along are you?" Sister Sarah asks Zodwa in a demanding tone.

Zodwa moans.

Sister Sarah grabs the stethoscope from around her neck, presses it against Zodwa's belly, and listens. She pulls a tape measure from a drawer and stretches it across Zodwa's belly. "The fetus is fifteen to seventeen weeks old. There is still a heartbeat, but this baby will not live. Can you stand?" she asks Zodwa.

Zodwa nods.

Sister Sarah sticks her head out the door. "Bring me a cup," she yells. She helps Zodwa to her feet, pulls her skirt and panties to the floor, and sticks the plastic jar between Zodwa's legs. "Pee in this. Now."

Sister Sarah turns to me. "Are you responsible for this girl?"

"Zodwa's aunt is in the car," I say.

"Go and get her. Now."

I hurry through the house, out the front door. Ruby's car is still there, but I don't see her. Feeling beholden to act like a parent for Zodwa, I race back to the exam room. "I can't find her," I say. "She can't have gone far. She should be here any minute."

"What have you taken to induce this abortion?" Sister Sarah snaps as she helps Zodwa back onto the table.

Zodwa keeps her eyes closed, silent. Blood pools on the white paper under her bottom.

"Zodwa!" I say. "This is not the time to hold back. Tell the nurse what happened."

Her voice is weak. "My sister's friend gave me the pills. I took two last night. Nothing happened so I took two more this morning. She did not tell me it would hurt."

"I suppose you thought you would just sit on the toilet and the baby would fall out?" Sister Sarah's question stings.

"Yes," Zodwa cries. "They did not tell me it would be like this."

Sister Sarah exhales a long breath. She turns to face me, her arms crossed. "It does not appear that Zodwa has an infection in her urine. This is good news. But she needs medical attention. Can you take her to the hospital straight away?"

Ruby sticks her head around the door, smiles. "How is it going?" she asks.

Her casual demeanor aggravates me.

Sister Sarah's cheeks flush with anger. "Are you this young woman's aunt?"

"I am."

"Come in here and close the door behind you," Sister Sarah orders.

I move to the head of the exam table to make room for Ruby, laying my hand on Zodwa's head to calm her—and myself. Sister Sarah pulls Zodwa's panties over her feet, up her legs, and packs them with thick pads before she pulls them the rest of the way up. She hands Zodwa her skirt off the floor and turns to Ruby, her hands on her hips. "Your niece is in very serious need of medical attention. The bleeding will only become worse as the fetus aborts."

Ruby's smile fades.

Sister Sarah addresses Ruby like an angry adult scolding a child. "You must take this girl to the hospital immediately. If you don't, she will hemorrhage and die along with the baby."

My heart pounds with adrenaline. I help Zodwa from the table and steady her while she pulls her skirt over her head. Sister Sarah scribbles a note on a piece of yellow paper and clips it to Zodwa's medical card. She glares at Ruby. "Go straight to the hospital and give these instructions to the admit clerk. Do not waste any time."

Zodwa stumbles back down the hill, doubled over, propped on my arm, groaning. Ruby follows ten paces behind. Her silence spooks me. She backs the car through the narrow opening in the fence and meanders down the road like we have all day.

"Are we going to the same hospital we took Granny GuGu to this morning?" I ask. We need to hurry. I glance at Ruby. She looks lost in her own thoughts. "Ruby? Ruby!"

She pulls to the side of the road and turns the engine off. She looks terrified.

"What are you doing?" I ask.

"What should I do?"

"What do you mean, what should you do? We should take the shortest route to the hospital."

"But what should I do?"

She's wasting time. She must be in shock. "Zodwa's bleeding. We need to get her to the hospital right away. Do you need to call JoJo to meet us there?"

"She cannot come. I do not know what to do."

"Ruby, maybe we should call an ambulance." I'd drive myself, but I don't know the way and Ruby seems too confused to help.

Zodwa writhes in pain in the back seat. Ruby stares through the windshield. I'm missing something. What in the hell is going on?

I take a deep breath and soften my tone. "Ruby, I don't understand why you're confused about what to do. Are you worried that they can't afford the medical care? Is that the problem?"

"No. Not that. The hospital will be free."

I'm losing patience. "Then what is it?"

Ruby grimaces with turmoil, her hands gripping the steering wheel. Her voice is so low I can barely hear her speak. "Zodwa's father has forbidden that she receive any care related to this pregnancy. I cannot go against his wishes."

Oh, my God! I close my eyes. Think, Karen. Breathe. You can't get mad at Ruby. She still has to live with these people after you go home. Exhale. Breathe again. You can't change it all in one afternoon. You can't let this girl die, either. Don't panic. Just breathe.

Ruby starts the car, makes a U-turn in the road. Oh, dear God, I pray, please let us be headed to the hospital.

"This is not fair," Ruby says.

"What's not fair?"

"None of this is fair."

We drive a short distance into the countryside. Ruby stops in front of a yellow stucco house that sits downhill from the road. She dials her cell phone, speaks a few words of Zulu, and waits. A man comes out of the house and saunters up the dirt driveway.

"Zodwa, get your things," Ruby says.

Oh, my God. We're not going to the hospital. Keep breathing, Karen.

Zodwa backs her way out of the car. Dragging her backpack on the ground, she wobbles down the grassy slope, into the house. The screen door slams behind her.

Ruby takes a deep breath and slams the car door behind her as she plods her way across the grass to meet Zodwa's unshaven father. They stand face-to-face on the slope, twenty feet from the car. He plants his feet wide, folds his arms across the dirty white T-shirt stretched over his bulky gut. Ruby leans in toward him, slashing the air between them with her arm. Her voice is low, rough like gravel. He sets his jaw, narrows his eyes in steely silence. Ruby turns and walks several feet back toward the car before she remembers more anger that needs to be voiced. She returns to face him again, closer this time. Close enough to feel his breath, tainted, I imagine, with alcohol. Her fist closes around her keys, her arms taught at her sides. Her fury feels raw. She takes one step backward, spits at his feet, turns and walks to the car. He waves his arm through the air in disgust as he heads down to his home.

Ruby drops into the front seat, closes the door behind her and leans over the steering wheel resting her forehead on her arms. Her chest trembles with each breath. There's nothing for me to say. Zodwa will die if she doesn't get to the hospital, and we both know it.

» » »   « « «

We head back toward town in silence. I feel sorry for Ruby. She lives a split life. In town, away from the men in her life, she's gregarious, flirty, opinionated, and seems to know everyone. I'd swear she could run for mayor with a landslide victory. With her family she's submissive, compliant, withdrawn. It's no wonder she has ulcers.

We pull into a gas station. She leans her head back, her arms fall limp. "Karen, I do not feel well. I am sorry I cannot go back to the conference this afternoon."

My own legs feel like rubber; my stomach twists with worry that Zodwa's father will take his anger for Ruby out on the girl. "That's okay, Ruby. We don't need to go back. We do need to eat, though. Is there anyplace nearby where we can get food? Let me treat you to lunch."

"Thank you, Karen. I appreciate your kindness." Her voice sounds weak from exhaustion.

I feel my own adrenaline collapse coming on.

"There is a shop around the corner that sells sandwiches," Ruby says.

"Let's go there. Let's relax for a few minutes before we go home."

While I inhale my roast beef sandwich, Ruby paces the sidewalk in front of the shop, talking on her cell phone.

"I have spoken with Rolina," she says, sitting down to her untouched sandwich. "Granny has not seen the doctor yet."

She pauses to wrap up her sandwich and stuff it into her already overflowing purse. "I am very tired, Karen. This seems to always be my life. There is never a time that I do not have to worry about something."

"I'm so sorry, Ruby. You're under so much stress. I don't know how you do it. I wish there was something I could do to make it easier for you."

"It is not your problem. It is my life." She cups her face in her hands, her elbows propped on the table. When she looks up again, she turns to me with a mischievous twinkle. "We shall go visit my friend, Simangele. She always knows how to make me feel better. And she wants to meet you, Karen. You will like her. We have been friends since we were young girls in Durban."

We could both use the distraction. "That sounds great, Ruby. I'd love to meet her."

» » »   « « «

We turn into the industrial park where Simangele and her husband own a factory. The asphalt parking lot, surrounded by an eight-foot high cyclone fence topped with rolls of razor wire, runs all the way to the doorsill of an old, two-story brick building. Most of the opaque windows look like they've been targets for batting practice. Ruby parks inches from the front door and, as soon as we step out of the car, I know why—the pavement is hot enough to melt our shoes.

The concrete floor inside feels cool by comparison. Light, streaming through the smashed windows, illuminates clouds of swirling sawdust. I hear the unmistakable hum of a sewing machine from an adjoining room. Ruby peeks her head around the corner to ask Simangele's whereabouts. "Ngiyabonga," she says, nodding her head in thanks.

We wind our way through a narrow hallway and turn the corner into an expansive, two-story factory room. The dust chokes me. I stop to cough and gape at the sight—coffins stacked from floor to ceiling. Coffins everywhere, in every stage of completion. Stacks of coffin tops and bottoms. Coffins with brass handles. Coffins with brass crosses embedded in the lids. Fumes from open, gallon-sized cans of shellac burn my nostrils. Men with white face masks, bent over sawhorses, rasp the edges of freshly assembled coffins. I run my fingers over the dusty, smooth wood. It feels eerie, but so practical. Of course they need to build coffins.

Then I see them—the tiny baby coffins. Ruby and Simangele hug each other for a long time, rocking back and forth in their embrace, while I wonder which of these tiny wooden boxes will hold Zodwa's unborn baby.

DAY 15

We arrive for day two of the AIDS conference in time to join the group for breakfast in the Royal Hotel dining room.

"Sanibonani," I say, to the women at my table. Their hostile stares bore right through me. Ruby makes no effort to introduce me. I feel stranded in unfriendly seas. My Durban rock star status is over.

There's no conga line this morning, but lots of singing. Standing by their chairs, the women toss the song back and forth across the room. They clap their hands over their heads, then down to the right, down to the left, voices raised to the ceiling. I desperately want for someone to take my arm and say, "Here! This is how you do it."

The young Zulu presenters from Durban, dressed in khaki slacks and blue denim shirts, work hard to maintain a professional attitude. It's not easy. They can't make it through a single sentence without being heckled. For Stanley's benefit, or maybe mine, they make occasional statements in English: "We must practice speaking freely here, with each other, so that we can take this important information to our students and their families." "We must try not to make judgments as to the character of those who are infected with HIV/AIDS." "We must not blame those who are infected for the ignorance that brought this disease to them." Each statement is met with loud interruptions that draw laughter from the teachers.

Stanley looks resigned to a day of misery. He walks down the side aisle and kneels next to my table. I'm sure his private conversation with me does nothing to endear either of us to this crowd.

"I must apologize," he says. "This is difficult for them. They are less welcoming than many of our audiences. We are doing everything we can to hold their attention."

"I don't think it's your fault." Where would one even begin to assign blame? There are far too many complications to unravel in a two-day conference where a white organization tells Zulus how to live their lives. History has instilled a lack of trust. Fear outweighs the logical need to make bold changes. I've heard that AIDS is robbing Africa of an entire generation. I see how that could be true. It seems clear that AIDS will get much worse before it gets better.

Stanley interrupts my downward spiral into despair. "You will speak this afternoon?"

"Sure. If you think it will be helpful."

"It can't hurt. Just focus on prevention."

At the morning break, Ruby sits hunched over our table making phone calls. I wonder if all these women have lives as dramatic as hers. I brave the food frenzy. "Here you go," I say, handing Ruby a plate of sandwiches and a cup of tea.

"Aye, thank you." She stares at her food. "I am worried, Karen. I do not believe my mother-in-law will come home from the hospital, and my husband refuses to go visit her. I know that it is difficult for him to see her in such a condition, but I worry that she will die before he visits her. If that happens, he will be very unhappy with himself." She turns to look at me. Her face, drawn with exhaustion and grief, oozes desperation. "I do not know what to do, Karen."

"I don't think you can do more than you already have. You can't make him go."

She heaves a sigh. "I know you are right. But he will not forgive himself if his mother dies and he has not had the courage to say good-bye."

"Maybe he just needs a little more time."

"I have told him already that he must not wait too long. I hope he has listened to me well."

Ruby holds her head in her hands, elbows propped on the table. I rub my hand over her back. She turns in my direction, just enough for me to see her tears. "I do not want to stay here, Karen," she whispers from behind her hand. "Do you want to come to the library with me? We will return in time for lunch."

"Yeah. Let's go."

We grab our purses and slip through the door into the heat of an African summer day. Palm trees along the front of the hotel sway in a warm breeze. Ruby pulls me into a bear hug. "Thank you, Karen. I need a break."

"I'm always up for a trip to the library."

"This is not the public library," she says, as we head for the car. "This is the educators' library. I want to check out materials for my classroom."

A few blocks away, we ring the doorbell on a small, yellow brick building. The librarian recognizes Ruby through the glass door. It never ceases to amaze me how many people Ruby knows. They all greet her as a long lost friend, tell me how much fun she is, what a great sense of humor she has, and how she always makes them happy. The librarian is no exception. She hugs Ruby and welcomes me to their country. While Ruby gathers her material from the elementary school section on the first floor, the librarian ushers me to the basement.

I'm in heaven! Rows and rows of books from horror novels to Greek mythology. I check out four books on Ruby's account: the history of African religions, the geography of South Africa, Zulu folk tales, and the tribal traditions of the Yoruba people. It would be fine with me if we skipped the afternoon session and just went home to read.

» » » « « «

After lunch, Stanley makes an inflated introduction of me. I walk to the front of the room, embarrassed, and turn to deliver my speech to seventy-five deadpan faces.

"Being tested is the single most effective weapon in the fight against AIDS," I say, trying to sound more confidant than I feel. "Knowledge is power. And knowing your status, positive or negative, gives you the power to make good choices. To be a leader in the fight against AIDS is to lead by example. Every person in this room should go for an HIV test. But it's not enough to just have the test. It's important to tell your family, your friends, your colleagues, and especially your students, that you've been tested.

"As educators and parents, we know that our children often follow our example instead of our words. And with HIV/AIDS, your example is a matter of life and death. Your action, and your willingness to be public about it, may be the very thing that inspires someone else to be tested. Your example could save a life."

They begin to chat among themselves. Teachers in the front of the room turn to talk to those at the back.

I continue. "If we tell children to do something, it's inevitable that they'll ask if we've done it ourselves. We have to be able to say 'yes' to gain their trust. I have been tested twice, myself. It's hard. There's a lot of anxiety waiting for the results. If you go for a test yourself, you will better understand the anxiety of the children you counsel.

"In America, in the beginning, there was a huge stigma attached to being HIV positive. It took a long time for that to change. And it only changed because people started to talk more openly about it. You can learn from America's mistake. You can start talking about it now. And you have an advantage in South Africa that we don't have in America. In my country, the drugs to treat AIDS are very expensive. You can get them for free. You don't need to die of AIDS.

"Being tested is the best way to fight AIDS. If you're positive, it's free to be treated. If you're negative, you can take precautions to prevent the spread. *Please* take an HIV test. *Please* show your children how to take care of themselves."

That's all I prepared. By the end they're so loud, I'm sure they didn't hear the last bit. It would be presumptuous to wait for applause. I head for my seat.

"Wait," Stanley says. "They might have questions."

They don't. They avoid eye contact with me for the rest of the afternoon. At the end of the day, a slender elderly woman wearing an orange shirt-waist dress approaches our table. She and Ruby exchange greetings in Zulu. She has a gentle smile and a soft voice. Even the way she holds her hands together in front of her body, with her modest purse draped over her arm, feels comfortable.

"Karen, this is my friend Busi," Ruby says. "We have been friends for a very long time."

"Sawubona," I say.

"It is a pleasure to meet you," Busi says. "It is my honor to greet you in your language. Welcome to our country. How do you like your time with Ruby and the children at Zinti?"

Busi, kind and gentle, is a breath of fresh air. I feel my shoulders relax. "Thank you. Your country is gorgeous, and Ruby takes good care of me. The kids at Zinti are the highlight of my visit. I'm so happy to have time with them."

"Ruby speaks very well of you. The children are fortunate to have you."

"I'm afraid I haven't made quite such a good impression today."

"Do not let them bother you," Busi says, laying her hand on my arm. "Sometimes it is hard to hear the truth. They will think about what you have said."

"Thank you. That makes me feel much better." I pause to examine the intricate lace beadwork that lies flat against her collar bones, fanned out in layers of color. "That's a beautiful necklace you're wearing."

She runs her long, thin fingers over the beads. "Thank you. If you like, I can take you to the woman who made it for me. She is not far from here. She will make one for you."

"I'd like that." I raise my eyebrows at Ruby, like a child begging for a favor. She and Busi share a brief exchange in Zulu.

"Come with me, Karen," Busi says. She slips her arm through mine. "Ruby has errands to do. I will introduce you to the bead woman on Church Street."

» » »   « « «

Two hours later, Ruby picks me up in the dirt parking lot behind Woolworth's. I hug Busi good-bye. "Thank you for everything. I had a great time. I hope to see you again."

She nods, smiles, and squeezes my hand. "You are most welcome. Thank you for being with me this afternoon."

I slide into the front seat next to Ruby. I'd love to show off my new treasures, but she's distracted. Besides, they're only exciting to me—she's worn this incredible beadwork all her life.

"I have good news, Karen," Ruby says as we drive off. "Zodwa is in the hospital. She will be okay."

"Oh, my God, Ruby. That's great news!" I exhale with relief, unaware until this moment just how anxious I've been, waiting for news of Zodwa's fate. "So her dad took her to the hospital?"

"No. That will never happen. After we took her home, Zodwa called her older sister. She came on the coombie to fetch Zodwa. It took them several hours to get to the hospital because they had to change coombie twice. My sister says by the time they arrived at the hospital, Zodwa was weak and needed a wheelchair."

I bet. She probably bled the entire way. "I'm so relieved that Zodwa's getting medical care. Do you know how she's doing?"

"She has not yet aborted the baby. The doctor is waiting to see if she will need to go to the operating theater. We will go now to the hospital to see her."

"Will I get to meet JoJo there?"

"No." Ruby hesitates. "Her husband will not permit her to go to the hospital. So we will take Zodwa her food." Her face lights up with a mischievous sparkle as she reaches into her purse and pulls out a bag of fat green grapes. It feels like we're two young girls sneaking around behind our parents' backs. Ruby's smile fades. "Zodwa's father will be angry if he knows we are caring for her. You must not say anything."

"I won't tell him." The bastard! I can't change how they

do things, but I can certainly be quiet long enough to help save this young woman's life.

We drive the rest of the way in silence, through town, over the freeway, past the Shekhina Nursing School into the hospital parking lot. Ruby turns off the engine and sits for a few seconds before she turns to look at me. "You should not feel bad about what you said at the conference this afternoon, Karen. What you have said is true."

Her calm but serious demeanor surprises me. It takes me a second to remember what I even said, to register relief from her support. "So why do they seem so angry with me?"

"I have a friend in this hospital," Ruby says. "She has AIDS and will die very soon. I visit her as often as I can. Her other women friends also visit. She is very sad because her husband will not come to the hospital and she will die without seeing him again. He is a fool. Instead of visiting his wife, he gives all of his money to a witch doctor who says he will reverse the curse that has been put on her. And when he asks the women who visit his wife if she is getting well, none of them will tell him the truth because it is not their place to interfere with his business."

I shake my head in disbelief. "I don't understand. Why does he go to a witch doctor and not a traditional healer? It seems like the healer would be the one who can help."

"The healers cannot do magic! They can only heal the ones who seek their help with enough time. The healers would tell her husband the truth. The witch doctors will lie and tell him they can help. This is how AIDS kills so many of our people."

"I still don't understand, Ruby. Why do people keep going to the witch doctors if they never cure anyone? Make me understand."

"Like my friend, they come to the hospital when the pain becomes too difficult and they need the drugs. The families are desperate and seek the witch doctor who will do nothing but lie and steal their money. And when my friend dies, the witch doctor will say it is because she went to the white man's hospital. He will say if her husband had just come to him sooner, or paid him more money for better spells, she would not have died. This makes many people stay away from the doctors who could help them. It is not good." She shakes her head.

I sit dumbfounded while Ruby collects her purse. She locks her door and comes around to open mine. "Come, Karen. Now you understand why they do not like to hear what you say."

» » »   « « «

We walk in silence through the tunnel of wire. As we step through the front door, Ruby hands me the bag of grapes. "I must go see my mother-in-law," she says. "You will go see Zodwa. We must not take too long. I must be home soon to make my husband's dinner." She hands me a piece of paper with Zodwa's room number. "Make her tell you what remedy she took to cause this abortion. She will not tell her sister. I will meet you back here, in the lobby."

Without even breaking her stride, Ruby rounds the corner, disappearing from sight. This was her plan all along! I feel manipulated as I stop at the information desk to ask directions. I'm eager to see Zodwa, but I don't want to ask her what she took. I understand why she wanted an abortion. Why would she tell me anything? I'm nobody to her. Even if I promised to keep it confidential—and I would— what would be the point? She'd know Ruby put me up to it.

"Follow the orange stripe on the ground," the information clerk says. "It will take you directly to the surgery ward. The sisters there will help you find her room."

There are no doors on the patient's rooms. There are no room numbers. The nurse at the ward station greets me. "May I help you?" she asks.

"Yes, please. I'm looking for a young woman who arrived yesterday evening. Her name is Zodwa." I don't even know her last name.

"She is a fortunate young woman," the nurse says as she leads me down the hallway. "She would surely have bled to death if she waited any longer to seek care."

Does this nurse realize that waiting wasn't Zodwa's choice? She peeks into one of the rooms. "Zodwa, you have a visitor."

Three beds line each side of the cavernous room. At the far end, late afternoon sun pours through the sheer white curtains. Shadows of the steel bars in the window create a checkerboard pattern on the floor. The room lacks any conspicuous signs of comfort: no television, no flowers, no bedside table, no call button, no chairs, no magazines, no color. Nothing to distract a patient from long hours of lying in bed. Today is Valentine's Day in the States. At home, red hearts would be pasted on every patient's wall. Bed tables would overflow with cards and flowers. It may be a silly holiday, but right now I miss it. Signs of love here would be reassuring.

Zodwa, the only patient in the room, occupies the bed nearest the door. She looks vulnerable, propped on pillows, her hospital gown far too large for her tiny body, her feet exposed at the edge of the bed. She rolls her head to look at me. Her expression is flat.

"Hi, Zodwa. My name is Karen." I didn't really introduce myself yesterday. "I don't know if you remember me. I helped you at the clinic, with your Aunt Ruby." That's ridiculous. I forget that I don't exactly *blend* here. What are the chances she actually forgets being taken to the clinic by a white woman—a complete stranger? "Your Auntie sent these grapes for you. Are you hungry?"

She nods, almost imperceptibly, but doesn't reach for them. She's probably weak.

I stick my hand into the bag and break a few free for her. I lay the bag on the bed, open her delicate hand and put three grapes in her palm. "Here you go. They're sweet and juicy. They'll help you stay strong."

"Thank you," she murmurs. Nothing more. She chews one at a time. It looks like an effort to move her jaw. She's pale and stops to rest between grapes.

I drag a heavy metal chair from the hallway into the room, next to Zodwa's bed. She grimaces in a spasm of pain, her head back, sweat on her forehead, without uttering a sound.

"I'm sorry that you have to go through this alone." I pause to consider what else I can say that won't sound stupid. "I'm really sorry. I can't even imagine how scary this must be." This feels like a safe assumption. Although her face shows no evidence of emotion, you can't be fifteen, pregnant, bleeding, hungry and shunned—and not be scared. "Are they giving you medicine to help with the pain?"

She nods.

"Your Aunt is worried about you. She'd be here herself, but her mother-in-law is also in this hospital, and she's visiting with her while I'm here with you." I hope that's true. I don't think I've misread Ruby's concern. She must care—she sent food. But this feels absurd. Why am I defending Ruby? Why can't she visit both of them?

"Your Aunt wants me to ask what pills you took to abort the baby. She thinks one of your friends at school has given you something dangerous."

Zodwa stares at the ceiling. She has no reason to trust me. I'm done questioning.

"I understand that you don't want to tell me. I'll tell Ruby you're too weak to talk."

She smiles now.

"So, how is school going for you? What are your favorite subjects?"

She turns toward me. Her words come with effort, but her smile is beautiful.

"I do not care for the study of math and science. They are too difficult for me. I am best at restaurant skills."

"You're learning to cook? That sounds like fun."

"Yes. We also learn how to operate a restaurant kitchen,

how to order the proper amount of food so that none of it is wasted."

"That sounds great. Having good business skills is so important."

Her smile broadens.

"What else do you like?" I ask.

"I like drama. I am learning to be an actress. I have a part now in our school play."

"And I bet you're good, too. I wish I could see your play. That would be a real treat."

There are no clocks on the wall, but I feel the pressure of being on time to meet Ruby. There's so much more I'd like to say. But how do you unravel so much pain in so short a time?

"I have to go now, Zodwa." I pause. What I want to say feels so much like a mother. I take her hand in mine. "Zodwa, I suspect you have plenty of adults lecturing you these days, so I'll be quick. You're a beautiful young woman. You have your whole life ahead of you. I hope it goes well for you. And I hope you protect yourself along the way. No man is worth getting AIDS. Please be careful." I lean over her bed and kiss her lightly on the forehead. "I hope I get to see you again while I'm here. Eat all your grapes. They'll help you stay strong. Bye now."

It feels cruel to leave an empty chair beside her bed. Just as I'm dragging it through the doorway, her faint voice reaches me.

"Thank you."

One hand on the door jam, I turn and smile—a mom kind of smile. "You're welcome, sweetheart." I cry all the way to the lobby.

"You must come with me," Ruby says. She makes no effort to conceal her agitation. "I have left Rolina in my mother-in-law's room. She wants to speak with you."

"Rolina? What does she want?"

"No. Not my maid." Her agitation grows. "My mother-in-law insists on speaking with you. We must hurry. I have errands in town before I go home to prepare my husband's dinner. I cannot be late."

We hurry down the outdoor corridor between rows of wards, following the green stripe to the respiratory unit. Granny GuGu's room, three doors down on the left, is indistinguishable from Zodwa's. A frail woman wearing an oxygen mask nods as we pass her bed. Granny GuGu lies on her side, in the bed nearest the window. She waves her arm and smiles as we approach.

"You must be careful," the nurse tells her. "You should not move your arm so much. It will disturb your IV line."

Does Granny actually understand the nurse's instructions?

Ruby stands behind me, her hand on my back, nudging me closer to Granny's bed. I take GuGu's hand in mine as the nurse lowers the bed rail and slides a chair under me. GuGu's paper-thin, wrinkled skin reminds me of my own grandmother whom I haven't thought of in years and suddenly ache to see again. Granny's eyes sparkle with enthusiasm as she speaks to me in the same animated way she always has since we discovered each other living in the same house. She rattles Zulu through her one-toothed grin, interrupted only by her raspy cough, as though we were old friends who speak the same language.

Eyebrows raised, I turn to Ruby for a translation. Her silence feels like punishment.

Gripping my hand with surprising strength, GuGu seems to ask for my undivided attention as she continues her mysterious monologue. I squeeze back, assuring her that I'm listening. The Zulu words roll from her lips, the hard guttural clicks softened by age. She stops with her familiar question mark expression that begs for my response.

"Yebo," I say.

"Thank you," she responds with a wide smile, as if I have given her a gift.

These are the only words we share in common.

"We will leave now," Ruby says.

My time with Granny is almost over. "GuGu," I say, "I'm happy that I got to meet you, if only for a very short time." She smiles.

"I hope you travel peacefully to the other side. And when you reach the other side, I hope you rest comfortably. It has been good to know you. Blessings to you on your journey."

GuGu closes her eyes and releases my hand. We've finished our good-byes. I stand, lean over and kiss her forehead. A narrow track of tears runs across the bridge of her nose onto her pillow. She opens her eyes and we smile at each other one last time.

» » »   « « «

Rolina flails her arms as she speaks to Ruby on the way to the car. She sounds hostile, her anger emphasized by spitting on the ground. I feel paranoid assuming I'm the center of every argument simply because I don't know the language. Rolina could be angry with Ruby for a million different reasons. But I would give anything to know what Granny GuGu said to me.

When we pull into the coombie depot, Ruby hands fare to Rolina who mutters under her breath until she's out of earshot.

"Come to the front seat," Ruby says. "We must make one stop in town before we go home. I need red pens for my classroom."

We park in an unfamiliar area of town where the unlit shops are rotted nearly to the point of collapse. One push and they'd topple like dominoes. Following Ruby, I peek into the dark shop. I don't need anything. We're both exhausted. Why can't this wait until tomorrow? "I'll wait outside," I shout in after her.

I press my forehead to the grimy window of the shop next door, cupping my hands around my eyes for a better view. Wooden cubby holes, about six-inches square, cover every

wall from floor to ceiling, each filled with items I don't recognize. I step through the door.

A man's deep voice startles me. "Can I help you?" he
asks.

I strain to see in the dim light. Tall, thin to the point of
emaciated, he sits eight feet away on an old three-legged
stool, his arms crossed in front of his chest. His filthy, wide-
brimmed hat and straggly gray beard nearly obscure his
leathered white face.

"No, I'm just looking," I say. "Waiting for my friend."

A low counter prevents me from wandering deeper into
the store. Eye-shaped shields lie on the floor, propped against
the counter. Made of white hides stretched between two
bowed arrows that are tied at each end with leather strips,
the shields are painted with red and black diamond patterns.
I recognize them as Zulu warrior shields from postcards at
the Johannesburg airport. But this isn't a tourist area. I
doubt these are souvenirs. Wrinkled heads, with long,
straight black hair that protrudes in a clump from the center
of the scalp, lie on the floor between the shields. They
remind me of the apple-core dolls my grandmother made
when I was little. These are much larger, though, perhaps
made from withered tree branches.

I squint at the unfamiliar objects that fill the cubby holes.
"What are those?" I ask, pointing to one.

"Tongues."

"Excuse me?"

"Tongues. Impala tongues."

I recoil at the disgusting thought, but can't resist knowing
more. I point to another cubby. "And those?" I ask.

Silence. I turn to look at him.

"Wild boar tails," he says, expressionless.

I can identify the contents of other cubbies myself: bones,
pig snouts, chicken legs, hooves. This is an animal parts
store!

Ruby grabs the back of my shirt and yanks me out of the

shop. On the street she lets loose of my shirt and grabs my arm so hard it hurts. "Get in the car!"

Her rage scares me. "What's wrong?" I ask.

"You should not be in that shop!"

"Why?" The shop doesn't look dangerous, just weird.

"That is not a shop you should be in," she growls. "Ever!"

"Okay. I promise. I won't ever go there again." Not that I could. I don't even know where we are. But my curiosity is piqued. I wait for Ruby to calm down, unclench her hands from the steering wheel. We drive in silence for a few minutes while I gather the courage to ask my next question. "Ruby, what kind of shop is that? He's selling pieces of animals."

"That is where the witch doctors purchase things for their black medicine. You have no business being in their shop."

It seems so ridiculous, but Ruby's not kidding. She's scared. Maybe I should be, too. My thoughts race to Alexander McCall Smith's *No. 1 Ladies' Detective Agency*, his tale of witch doctors in Botswana using young children's finger bones for their curses. Maybe it's not fiction.

With a flash of nausea I remember the heads on the floor. No! They can't possibly be *real*. I struggle to remember details that could assure me they're fake. I can't think of one. I have questions that need answers. Ruby will never bring me here again. Maybe Thulani will ride the coombie with me. Is he old enough to protect me? Maybe Ruby has already protected me and I shouldn't push my luck.

» » » « « «

The boys enjoy my sloppy joes. Ruby refuses to eat; says her ulcers are acting up. Mhambi arrives home later than usual. He looks exhausted. We're all exhausted.

"Karen, I have found the music paper you asked for," Mhambi says, pulling a pad of staff paper from his briefcase before he plops into his armchair. He slides his feet out of his shoes, lights a cigarette and rests his arm across his head. "But I am too distracted for a lesson tonight," he continues. "Perhaps we can begin tomorrow. Tonight I am worried. I have just come from the hospital. My mother is very sick."

"I'm so sorry, Mhambi."

"Thank you for your concern, Karen." He takes a deep drag on his cigarette. "My mother told me that you spoke with her this afternoon."

I nod.

"She was very pleased to see you."

"I feel honored that she asked for me. She's a special woman."

"Indeed." Mhambi's eyes have sunk deeper into his face since yesterday. His lips tremble as he speaks. "The doctor did not have a good report for me this evening. I do not know how I will continue to live without my mother. She is the inspiration for my life."

DAY 16

FRIDAY, FEBRUARY 15, 2008

I close my eyes for the ride to school. If anyone asks, I'll tell them I'm meditating. The combination of coombies whizzing in and out of traffic and the build-up of condensation on the windshield is more than I can handle today. Phyllis and Ruby banter with the radio talk show. Their conversation flows smoothly between English and Zulu. Each time Phyllis slams on the brakes, I scrunch my shoulders and Pamela gives my arm a gentle squeeze.

As we climb the steep hill toward the Drakensburgs, the car slows to a crawl. A nearly imperceptible gasp comes from the front seat. Someone turns the radio off. I open my eyes to see what has silenced them. A long line of cars creeps up the hill. Kids huddle together in groups of six or seven along both sides of the road; the older children with their arms around the younger ones—their faces filled with terror.

"Haybo," Ruby whispers under her breath.

Phyllis mumbles something about a disabled car blocking the roadway. A somber silence engulfs the three women. As usual, I struggle to understand the events taking place around me.

As we creep forward through the throngs of children, Phyllis and Ruby share hushed Zulu words. Pamela stares out her window. We pass the guardrail that separates the roadway from the steep decline into the valley. Phyllis pulls onto the dirt shoulder, behind a parked blue sedan. Its doors hang wide open. My heart pounds. Something is very wrong.

"What's going on?" I ask.

"There has been an accident," Phyllis says.

I look around as we climb out of the car. No smashed vehicles. No dent in the guardrail. I peek over the steep embankment, fearful of what might lie at the bottom. Still nothing.

Phyllis, Ruby, and Pamela walk back down the hill toward the children. In their low-heeled sandals they pick their steps through the loose gravel. I follow behind, like a child, silently waiting for the nature of the trauma to be revealed.

We pass a middle-aged woman sitting on the uphill end of the guardrail. Bent over, her head rests in her hands, one elbow on each knee. Another woman stands in the center of the road directing the steady flow of traffic through the crowd. She motions for the kids to stay on the far side of the road. They line up, two or three deep along the hillside, staring at us.

Then I see them. On our side of the road. Two skinny legs protrude from under the guardrail into the gravel shoulder. Spattered with red dust and pebbles, they lie very still. His toes point away from each other. He wears only one shoe. My stomach turns as I understand what has happened. As I move closer I see the boy's khaki shorts and the bottom of his navy blue sweater vest. The rest of his body is hidden from view, behind the guardrail in the tall grass.

Phyllis leans over the guardrail and takes his tiny wrist in her hand. She takes a deep breath and closes her eyes as she feels for a pulse. She lays his arm across his belly and stands.

"He is dead," she whispers. "There is nothing to be done for him."

She mumbles something else. Pamela hurries to our car, pulls a blanket from the trunk, and hurries back. Phyllis spreads the blanket over the boy's upper body. His legs are still visible. I reach for the guardrail to steady myself. I feel sick. Scared. Anxious. Numb. Everything. Nothing. I want to scream.

Phyllis pulls her cell phone from her bra and makes a call. "I have notified the officials," she says. "They will come as soon as it is possible."

I'm not sure who she's addressing. Me? Pamela? The kids? It doesn't matter. She gathers the boy's other shoe and backpack, laying them neatly next to his body. Ruby walks back up the road. She sits down on the guardrail next to the woman we passed earlier. Pamela opens her arms. Little kids rush to hug her legs. Phyllis motions for the kids on the other side of the road to be on their way. Gradually, the older ones take the little ones by their hands and climb the hill. At the top, they turn back for one more look.

I feel frozen in place. Stupid for doing nothing. Painfully aware of my status as an outsider. I need to do something. Anything. I know how to hold children. Rock them. Comfort them. They'll let me in, even if we don't know each other. I move closer to a cluster of kids. They move closer to me, relieved to have an adult body to lean against. I stretch my arms around them. Touch their warm heads. Rub my hands over their backs. They hug my legs. It isn't much I offer, but it's all I know. We cling to each other. Cry.

A screeching howl floats up the hillside from the valley below. Phyllis seems in a hurry to send the kids off to school. She motions for the cars to stop, to allow me to escort the kids across the road. On the other side, I lean over to kiss the top of each head. Their hands slide down my legs as they move away. Heads down, they climb the hill with slow deliberate steps.

The strange noise grows louder. Nothing tucked away in my memory identifies this horrid shriek. Could it be a wounded animal? I shield my eyes against the glint of sunlight on the dew. I don't see anything in the tall grass. The muscles in my legs tense with a surge of adrenaline as I instinctively prepare to flee.

No one else looks alarmed. They stand silently at the guardrail, gazing down the embankment. Again I shield my eyes against the glare and squint into the distance. This time I see movement in the tall grass. As the creature grows closer, Phyllis and Pamela motion for me to follow them back to the car. As we approach the car, I stop to join Ruby and the woman who still sits with her head in her hands.

Ruby places her hand in the middle of the woman's back, gives her a gentle push. "Go." Ruby says. "Go now." The woman hugs Ruby, walks to the blue car, shuts the door, and pulls away.

I can't leave now. I need to know what this creature is. Certain that Phyllis won't leave without me, I turn back to look down the embankment. As the wailing grows louder, I make out three heads just above the grass. Three women. The one in the center thrashes her way up the hill. She stumbles. Disappears in the tall grass. Stands again. Throws her arms violently over her head, thrashing the air with every step.

Warm breath falls on the back of my neck. A palm rests on my shoulder. "It is the boy's mother," Ruby says, her voice soft, tender. "She has come from the village to collect her son's body."

I can barely see through my tears. Every few steps the mother throws herself to the ground, writhing in agony. The sounds that escape with her sobs pierce my soul. I have never heard a human being screech like this—the cry of a tortured animal before the relief of death. My heart cracks. I sob with her. I remind myself that *my* boy is safe at home. That does nothing to relieve my raw agony.

As they draw near, I hear faint, husky voices. The two women walking alongside the mother kneel on either side of her as she pounds the earth with her fists. Their lilting chants make me want to run into their arms. Let them hold me.

All three stand, walk several paces closer to the boy's body. The mother throws herself on the ground again. Her screams shred me. I let go a violent sob.

"She will be fine," Ruby whispers in my ear. She wraps her arm around my waist and leads me away. "The women will care for her. They will feed her and keep her safe while she grieves for her son."

» » »   « « «

We ride the rest of the way to school in silence. My legs are too weak to climb the hill to the classrooms. I collapse into a chair in the library, fold my arms on the table, bury my head in them, and sob. Somehow Phyllis, Ruby, and Pamela can move on with their day. I feel wrecked.

Every death I've ever attended at the hospital flashes through my mind. Why have I never seen a mother grieve like this before? How do American women contain their grief? I've never questioned before now. *This* is what grief looks like. *Sounds* like. *Feels* like. There's no hiding this grief. No shame.

Reality begins to take hold of me. Half the kids at Zinti have watched their parents die. How do they carry on? How do they come to school every day? How do they laugh? Play? How do they go home to an empty house? How do they go to bed at night without anyone to tuck them in? Into what? A mat on a mud floor? My tears turn to anger. Numbness. I need relief.

Missy opens the library door with her butt, her tea tray in hand. She stirs two teaspoons of sugar into my cup, sits next to me with her arm around my shoulder, and motions for me to drink. I lean against her shoulder in silence. Phyllis comes in and sits across from us. I stare at her with blank, swollen eyes.

"The women will care for her," Phyllis says, her voice tender. "She will be fine, Karen."

"Do you know how it happened?" I ask.

"Did you see the woman who sat with Ruby on the guardrail?"

I nod.

"She is the one who struck the boy with her car. The children were playing at the edge of the road. They were not being cautious."

"What will happen to her?"

"Ruby sent her home. She was too upset to teach at her school today."

Of course she was upset and couldn't go to work; she just killed a seven-year-old boy. "I mean, will she be arrested, or go to jail? Will she be punished for killing him?"

Phyllis shakes her head. "She did not wish to strike him. There is no reason to punish her. The children were being reckless and it could not be avoided. These things happen."

These things happen? Like children are disposable? My stomach churns.

"Come now, Karen," Phyllis says. "It will be good for you to teach your lessons."

Missy follows me up the hill. She sets a second cup of tea on my desk and hugs me before she leaves. The kids stand to greet me with subdued voices, "Good morning, Mees Karreen."

Do they know what happened? Or do they just sense my somber mood?

"Good morning, learners. Today we will practice our verbs."

I will collapse any second.

"Yesterday I prayed for rain," I say, writing the sentence on the chalkboard.

"Yesterday I prayed for rain," the kids repeat in unison.

"Today I am praying for rain."

"Today I am praying for rain." Thirty-six tiny voices work together to please the teacher from America.

I smile. "Tomorrow I will pray for rain."

"Tomorrow I will pray for rain."

My imagination drifts to a place where rain is soft and soothes the harsh edges of life.

» » » « « «

During my second hour of teaching, a third grade girl delivers a message from Phyllis. "It is private," she says. I lean over so she can whisper in my ear. "Ma'am wants you to come to her office, please. She says 'come now,' please."

I assign Nandi's class the task of copying sentences from the chalkboard into their notebooks. I take the girl's hand. She holds her head high and leads me down the hill, proud that she's accomplished her mission.

In Phyllis's office, all the teachers huddle around Ruby. I stand at the periphery of the circle, waiting for a glimpse of understanding. Ruby presses her phone to her ear, listening with a solemn expression. When she hangs up, she speaks to the teachers in Zulu.

Thank God for Pamela who leans in close to translate. "Ruby has just learned from the hospital that her mother-in-law has passed away. We think it happened about an hour ago, but Ruby has just received the news. Now she must call her husband to tell him."

I feel selfish—uncertain that I can handle another death today; relieved that I said good-bye to Granny yesterday. Ruby dials her phone and hands it to Phyllis. When Mhambi answers, Phyllis delivers the news.

» » » « « «

Our silence is interrupted only by Ruby's occasional whisper of "Haybo!" followed by a round of soft mumbles from Phyllis and Pamela. Phyllis drops Ruby at the gas station so she can take her car to meet Mhambi at the hospital, leaves Pamela at the end of her street, and takes me across town to Ruby's house. Rolina looks sick when Phyllis delivers the news about Granny.

"Aye, Karen," Phyllis says, collapsing onto the sofa. "This is a difficult day."

"It sure is." Unbearably hard. A day that warrants withdrawing into a cocoon of grief. "What can I do to help Ruby?" I ask.

"Your presence will be very helpful to her," Phyllis says. "Ruby is married to a traditional man and now she becomes the mother of the entire Ndlela family. It will be very difficult for her. Now she must follow the traditional ways."

"So what should I do?"

"You do not need to do anything special. Your presence alone is good for Ruby."

» » » « « «

There must be something practical I can do. I boil the water in the kettle over and over, keeping it hot for when Ruby arrives home.

"Haybo!" Ruby sits on the sofa, a blank expression pasted across her face. "I always knew this day would arrive. Now it is here and I am not ready to be the mother of my husband's family. I have many responsibilities now, and still I am supposed to sit here on the floor and receive visitors."

"Sit on the floor?"

"Haybo! It makes my back hurt just to think of it. Our custom is that the women sit on the floor for a week—a whole week—while mourners come to express their sorrow. But I need to make sandwiches, cakes, tea, fruit. They will all be here tomorrow and I must be prepared."

"I can help. What do you want me to do?"

"You cannot do anything. It is I who must make them. It will not be accepted for anyone else to prepare the food."

This doesn't feel right. I can't just sit here and watch her work. Not now.

"Tonight will be easy," Ruby says. "It will only be the teachers from Zinti. They will not stay long and will not expect to be fed."

"Can I make dinner for you and the boys?"

"Yes, Karen. My husband will be home very late, and he will not eat tonight. So you do me a great favor."

I'm relieved to be able to do *something*.

The kitchen door slams. Ruby sighs, fixing her gaze on her lap as Siphelele bounces into the living room. Alarm crosses his face when he sees his mother.

Siphelele shakes his head. "No." He drops his backpack to the floor next to his feet. "No. Do not tell me that Granny has died."

Ruby lifts her head to answer him. "No," she says. "Granny is okay. She is in the hospital."

My head spins toward Ruby, my mouth agape. I look

back to Siphelele. He doesn't believe her either. He storms off to his room. I stare at Ruby in confusion.

"It is his father's responsibility to tell him," she shrugs. "Not mine."

I sit in stunned silence while Ruby makes phone calls. I can't even pretend to understand.

» » »   « « «

After dinner, Ruby sits on the living room floor in mourning attire: layers of scarf wrapped around her head, another scarf draped around her neck, sleeves that cover her shoulders and elbows, and an apron. Sweat pours down her face.

The living room fills with teachers from Zinti and other rural schools. They smile as I greet them in their language. I sit on the sofa next to Pamela, content to float in the Zulu conversation. When I can't stay awake another minute, I excuse myself for the evening and crawl between my sheets, where the sweet, soft music of the women's chants—just like I heard on the hillside this morning—drift across the patio to lull me to sleep. This surreal day of loss is finally over.

DAY 17
SATURDAY, FEBRUARY 16, 2008

"Haybo, Miss Karen," Thulani says, perched on his stool at the kitchen counter. "This is fantastic!" He wipes the last drop of Aunt Jemima syrup from his plate and licks his finger. "I could eat these every morning."

Ruby declares her pancakes too sweet before she rushes off to the market for sandwich supplies. Mhambi shuffles into the kitchen in his slippers, his white T-shirt tucked into belted khaki shorts.

"Can I make you some tea, Mhambi? Some pancakes?"

"Thank you, Karen, I will have tea. But I will not eat again before I bury my mother."

I join him in the living room where he slumps in his armchair without television or radio for distraction. His legs, stretched out in front of him, look limp. One arm lies across the top of his head. Depleted, every muscle in his face quivers. His half-empty teacup sits on the coffee table next to the ash tray. He takes a long drag on his cigarette.

This is the first opportunity I've had to talk with him since Granny died. "I'm so sorry for your loss, Mhambi."

He sighs hard. His voice trembles on the edge of tears. "Thank you, Karen. I apologize that your visit with us is interrupted by our grief. This is not fair for you."

"Oh, Mhambi, no. Don't say that. Please, don't even spend one minute worrying about me. I feel bad that I'm in the way at such a personal time. I don't want to intrude."

"You must not think that way. Your presence is most helpful to Ruby. I will need to be in Ntwana much of this week to make arrangements for my mother's funeral. It is good that you are here to keep my wife company."

We sit in silence as Mhambi finishes his tea and lights up another cigarette. When he turns his head toward me to speak again, I'm surprised to see him cry openly.

"This is very hard for me. I cannot bear the thought of even one day without my mother," he says, his pain raw, honest. "I want to give a proper farewell to my mother. I must honor the sacrifices that she has made for me. She was a humble woman. I want to be strong for her. I will not be able to do that if I break down like this at her funeral. That is my biggest fear."

"I can see that you really love your mother."

"She was a very strong woman, Karen. Do you know that my mother was illiterate? She preferred that I be educated rather than herself. She insisted that as her eldest son I learn to read and make my life important to our people. She made many sacrifices for me."

"She sounds like an amazing woman. I bet she was proud of you."

"Not always." He speaks slowly, in a pensive tone, allowing his emotions to ebb and flow. "When I was a young man I made many mistakes. I gave my mother many reasons to be disappointed with me. When I was a young man of Siphelele's age, my father took a second wife. When he left my mother's home to live with his other wife, I became the provider for my family. I was very angry. I drank too much. I did not honor my mother as I should have."

I draw a long, silent breath and exhale slowly. I'm touched that he trusts me with such intimate pieces of his life.

"There was a time I was not welcome in my mother's home. I became very ashamed of myself. I quit drinking. I took a job as a coombie driver. It must have been very difficult for her to watch me risk my life every day at the most dangerous job in all of KwaZulu-Natal. But she was a strong woman. I worked hard to earn enough money to provide for my mother and finish my education. I have spent most of my life working to make her proud of me again."

His vulnerability endears him to me. "She just wanted what was best for you, Mhambi. It must have made her very happy to watch you turn your life around, become success-ful."

He looks in my eyes as though he's about to tell me his deepest secret. "It is the women who have the greatest strength. Your ability to make personal sacrifice to improve the lives of the children makes you much stronger than any man. I admire you, Karen. It is an enormous sacrifice that you make to be away from your family and your country to be here to help our children. They are not even your own blood, and still you are willing to make sacrifices for them. I would never be able to do what you have done."

I struggle to hold back my own tears. I've never consid-ered this journey a personal sacrifice. "I do miss my son and my friends," I say. "But I'm only here for three months. That's not too long to be away from home for something that makes me happy."

"You are too modest, Karen. Your son must be very proud of the way you live your life. What does he say about you coming to Africa to help our children?"

This stranger from a foreign culture opens a new window for me. He encourages me to see myself from a different view. Although we are from opposite sides of the world, our roles—me as a mother and him as a son—erase our differ-ences. I pause to remember what Kevin has shared about me undertaking this journey. He asked me to be careful, stay safe. He wants to see my photos. Being a teacher himself, he's curious about the African schools. But I don't know how he feels about *me*.

"I don't know, Mhambi. We've never talked about how he feels about me coming here. I hope he's happy for me that I'm living my dream."

"He is proud of you. I am certain of this. You must inspire him in ways that he is not yet ready to tell you."

"I hope so." I really do.

I want to hug Mhambi. Thank him for encouraging me to trust that my son understands my good intentions, that he might see past the mistakes I've made. "I hope that Kevin is as proud of me in my old age as you are of your mother."

A knock on the half-open front door interrupts our conversation. We both wipe our eyes.

"Hello? May I come in?"

Neither of us expected Phyllis. Mhambi jumps up from his armchair and transforms himself into the proud magistrate I'm accustomed to seeing.

"Come in, Ma'am. It is good to see you," Mhambi greets her at the door.

"How are you keeping today?" Phyllis asks.

"It is a very hard time. I am as well as can be expected." He glances at his watch. "My cousin will be here soon to drive me and the boys to Ntwana. We must mow the lawns and prepare the grounds. I am sorry that Ruby is not home. She has gone to the market and will not be long."

"I came to collect, Karen," Phyllis says, smiling at me. "I am going to town and I know how much she enjoys the Internet café."

I feel like a little kid who's just been invited to the ice cream shop.

"That is very kind," Mhambi says. "It will be good for Karen to speak with her family."

» » » « « «

"Hey, Patrick," I say, slipping into the front seat. I haven't seen him since they picked me up at the airport. "Are you going to town with us?"

"Yes, Ma'am. I will stay with you while my grandmother does her errands."

I secretly long for time alone to do my errands and explore. "You must have something more fun to do than hang out with an old lady."

"Patrick does not mind," Phyllis says. "You should not be alone."

We drive the same wide road that Ruby took on our first

trip to town: massive estates on one side, tenement homes on the other. Except, half-way to town we turn left down a steep hill, drive through the tenements, and spill out into a modern strip mall. Phyllis drops us off on the top deck of a parking structure.

"I will be busy for nearly an hour," she says. "Will that be too long for you?"

An hour for email? "No! That's not long at all. Are you sure you're not rushing yourself?"

"If I return at 12:30, it will allow me to finish all of my errands."

Two hours! "That sounds perfect. I'll see you then."

"Patrick, are you sure you don't want to go do something fun?" I ask, after twenty minutes in line at the post office. You're kind to stay with me, but I'll be fine. Really. We don't have to tell your grandmother."

His face lights up. "Are you certain?"

"Positive. Just point me in the direction of the Internet café and we'll meet at 12:15 right where your grandmother dropped us off."

"Thank you, Miss Karen! My mates will be very happy about this."

It's good to know my friends haven't forgotten about me, but the news from home feels foreign.

> *... Clinton and Obama are neck and neck in the primaries ... workers at a Georgia sugar factory are sick from inhaling too much sugar dust ... Lucie has a new job ... Disneyland was fun ... is Ruby's son keeping you company so you don't miss Kevin too much ... can you set up a pen pal exchange between Zinti and a California school ...*

Even here, in a modern Internet café, I can only send brief messages. I post to my website.

What I Miss Most:

Showers
Salad
Electric fans
Windows without bars
Dish soap
Easy access to books
Condiments
Ice cubes
FAMILY & FRIENDS !!!

The strip mall reminds me too much of home—shoe stores, soccer clothes, costume jewelry—except for the spice shop, where five-gallon buckets of spices are lined up on wooden planks stacked atop concrete blocks. A hand-written sign stapled to a yard stick, planted in the center of each bucket, identifies the spice. The colors alone—rich oranges, deep yellows, and reds—are enough to satisfy my senses. I squeeze through the narrow aisles and stick my nose in each bucket for a whiff of the tantalizing aromas: cinnamon, paprika, ginger, cardamom, saffron and curry. Dozens of curry varieties. I scoop from several buckets into tiny paper sacks, collecting exotic gifts for Ruby and my friends at home.

"Ah," Phyllis says when she picks us up. She raises her nose to sniff the air in the car. "So you have discovered the spice shop!"

"I've never seen anything like it. At home we buy spices in tiny little jars that cost a fortune."

"How impractical."

Phyllis tells me about her errands. She and Pamela hope to retire from teaching and open a bed and breakfast in town. "The paperwork is difficult, even though we are colored, not Zulu."

"Not Zulu? What do you mean?"

"Pamela and I are not Zulu. Our father was a Zulu man, but our mother was white. So we are colored."

"Why does that make paperwork difficult? I don't understand the connection."

"Even though we are not Zulu, and do not follow the traditional ways, Natal is still Zulu. Without husbands to sign the papers we cannot open a bank account or have a bank loan. It is very difficult to borrow money. We must go outside of the banks."

"Are you serious?"

Patrick sits silently in the back seat. I wonder how he takes in this conversation.

"Aye, Karen," Phyllis says. "Without a husband it is very difficult to be a business woman. I can tell the bank that I no longer live with my husband, that he is still in Dundee where we come from, and the bank manager says, 'No problem. We will wait for him to come here.' I can tell them that he has taken another wife and they will say, 'What a lucky man.' It is no use trying to convince the bank, so I must find private individuals who will lend us the money."

"That's awful. I'm so sorry."

"It is very unfair. But what can you do? We would like for it to be different for our daughters. They cannot even have a driver's license without a father or uncle to sign for them."

I shake my head. "Oh, my God. That's paralyzing, Phyllis."

"This is why I feel sorry for Ruby. Now that her mother-in-law has passed, she must observe the traditional ways. It will not be easy for her."

We pull up to Ruby's; I turn to hug Phyllis good-bye. "I hope you find funding for your B&B. You and Pamela would be good inn keepers. Thanks for taking me to town. It was great."

"Ruby will not come to school this week," Phyllis says. "I will pick you up here on Monday. Can you be ready by quarter to seven?"

"Sure."

"And Karen, do not worry. Even though Ruby will not be able to take you to town this week, I will see to it that you do not grow bored."

Bored? Not a chance!

» » »   « « «

Ruby sits on the edge of the sofa, legs outstretched, mopping sweat from her forehead. The furniture has been pushed against the walls to make space for the white plastic lawn chairs scattered around the room. Platters of egg salad sandwiches and cookies fill the coffee table. Dozens of empty glasses sit next to pitchers of cold tea and orange soda on the sideboard.

"Haybo!" Ruby says. "I am glad you are home, Karen. I do not like sitting here alone."

"Sorry, Ruby. I didn't know you were waiting for me."

"This is what I must do all week. Sit, sit, sit," she says, irritated. "When I go to Ntwana later this week, I will sit on a straw mat in the middle of the rondavel, in the dark, under a wool blanket." She shakes her head. "My back is already sore just thinking about it. I do not know if I can do this."

"Haybo! That sounds miserable. Is there anything I can do to help?"

A car door slams in the driveway. Ruby slides off the sofa, onto the floor.

"When my guests arrive you can serve them food and something to drink. It will be easier for me if I do not have to get up and down from the floor."

Ruby drops her chin to her chest as the first mourner walks through the open living room door. She speaks to Ruby in Zulu. Ruby nods, without raising her head, without speaking. Another woman arrives. And another. Soon the living room is filled with Zulu women. I jump into action, silently serving sandwiches and soda, washing plates, making sure everyone is fed. Except Ruby. She's not allowed to eat in front of her guests. They talk among themselves while she sits on the floor, head bowed. Despite my "sawubona" to each of them as they entered, none of them speak to me. Instead, they take turns pointing at me during their conversations with each other.

Ruby pushes herself up to the sofa when they leave. With her hands pressed into the small of her back, she stretches from side to side, exhaling a loud puff of air. "At least here I can take comfort on the sofa between visitors. In Ntwana all eyes will watch me and I will not leave the mat except to use the bathroom."

"Ruby, would it be easier for you if I wasn't here? I mean if I filled all the trays and then went to my room while you visit with your guests?" I'm not sure if I ask for her relief or mine. Being the invisible servant, the object of gossip, makes me uncomfortable.

"No, Karen, you must stay. I am not ashamed to have a white person in my home!"

Her answer hits me hard. It never occurred to me that *shame* over me—for being white—was a possibility. Do her friends give her grief for housing a white woman? My discomfort escalates.

The next group is more friendly. At least they're willing to return my greeting. Except for one woman, with a permanent snarled expression, who looks like a linebacker in a skirt. As she's preparing to leave, she towers over Ruby with one hand on her hip, the other pointed at me. Speaking to the top of Ruby's head, she nudges her foot into Ruby's thigh to evoke a response.

"Karen," Ruby says, pointing to the linebacker, "this is my college professor of education. She is impressed and wants to know if you will come to her house for tea."

Knock me over! It would have taken a lifetime to guess that one. I break into a smile for the professor. "Of course."

The professor nods at me. "Very good," she says. "I look forward to having you as a guest in my home."

She speaks English!

"I look forward to it, too," I say.

» » »　« « «

Ruby and I sit on the floor in silence. I envy these women.

They wear bright, clingy clothes that reveal every roll of skin. No one struggles to hold in their stomach. Strong and substantial, they strike a stance of power, their feet spread wide on the ground. They ooze confidence, seemingly unaffected by concerns of body image, even with the scars on their faces. If I needed to be held, nurtured, I'd feel comfortable in their solid arms.

"I do not think you listen to me," Ruby interrupts my wandering thoughts. "Do you have something on your mind, Karen?"

"Honestly?"

"Yes. Honest. Like my sister. What were you thinking?"

"How free you all are with your bodies. How nice that must be. In my country, women are supposed to be thin, not have bellies. Big women are encouraged to hide their bodies. It causes a lot of stress and we end up being ashamed of our bodies."

"Haybo! If you are thin there is something not right with your body," she grins. "Or you are a very bad cook!"

She makes me laugh. "We're supposed to be thin—and good cooks!"

"Many of my friends have asked why your clothes are so large, three sizes bigger than necessary. You must not be ashamed of your body, Karen. Before you leave, we will help you become a traditional woman."

I grab my breasts, one in each hand, and jut my chin into the air to mimic one of Ruby's favorite poses. "This is my body, and I am proud of it!" I say.

Ruby rolls on the floor in fits of contagious laughter. I join her on the floor, leaning against the sofa. Her arm rests over my shoulder. "I like making you laugh, Ruby."

"It is good for me. It is good for you, too." She pauses, slipping back into her somber mood. "There are many things that make me very sad, Karen."

"The boy on the road to school? Thinking about him and his mother makes me sad, too."

"It is not only him." Her eyes look empty. "Can I tell you something?"

"Of course." I hope I can handle what she wants to share.

"It is Zodwa's baby that makes me sad. Sad that I was not a stronger woman. I knew long ago that Zodwa was pregnant. I wanted to offer to her that I would take her baby and raise it as my own. But I was afraid that her father would be angry with me. It was a baby girl," she cries. "I could have had a baby girl. If only I had been more brave."

I exhale a deep sigh. Ruby cares more deeply than I realize.

"And watching my husband grieve for his mother reminds me of my own mother's death." She takes a deep breath and dries her face with her apron. "It was many years ago. But now it feels new again. She was in Pietermaritzburg on an errand for me, an errand that now seems very unnecessary. She did not come home, even when it became very late. I knew something was wrong. I drove all over town to look for her and I could not find her anyplace."

I feel it coming. This story's going to be brutal. Keep breathing, Karen.

"The next day my sister heard on the radio the description of a woman who had been found stabbed on the street. She called me to tell me that it sounded like our mother. I went to the morgue with my sister and my brother. It was my mother. I told my brother and sister that I must see her wounds. They could not look. But I lifted the sheet away from her body, and there they were." She points to the top of her thigh, near her groin. "Three holes where the screwdriver punctured her artery. She bled to death on the street." She turns to look at me. Tears streak her face. "It was awful, Karen."

"I'm so sorry, Ruby. What a horrible way to die. What a horrible way for you to find out."

"I have never forgiven myself for sending my mother on an errand that night. If it were not for me, she would be here with me today. I miss her still."

Ruby lays her head on my shoulder. The brief silence allows me to think about my own mother. How will I handle her death?

DAY 18
SUNDAY, FEBRUARY 17, 2008

I peek my head through the doorway of Granny's bedroom to see if Thulani wants pancakes again this morning. He lies on the bed, curled in the fetal position, his eyes swollen and red. I sit next to him, rubbing my hand back and forth across his back.

"What can I do for you, Thulani?"

He shrugs his shoulders as he pulls the neck of his T-shirt up to wipe his face. "I do not wish to dishonor my grandmother, but I do not like sleeping in her room. It is as though she is still here. It feels, how shall I say? Creepy."

I nod. "I bet it does."

"I am not permitted to complain. My uncle would not understand. And Siphelele is not to cry. My uncle will not hear of it. This is very hard." He struggles to maintain his composure.

"I'm going to make breakfast. Will you come and eat with me?"

"Thank you, Karen. I will come after my uncle has left for Ntwana. He must go today to buy a cow for the funeral. At least he does not take me and Siphelele with him this time."

Through the kitchen window I watch Mhambi and Ruby in the driveway. He listens to her, his arms relaxed at his side, cigarette in hand. She stands facing him, occasionally glancing into his face. They both appear unhurried, and although they never touch, I sense an intimacy between them—something I've not seen until now. They nod at each other as Ruby slides into her car. Mhambi unlocks the chain and opens the driveway gate for her before he returns to the house.

"Would you like some tea?" I ask.

"That is not necessary," Mhambi says. "I have already had my tea this morning. I am off to Ntwana now to make additional preparations for my mother's funeral."

"Thulani says you're buying a cow for the feast."

"Yes. We will have three-hundred guests so I must find a very fat cow," he chuckles.

I smile as my imagination conjures up a picture of Mhambi in a field of cows looking for the fattest one. I have no idea how many people one cow will feed. A rump roast serves six to eight.

"I have spoken with Ruby," he says. "We would like very much for you to be our guest at Ntwana next weekend. You will do me a great honor by attending my mother's funeral."

"I would like that very much." Actually, I would hate to be excluded.

"Ah. Then it is settled! You will come to Ntwana with me and the boys on Thursday night. I have spoken with Ma'am. She will release you from your duties at Zinti on Friday. Ruby will go to Ntwana tomorrow to receive the women. You will sit with her when you arrive."

I get to participate! This is more than I ever could have hoped for. "I feel so honored that you would include me. Is there anything special I need to do to prepare? Will it be okay if I take pictures and movies in Ntwana?"

"Sitting with Ruby will be a great help to her. You do not need to do more. My mother would be very happy to know that you wish to remember her burial with your cameras."

» » »   « « «

Ruby sits on the floor all morning receiving mourners. Between visitors she creeps up to the sofa, moans about her aching back, how she dreads sitting on the hard floor of the unlit rondavel all week where she'll sleep on an old rotten mattress and be allowed to get up only to go to the bathroom. She assures me that I won't enjoy sitting with her, that it's much harder and lonelier than I imagine. She's probably right. But I may never attend another Zulu funeral in my life, so I plan to soak it all in.

"Ah," Ruby says, as a green sedan pulls into the driveway, "this is my Uncle Leonard and Aunt Rose from Durban. They are eager to meet you. You will like them."

She slips back to the floor as I stand to greet them at the front door.

"You must be Karen, from America. It is my great pleasure to meet you," Leonard says, extending his hand. He towers over me. As he clasps my hand in both of his, a soft smile spreads across his face, all the way to his dimples. I like him already. He steps back to allow his wife to enter.

"And you must be Rose," I say. "Ruby's pleased you're here."

She offers both hands, covered with perfectly pressed white gloves trimmed in lace. A small, plain white purse hangs over her arm. Her gray hair, coiffed from a fresh visit to the beauty parlor, tops her petite frame. She reminds me of the refined, country church ladies from my grandparents' Kentucky.

"Ruby," Leonard says, "you must sit with me while I am here. Come, let me give you a hug."

Ruby rises from the floor and steps into Leonard's open arms. She buries her face in his shoulder while Rose and I watch. They whisper in each other's ears before Leonard pulls a crisp handkerchief from his shirt pocket. Ruby dries her face as we all take our seats. Leonard sits on the long sofa, flanked by his wife and Ruby.

"You will be okay," Leonard assures Ruby, in a gentle tone. "Even though it is hard now, it will become easier with time."

Ruby nods, leans her head against his shoulder, and releases her held breath as she twists his handkerchief through her fingers.

Leonard turns to me with a wide grin that reveals his perfect, brilliant white teeth. "So tell me, Karen, where are you from in America?"

"California. The San Francisco area."

"Ah. I have seen the photographs. It is beautiful.

Unfortunately, it is one of the places we did not visit in your fine country."

"You've been to America?" I try to reel my voice back from sounding astonished.

"Many times. Atlanta. Chicago. Dallas. New York City."

"You've been to New York City? I'm jealous! I've never been there. What brought you to my country so many times?"

"Before I retired, I was a preacher for the Seventh-Day Adventist Church. In my later years I was a member of the international council of leaders. When my wife retired from being a school teacher, we were fortunate to travel the world to see how people live in many other places. Your country is one of our favorites."

"If you ever come to California, I'd love to show you my home."

"I can see from your face that it is a wonderful place," Leonard says with a wistful sigh. "But I'm afraid that our traveling days are over, except here in our country. Traveling is much more difficult now that we are elderly."

He reaches to pat Rose's leg. The look they exchange speaks of a tender relationship that's been nurtured by mutual respect for a half-century. Rose and Ruby seem content to sit silently through our conversation, happy just to be near this man who radiates warmth and compassion.

"Ruby tells me that you will attend Granny GuGu's funeral," Leonard says.

"I am. I'm so pleased to be included."

"There will no doubt be many aspects of the traditional funeral that are unfamiliar to you," he says. "Many of the rites are based in superstition and black medicine."

My mouth falls open. I swallow and try to appear unaffected. I'm not sure if I'm more surprised to learn this news, or that he speaks about it so openly.

"The old ways are no longer practiced in my religion," he says. "But in the rural areas they are mingled with the new religions in ways that are hard to separate. If you will allow me, it will be my pleasure to explain the meaning of the rituals to you as they occur."

"That would be great!" What a fantastic stroke of good fortune to be tutored by an educated man who's willing to address the traditions without any apparent attachments. Granny's funeral will be even more interesting than I imagined.

"Very well then, Karen. You will find me on Saturday and I will educate you in the Zulu ways."

"Ruby," Leonard says, "before I go I would like to see Siphelele. Is he home?"

Ruby lowers her chin to her chest as she heads toward Siphelele's room where he's been secluded all day. She nudges him down the hall, ahead of her, into the living room. Leonard stands to greet Siphelele, who takes his great-uncle's hand, keeping his head tilted downward to hide his red, swollen eyes.

The two of them exchange quiet words in Zulu before Leonard pulls Siphelele to his chest in a bear hug. "It will be okay, son," he says.

His tenderness brings me to the edge of tears. Siphelele needs this. He's only fifteen. He needs to be hugged and allowed to grieve. This is the first physical expression of comfort I've seen since Granny died on Friday. Leonard holds Siphelele for a long time before he pats his back and releases him. Siphelele nods, turns, and retreats to his room, unable to speak.

» » »   « « «

The grief exhausts me. I'd like to curl up in a ball and sleep the rest of the day away. Instead, Ruby and I sit in silence, munching on egg salad sandwiches and store-bought cookies washed down with flat, warm orange soda. The front door hangs open, an invitation for a breeze to move the heavy, stale air. Flies feast on our platter of sandwiches. My stomach churns. Just as I'm about to make my escape to the backyard for a nap, several cars pull up to the curb.

Ruby slides to her place on the floor and sends me to the kitchen to wash glasses and refill the soda pitcher. The front door slams shut. I hear the low drone of male voices from the other room. I wish I could set the drinks on the dining room table and escape unnoticed. When I return to the living room, eight men about Mhambi's age, dressed in khaki slacks and golf shirts, turn to address me.

"Ma'am," they say in unison, reaching to shake my hand.

I'd like to run away and hide. Plug into my iPod. Disappear in my music from home. I set the tray of glasses and soda on the coffee table, and reach to accept their handshakes.

"Hello," I say. "It's nice ..."

"Karen!" Ruby shouts. "Do not be so lazy! Do not insult these friends of my husband by greeting them in your language. Greet them again with respect, in their mother tongue."

My face flushes with humiliation. "I'm sorry, Ruby."

"Do not waste your time being sorry! Greet them properly. Now!"

» » »   « « «

Thulani fetches me from my room for the evening mourning. This afternoon was a disaster. I feel bad about screwing up, greeting in English instead of Zulu, but none of the men seemed to mind. Ruby, sour with me all afternoon, ordered me in and out of the kitchen, speaking only Zulu even though the men used English. My nap hasn't helped. I feel like I'll never be rested again. I resolve to fit in better: try to remember all my Zulu, try to smile more and talk less. In an effort to be more Zulu, and make Ruby happy, I wear one of the necklaces I bought with Busi.

Mhambi's sister-in-law sits in absolute silence on the floor, tucked away in the dining room among the chair legs, almost under the table. With a glazed look of hopelessness, she never speaks.

Ruby sits on the floor across from my seat, her back resting against the sofa, playing with her three-year old nephew. She silently monitors my every move without ever making eye contact. Mhambi's brother, Mr. Happy-Go-Lucky, behaves as if I'm the only person in the room. He flashes a Hollywood smile, admires my necklace, and tells me what a beautiful wife I'd make. His conversation, totally without substance, lacks the gentlemanly reserve that Mhambi offers me. He makes me squirm.

Ruby seems oblivious to his flirtations. I'm concerned that my polite smile and conversation gives him—and his wife—the wrong message. I'm even more afraid that if I tell him to back off, Ruby might take my head off.

I retreat to the kitchen with Thulani and his young cousin, happy to wash dishes and play Rock-Paper-Scissors until I can escape to my room. Sleep comes hard, wondering how I will manage to make it through the funeral under Ruby's critical glare.

DAY 19
MONDAY, FEBRUARY 18, 2008

"Good morning, Karen. How are you today?" Phyllis asks as I close the car door. "I have a surprise for you today. A great surprise you will enjoy very much."

Her upbeat demeanor is a welcome relief. I feel free, like a young school girl skipping off for the day without a watchful parent. "What?" I turn to smile at her. "Tell me. I'm no good at waiting!"

"There is a rock not far from Zinti that I have been wanting to show you. It is a very special rock. Today we shall visit it before we go to school."

"I love rocks! I can't wait to see it."

We swing by Pamela's house. "Sawubona," I smile as she slides into the car.

"Good morning, Karen. How was your weekend?"

"It was okay. Ruby had lots of mourners. It's hard for her. One time I forgot to greet in Zulu and she snapped at me. I think I embarrassed her. I really enjoyed meeting her Uncle Leonard, though. He invited me to spend time with him at the funeral."

"I am sure Ruby is not angry with you," Phyllis says. "She is under a great deal of stress now that Granny has passed. It is not you she is unhappy with."

"You keep saying how Ruby's life is going to be so different now. What's that about?"

"It would be very hard for you to understand, Karen," Phyllis shakes her head with an exaggerated sigh. "Sometimes, I do not understand it myself."

I'm tempted to press for more information. I turn to look at Pamela in the back seat. She purses her lips, shakes her head and says "don't even ask" with her eyes.

"Ruby's Uncle Leonard is a good man," Phyllis says. "You are fortunate to keep company with him at the funeral. He will teach you much."

199

We begin our ascent up the road toward the village. The morning mist has risen early today, leaving behind shards of light glinting on the broad leaves of the pygmy palm trees that dot the hillside.

"It was not that long ago that we were not able to take this ride to school in daylight," Phyllis says.

I scrunch my eyebrows. "What do you mean?"

"For many years, Pamela and I—and all the colored teachers—had to come to school very early in the morning while it was still dark. And we had to ride the coombie so we could hide among the Zulu teachers and not be discovered by the Indunas."

"Indunas?"

"The chiefs. The men who control the tribes. They were always at war with each other, killing anyone who dared to cross the creek or the road onto their land. They killed even another Zulu who did not belong to their own tribe. They would have slaughtered a colored woman without even one question." Phyllis slides her finger across her throat, her face distorted with anger. Or is it fear?

The muscles in my face tense. I turn to see Pamela's reaction.

"It is true," Pamela says. "One time, during a long and bloody war for land, one of the Indunas stopped the coombie we rode in. My sister and I were very frightened when the Induna's men came into the coombie to inspect the passengers. We were the only two colored teachers that day. They made us get off and stand by the side of the road while the Induna asked us many angry questions. We were certain that they would kill us right there by the road."

My stomach tightens in a knot. I take a deep breath to loosen the constriction in my chest. "I can't even imagine how terrified you were."

Phyllis shakes her head. "We do not know why they let us live that day."

We all pause. I hesitate to ask my next question, but I can't help myself. "Were the turf wars related to Apartheid?"

"No," Phyllis says, emphatically. She pauses, as if to reconsider her answer. "The incident we speak of happened about ten years ago, well after the end of Apartheid. The Indunas have always fought among themselves for control of the land. It has actually been more peaceful since the end of Apartheid. Even so, before you came to Zinti, it was necessary for me to visit every Induna who controls land between Zinti and the paved road to obtain their permission to bring a white woman across their territory. The Inspector said it was best that we did not take a chance."

So *this* is what they were talking about at the beginning when they said they wanted me to have "the best possible experience." Would I have even come if I knew this little detail?

"Am I safe?" I ask.

"Yes, Karen. They are pleased to have a white woman to teach their children now. It has been a very long time now that we are able to come to school safely."

I don't even want to ask how long. If she needed permission to bring me to school, it hasn't been long enough. Still, she sounds confident. Surely she wouldn't tell me this if she wasn't.

We bump down the dirt road toward Zinti in silence. I wonder where the boundaries are between Induna territories. The row of trees along the creek? The ridge on the other side of the valley? Nothing looks obvious. Would I recognize an Induna if I saw one? I never see anyone in the village except the children and an occasional woman walking alongside the road with a bundle perched on her head. Where are the men? Why don't I see them? Maybe it's best I don't.

"We are very near the Zinti rock now," Phyllis says. "I am excited for you."

We drive on, around the bend, following a narrow road cut into the slope. On the back side of the hill, I draw a deep breath, in awe of the magnificent view. Rolling emerald hills fan out before me. Tall grass, undulating in the soft breeze, drips with shimmering light. Off to the right, a solitary rock formation juts hundreds of feet into the air from the center of the hill—a sandy crystal formation framed by pure blue sky. The morning sunlight plays on the rock, illuminating narrow red streaks from the tip to the ground.

Phyllis stops her car. Mesmerized by the beauty, I walk in a trance along the road.

"Is it not wonderful?" Phyllis asks, as she and Pamela approach behind me.

"There are no words to describe it."

"We knew you would like it," Pamela says, pleased. "This is the Valley of Green."

My eyes fill as I turn a complete circle, trying to absorb the spectacular beauty. "It's incredible."

"There is a great legend to the rock," Phyllis says. "A magical underground river runs to the valley from a cave deep inside the rock. This water has the power to grow crops that cannot be matched anyplace on this earth."

I believe her. This shade of green cannot be equaled.

"You can climb through an opening in the side of the rock to reach the cave. But the legend says that there is a snake that lives there who will curse your camera if you try to capture its spirit in a photograph. And look, Karen, at the side of the rock. Water runs down the side even when there is no rain. For many years the water was clear. Now, the spirits have become angered at how much blood has been shed for useless reasons, and the water runs red. Can you see the dark stains on the side of the rock, Karen?"

Squinting against the glare, I nod. Rivulets of water glide down the surface of the rock. The deep red lines may be caused by iron in the water, and cameras messed up by a magnetic field, but the myth captures my heart.

"It is only the young girls, the ones who are still pure virgins, who may tend to the crops here in the Valley of Green," Pamela says. "The Zulu king comes all the way to this valley every spring to receive gifts of crops from the villagers. It is when they have the offering ceremony that the king also inspects the girls who have reached puberty during the year."

Her words jolt me out of my reverence. "Inspect them? What do you mean?"

"How shall I say?" Phyllis pauses. "He inspects to determine if they are still virgins."

"So they can keep tending the crops?" That seems a bit extreme.

"No, Karen. That is not the reason."

I raise my eyebrows to her, begging an explanation.

"The girls who are virgins will have their clitoris removed. The girls who are no longer virgins, will not."

"Damn! Why?" My arms tense with fury. I want to stomp; scream. "Why do they do that?"

Phyllis sighs. "It is the traditional way, Karen."

"But why? It's so brutal. Why can't they just let the girls be whole and beautiful? And only the virgins? The most innocent? I don't understand."

"It is the way to show that a woman is worthy of a husband," Pamela says, without emotion. "When a man is ready to take a girl in marriage, he may inspect her to see whether or not she was a virgin when she reached puberty."

"Shit! I don't suppose *he* has to be a virgin! That's so unfair."

Phyllis and Pamela stand motionless and silent as they watch me flail my arms through the air, ranting at the inequities.

"It is also unfair," Phyllis says, her voice calm and even, "that a woman without a husband has no rights. No freedom. No voice."

My heart sinks. Resolving the women's issues is not as simple as I would like to believe. Phyllis and Pamela watch with stoic expressions as my attitude of righteous indignation transforms into despair. Without another word, we return to the car and head for school.

» » » « « «

Phyllis assigns me to Ruby's class while she's out this week: forty-eight students—double the size of the Grade Four classes—with only six weeks of English instruction. Their command of English equals my command of Zulu. I feel lost. They won't stay in their chairs; poke each other; throw pencils, rulers and chairs across the room; and shout to be heard above the chaos. I might call it over-the-top playground behavior, but I sense an undercurrent of terrorism.

"Quiet!" I scream in frustration, embarrassed by the oxymoron.

A few girls whom I suspect have moved to the village from the city, turn toward me revealing scolded expressions. I'm relieved that *someone* knows the meaning of "quiet." But their attention is short lived. Within seconds they return to defending themselves against the makeshift weapons.

I make eye contact with one of the ring-leader boys at the back of the room. "Wozala!" I say forcefully, pointing at him. "Wozala!"

The entire class spins toward me this time, shocked that I can demand that he approach me. Too bad I don't have another attention grabbing word in my repertoire. The boy smirks at me, but saunters to the front of the room as the others calm to a dim roar. He seems remarkably content to stand at the front of the classroom, holding my hand for the rest of the day. I hope he doesn't feel me tremble.

Using sign language, I manage to have them open their workbooks and copy the list of sentences I write on the board: I WILL LISTEN TO MY TEACHER. I LOVE MATH. IF I CAN READ, I CAN DO ANYTHING. I LEARN MY LESSONS WELL. Clueless how to make them understand what they're writing, I pray it will sink in by osmosis.

I make a lousy instructor for Ruby's class, but a fair babysitter—no one gets hurt. I'll never hand out the plastic recorders I've brought. They look too much like weapons now.

» » »   « « «

"Thulani?" I whisper, poking my head into his room. "Can you help me?"

He steps across the hall with me, into the bathroom.

"I'm embarrassed," I say. "I can't get the toilet to flush."

"Aye, no problem, Karen," he smiles. "I will show you how." He removes the single knob from the sink and screws it onto the rusted metal stem protruding from the wall under the toilet. As he opens the shut-off valve, water gurgles into the tank. I press the flush lever. A spray of water shoots from the bowl, against the closed lid, over the rim, onto the floor.

"You see," Thulani says, "it works fine. When you are finished, you turn it the other way."

"Thanks," I say, shielding my face from the spray as I bend over to turn the knob.

Hands on my hips, surveying the mess, it seems obvious that peeing in my bedroom sink will be easier. I head to my room, ready to sacrifice an old T-shirt as a bathroom mop.

Ruby stops me in the hallway, her face darkened with dismay. She holds her hand in front of my face, her fingers spread wide. Her middle finger is wrapped in a beehive of gauze.

"Oh, my God, Ruby! What happened to your finger?" The bathroom floor can wait.

"My finger is on fire."

"Did you burn it on the stove?"

"It is not like that. It burns from the inside."

I watch with anticipation as she loosens one end and, like a magician with scarves, pulls yards of white gauze off her finger.

"It is my punishment for believing that my husband's mother has been a burden to me," she says. "The spirits of evil are trapped in me now, burning through my finger."

The American expression of something irritating being "under my skin" pops to mind. As the last layer of gauze falls to the floor, Ruby sticks her finger out for me to inspect. To see better in the dim light of the hallway, I pull her hand closer to my face.

"You have a hangnail, Ruby! An infected hangnail."

In the kitchen, I prepare a bowl of warm salt water. Between packing clothes, candles and cooking supplies to take to Ntwana, Ruby pauses to soak her infected finger.

"This is magic, Karen!" she says, amazed at the speedy results.

Effective? Yes. Magic? Only in Ruby's world.

» » » « « «

"Mhambi, you look tired," I say.

Slumped in his armchair in a white T-shirt and black shorts, his court ID badge still hangs from its lanyard around his neck. With one arm resting on his head, he drags on the stub of his cigarette. Mhambi looks worn out already, and this is only Monday.

He reaches for the remote to turn down the sound on the soccer match. "Haybo, Karen," he says, exhaling blue smoke into the living room. "It was a very difficult day."

"More vagrants than usual?" I ask, hoping my perky tone will lighten his mood.

He turns to me, sullen, his eyes empty. "Today I had some very bad news, Karen."

I instantly regret my flippant response. He takes one last drag before he stubs his cigarette out in the ash tray on the coffee table. "Today I learned that my nephew was shot in the back of the head at the coombie depot."

"Oh, Mhambi!" I slap my hands to my cheeks, my mouth open in shock. "I'm so sorry."

He shakes his head and exhales a long sigh. "I am not surprised, Karen. Still, it is sad."

This is way too much loss: Zodwa's baby, the boy on the side of the road, Granny GuGu, and now, Mhambi's nephew. I want to lay my hand on his arm, comfort him. But I know I can't. Unsure what to say next, I wait.

"This coombie business is too dangerous," Mhambi says. "I warned my nephew that his days would be short if he continued." He leans forward, resting his head in his hands, his elbows on his knees. "There is a lot of money to be made driving a coombie. Even for an uneducated man. It is very tempting. I know. I drove a coombie when I was young and foolish. My nephew said he would quit, but now it is too late."

"Do they know who shot him?" I ask.

He shakes his head. "It was dark. No one can say for sure. But I know it was another driver who was angry that my nephew strayed into his territory."

I furrow my eyebrows. "What do you mean?"

"This happens all the time, Karen. The competition for coombie territory is fierce."

"Drivers kill each other over passengers?"

He nods, lights another cigarette.

"It seems like there are plenty of passengers to go around," I say.

"Aye, Karen, that is just it. There are many passengers and not enough coombies. The government issues only a certain number of permits. It is, how do you say? A corrupt system. The officials take bribes from men who want to run the coombies in particular areas of Natal. Then these men decide who may drive a coombie in their territory."

This sounds like mafia drug territories in the States.

"If you want to drive a coombie, you must give a portion of your passenger fares to the one who controls the territory. It is not right, but the drivers do it because they still make a great deal of money. And they want to live."

"Dang! That's brutal."

"Yes. I am afraid it is. If a driver intrudes into another driver's territory, he will be killed," he snaps his fingers, "like that. Then the man who runs the territory will have a new coombie—for free—to give to his mate to drive, and he will make even more money."

I shake my head. Apparently no place on earth is safe from greed.

» » » « « «

The rock and its myths. Virgins and clitorectomies. Hangnails and evil spirits. Coombies and the mafia. Just when I think I'm beginning to adjust, I feel slammed. I can't even have a glass of wine to numb my racing mind— Mhambi doesn't allow alcohol in his home. Locked in my concrete room in the backyard, I recite a familiar prayer, over and over, out loud, hoping my words will drown my thoughts. Hoping to sleep.

DAY 20

I fear that in the frenzy of boys leaping from desk to desk in stocking feet, one of them will slip and break an arm. My shouts of "Quiet!" can't be heard above the crash of chairs flying across the room. Maybe this is how the windows broke. With uncanny accuracy, the boys fling pencils and rulers at the girls who sit huddled in small groups. Some of the girls shield their heads with their arms; others giggle like this is just an adolescent prank.

Yesterday's method of coping falls flat today. The ringleader boy either can't hear my demand of "Wozala!" over the roar, or he chooses to ignore me. I refuse to dodge chairs to walk to the back of the room. It would be pointless anyway. I can't hold his hand and confiscate makeshift weapons at the same time. I've lost control—and they know it.

» » »   « « «

"Phyllis," I say, hunched over the lunch table, "I can't handle Ruby's class."

Pamela lowers her head and looks away.

"What is the problem?" Phyllis asks.

She can't hear the din from her office? I search for kind words. "They're out of control."

"In what way do you mean 'out of control'?"

She sits quietly through my description of the chaos. I can't tell if she's disbelieving, or trying to buy time.

"It is true that many of the boys who misbehave are in Ruby's class. You must tell me the names of those who have not obeyed you."

I shake my head. She knows I can't do that. I don't know one single boy's name. Unlike the girls, they aren't patient enough to repeat their names over and over until I understand.

209

Phyllis pushes her margarine sandwich away. Crossing her arms on the table, she purses her lips. "There is one boy in particular who worries me," she says. "I must know if he is involved. I have spoken several times with his grandmother. She is not able to control his behavior."

"I don't know their names, but I can point them out to you."

"I must know if this boy is one of the learners who gives you trouble. I worry that if we do not stop him, he will become a serious problem for Zinti."

"What kind of problem? Is there something I should know?"

Pamela's face radiates concern. She glances at Phyllis without turning her head.

"Not long ago," Phyllis says, expressionless, "this boy stabbed a man in the village because he would not share his food."

My mouth falls open. My stomach sinks.

"When lunch has ended you will show me the boys. I will speak with their parents this very afternoon." She pushes her chair away from the table and stands to brush the bread-crumbs from her skirt. Her heels click across the concrete floor as she heads for her office.

That's it? That's all she's going to say about this stabbing? Did he kill the man or just injure him? That's absurd! Like one is more acceptable than the other? Do I want to identify these boys now? I don't think so. They'll know I ratted on them. Why the hell is this boy still at school? I need to know which one she's talking about so I can—what? Keep my distance? Watch my back?

"Pamela?" My voice feels thin, desperate. "Did he kill the man?"

She nods. "In the man's rondavel. While he slept."

This is way beyond adolescent pranks. They're dangerous. I can't go back to Ruby's classroom alone, afraid to turn my back on an eight-year-old boy. I have to make Phyllis understand.

» » » « « «

"Is there anything else you need me to do for you?" I fol-low Ruby to her car, my arms loaded with a stack of plates, a plastic bag of silverware slung over my shoulder. I don't want to tell her about the problems at school today. She has enough on her mind.

"No, Karen. I have taken everything from here that I will need for the funeral." Ruby opens her trunk to reveal boxes of dishes and enormous aluminum pans.

"Holy cow, Ruby! Where did you get all those dishes?" I know I haven't seen them in the kitchen.

"They are in my bedroom closet," she says, turning to face me. "All Zulu women have many dishes as I do. We must be prepared to feed our families."

Ruby tosses her purse onto the front seat of the car. We hug each other good-bye.

"Haybo, Karen. I will miss you. It is a long time to sit in the dark, under a heavy blanket. I wish you could come with me tonight."

"I'll miss you, too, Ruby." I rub my hand across the small of her back. "Take care of your back. I'll see you Thursday night. Drive safely."

I slide the chain through the gate and wave as Ruby's headlights flash across the fence.

DAY 21

The mornings turn cooler and more damp every day. It reminds me of home and, in an odd way, makes me feel more comfortable here in my home away from home. I left California three weeks ago. One-quarter of the way through my trip, I'm adapting to my African life. The unexpected twists and turns still surprise me, but the disturbance to my equilibrium feels shorter each time.

I climb the hill to the classrooms, my windbreaker zipped over my chest. Sindiswa races past, her fleece scarf tied in a cute bow around her neck. She turns at the top of the steps to blow me a kiss. I wonder if the kids without track jackets are hearty—or cold. Nomusa and I hunt for each other every morning now. I greet her with a hug. She loves me back with her gorgeous smile.

Phyllis seems annoyed that I don't want to return to Ruby's classroom—but she doesn't argue with me. I can't imagine the classroom still standing after an unsupervised morning, but I don't ask who's watching the kids. I don't want to feel guilty if they spend the rest of the week without a teacher.

Happy to be back with the Grade Four students, I question them about the hand-drawn poster I've admired with curiosity. With most posters printed in Zulu, it seems odd that the symbolism of the South African flag is taught in English. Like a game of charades, we laugh together as the kids enact the various meanings. I point to the white stripe. Two girls put their arms over each others' shoulders, one kisses the other on the cheek: peace. Next are the blocks of yellow. One boy opens his mouth wide and points to his gold-capped tooth: wealth of the gold mines. The girls giggle as another boy flexes his bicep muscle and twists his face into a fierce grimace to explain black: the people's strength.

When I move to the red section two boys point their fingers at each other, mocking a gun fight. One takes his red ink pen and scribbles on his arm: blood, shed for freedom. I point last to the massive blocks of blue and green. Smiling faces swivel to the windows, pointing toward the hillside and sky: green land sustained by rain, the sustenance of the people.

I'm touched by their proud desire to demonstrate their understanding. I don't have an American flag to show them. I'm clueless about the meaning of the colors, anyway. Stars and stripes I know, but how would I define "colonies?" I show my appreciation by singing *America the Beautiful*. I'm surprised by how many of them sing along. They don't know the words, but they sure know the tune.

Our math lesson is smooth. The kids seem much more comfortable with numbers than with English. I draw dozens of lines on the board, circling groups of ten and counting the remaining leftovers, writing the number below each group. Three groups of ten, with seven leftover, translates to 37. They catch on quickly to this system and take turns coming to the blackboard, solving the grouping problems as quickly as I can draw them. I expect that next week we'll be using this method to add columns of single digits. They excel at math.

"Karen," Phyllis says at lunch, "I have a meeting in Maritzburg this afternoon. There is a museum I believe you would like. The Tathum Art Gallery. Would you like to see it today?"

"An art gallery? I'd love it!"

"Very well. We must pack our things and leave straight away. My sister will have a ride home with one of the other teachers."

With raised eyebrows I glance across the table at Pamela, looking for confirmation that she's okay about being left behind.

She smiles. "You will like the museum, Karen. They have very nice art for you to enjoy."

Maybe Phyllis isn't angry with me after all. I'd ask, but what's the point? It seems there's a cultural taboo about telling someone something they don't want to hear. When I ask questions that cross that line, I don't get rolled eyes, sarcastic comments, or sighs of exasperation. They stare at me with blank-eyed expressions that look right through me, like I don't exist.

Besides, I don't want to spoil my afternoon of pure pleasure.

» » » « « «

The Tathum Art Gallery sits across from the park in the center of Pietermaritzburg. A flight of concrete steps as wide as the old stone building leads from the street to the massive glass doors. Phyllis holds her head high, looking proud and regal as she climbs the steps, as if this were her own personal museum. The guard swings the door open and greets her by name. She must be a regular! Inside the air-conditioned lobby, we sign the guest book and step through the metal detector. Another guard greets us, handing us a museum map.

On the rear wall of the lobby, three enormous portraits, at least as tall as I am, hang side-by-side in gilded frames: Jacob Zuma, a Zulu man, current President of the African National Congress; Nelson Mandela, South Africa's great anti-Apartheid activist and first elected black president; and Bishop Desmond Tutu, recipient of the 1984 Nobel Peace Prize and the 2005 Gandhi Peace Prize. Chills race through my body as I realize the profound history these men represent.

Phyllis stands silently at my side in the first gallery room as I marvel at baskets woven from thin telephone wire, in intricate, swirling patterns of bright lime green, purple, and turquoise. They hang on the fractured branches of a dead tree trunk that's been polished to a high sheen. The rich mahogany-colored wood contrasts the simple elegance of nature against the gaudy colors of technology.

"Oh my gosh, Phyllis! Look at this!" I say. With one hand thrown over my open mouth, I point at a floor to ceiling depiction of Nelson Mandela hanging on the wall behind the tree of baskets. I turn to see Phyllis reveal a smile of deep pride. When I step closer to the portrait, I realize it's created entirely from tiny pieces of dirty and crumpled trash recovered from the street gutters. For the first time since my arrival, I sense the breadth of South African culture.

As we move from room to room, exploring the unique art, I feel the tension drain from my body. Here, in the universal atmosphere of reverence for art, protected from the frenzy of daily life, I let my guard down. Without the need to be vigilant in my surroundings, I feel soothed by joy for the art; lost in my own internal world.

In one room, a single, aluminum-shaded light hangs from the ceiling, similar to those I've seen shined into a suspect's face during interrogation in movies. The lamp illuminates a full-length coat hanging on an iron stick-figure man. Fashioned in patchwork style, the coat is made from thin layers of tire tread, splattered with red paint that drips from the hem of the coat onto the floor.

Another room, decorated with brightly-colored, 60's-style furniture, features enormous coffee table bowls that look like woven silver. As I lean in to examine them, I see they are actually made from tinfoil gum wrappers.

"Our people have great talent," Phyllis says. The quality of her voice—tender, without the usual brash edge—implies that she longs to experience this raw talent in her daily life. "It is a shame that they do not have money to purchase proper art supplies. They must find other ways to create their art."

"It is a shame. That's true. But if they bought paint and canvas their art would look like everyone else's. This is so remarkable because it's so resourceful. So creative."

"Come, Karen. I will show you where you may have tea and rest while I am at my meeting. We shall meet at my car at half-past four."

The café on the second floor is spectacular: high ceilings, small round tables covered with white linen cloths, soft music, and a menu of delicate Indian pastries. I linger over black tea with cream and sugar and a fabulous almond cake dipped in honey. I marvel at the traditional Zulu beaded ropes that hold the curtains open. This tiny haven of calm that feeds me, instead of depleting me, will become my respite from chaos in the coming weeks.

I cross Jabu Ndivu Street, headed for the Internet café, past small wood-frame shops painted garish colors, squeezed between brick office buildings with enormous glass windows. Nearly every office door sports the international symbol for forbidden access—a red circle with a diagonal slash—containing the disconcerting images of a rifle, sword, and hand grenade. With the Kevlar strap of my practical brown travel purse slung over my neck, my hands are free to inspect the fine woven scarves offered by the street vendors.

"Pretty white lady," the men call, enticing me closer. "This one beautiful for you." I give in to a gorgeous black scarf embroidered with lush red roses and fringed with gold tassels.

As I round the corner onto Burger Street, I hear a woman's voice from behind shout, "Karen! Karen!" It takes a second to register that she must be calling after me. Without turning around, I slow my pace, trying to recall her voice. I spin around as my heart leaps. I've only met Phyllis' daughter once, but she feels like a long lost friend greeting me half-way around the world from home.

"Paula!"

A modern, professional woman in her mid-thirties, Paula plods up the street, her hips in full swing. A huge grin spreads across her face as she catches up to me.

"Aye, woman!" she pants. "You must learn to walk the traditional way. Not like you are running a race!"

"It's good to see you," I say.

We share a long hug before she slips her arm around my waist to keep me at her pace as we head up the street.

"Do you have time to shop with me?" Paula asks.

"Sure. What do you need?"

"It is not for me." She stops and turns to face me. "It is for you. Look at you." She waves her hand up and down my outfit.

I've already heard plenty about my pitiful wardrobe. "What do you mean?" I grin. "There's nothing wrong with my clothes!"

She takes my hand. "Come with me. Everyone talks about how you hide your body behind clothes that are three sizes too large. You must learn to dress like a traditional woman."

We laugh as she drags me through the tiny dress shops overflowing with bright, stretchy jersey skirts and blouses. She reaches one hand inside my dressing room and confiscates my faded cotton shirt, refusing to give it back until I've promised to buy at least one outfit of her choosing. Captive, half-naked at the back of the shop, I listen to Paula and the shop owner giggle as they decide what to have me try on next. I leave with a strapless yellow and brown flowered dress and a skirt that feels painted across my bum.

"You know I can never wear these at home," I laugh, back on the street.

"Aye, but you are not at home. You are in Africa." She wags her finger at me. "I am going to tell Ruby that you have bought these beautiful dresses and that if you refuse to wear them, she must steal your old clothes!"

"Oh, Paula, this has been so much fun." I fling my arms around her in a bear hug. "Can we do this again?"

"Aye. Any day, Karen. I work here in Maritzburg. I will tell my mother that she must bring you here often."

» » »   « « «

"Miss America!" Ronald says, opening the door for me. He kisses me on each cheek as a blast of stale, hot air rushes out of the Internet café. "It is good to see you again."

"Good to see you, too. I have lots of time today. Can I have a computer for a whole hour?"

I wait my turn, perched on a swivel stool, the seat covered with clear packing tape to hold the shredded red leather in place. My bag of new clothes dangles between my legs. Within minutes I feel sweat running down my back. Ronald brings me a Styrofoam cup of cold water and pushes a floor fan in front of me—six inches from my face.

"Thank you, Ronald," I smile. "I wouldn't want to pass out on you."

"It is no problem, Miss America. I take very good care of you."

I watch an adolescent girl across the room as she makes her way down the row of computer users, stopping only to chat with the guys. Young, maybe fourteen, she wears a low cut, white lacy blouse stretched over her well-developed bust, and a ruffled ultra-mini skirt that barely covers her butt. A slight baby-bump protrudes from her otherwise petite frame. It's hard to say if she's a shop employee, Ronald's girlfriend or sister, or just a flirty girl off the street.

She approaches me from the back of the shop, her hands clasped behind her back, until she stands in front of me with her chin held high.

"I want you to give me a job," she announces with determination.

"Excuse me?" She must have me confused with someone else.

"I want you to give me a job!"

"I'm so sorry, but I don't have a job to give you."

"You are American lady. Yes?"

"I am. But I don't live here. I'm just visiting. I don't work here. I don't have a job to offer."

Suddenly downcast, she hangs her head.

I hate to disappoint her. "What kind of work are you looking for?" I ask. "Maybe we can come up with some ideas for you."

She stands up straight, her shoulders back. Her eyes brighten as she lists her skills. "As you are able to see, I am very good with English. I have finished my exams at school. I can write. I can do math. And I am very honest."

"Those are all good skills. How old are you?"

"Twenty. Nearly twenty-one."

I seriously doubt that. "Have you ever had a job before?"

"No, ma'am. The jobs are taken by the boys." She turns and points at Ronald. "It is good for him, but it is very difficult to be a girl and have a job."

I'll brainstorm with her like I would with the teens at home. McDonalds, bagging at the grocery store, answering phones—anything to generate self-esteem and an income. "Where would you like to work?"

She beams. "In America. With you."

Dumbfounded, I struggle to take this in. She wants me to take her home with me? My heart sinks as I realize this young pregnant girl—she can't be a day over fifteen—wants to entrust her life to a total stranger. "You want to work for me in America?"

"Yes, Ma'am!" she says, excited that I've finally caught on. "I will work very hard. I will clean your home and wash your clothes. I will cook. I will take very good care of you."

My question wasn't intended to be literal—simply an expression of my ah-ha realization of what she wants. Now that we understand each other, I feel shaken. I can never give her what she wants. I don't want to crush her, either.

My eyes fill with tears. "Sweetheart, I wish it was that easy to take you home with me. I know you would work hard, and you'd be good, too. But there are laws about taking children from one country to another. Your country won't let you leave, and my country won't let you enter."

"That is not true!" She crosses her arms and stomps her foot. "I have heard that *anyone* can go to America."

She probably *has* heard that. We preach that. But the hard, cold reality is otherwise.

"Anyone can come to America. But it's not easy. You would need permission from your government to leave South Africa, and you'd need legal papers to live in my country. That takes a long time and a lot of money. Money I don't have."

"I will pay you to take me home with you."

I hate crushing her dreams. "I'm sorry. Really, I'm so sorry. I wish I could help you."

She stares at me in angry disbelief, cinching her arms tighter across her chest. Daggers stab at my heart as though I have personally condemned her to a life of poverty, hardship, and abuse. "I'm so sorry."

Her arms drop to her side as she turns and sulks away. My heart sinks. How much courage did it take for her to stand before a total stranger and ask to be saved? I feel like a coward for saying no. Her act of desperation tugs on my heart; touches me in a way I can't quite name. I'll never be able to forgive myself for disappointing her. Somewhere, deep in my soul, she has changed me.

I scroll through my emails without enthusiasm, suspended between the life I live at home and my life here. My friends and family from that other life, half-way around the world, are writing to the woman I was when I left California. She's not here.

» » » « « «

I stand on the dusky street, swaddled in my new scarf, shielding myself from the chill. In a stupor, I watch Phyllis come down the steps from the building across the street. I pick my way through rush hour traffic to meet her.

"Are you feeling unwell, Karen?" she asks.

"I'm okay."

"Did you not enjoy your afternoon in town?"

I don't know how to talk about what just happened. At

the same time, I want Phyllis to know how much I appreciate the gallery, having a whole afternoon in town. As we meander back to the parking lot, I show off my new clothes and tell her about tea at the Tathum Café.

"Still, something is not right, Karen. What has happened?"

Nearing the parking lot, I begin to relay my encounter with the young girl at the Internet café. Looking at Phyllis across the roof of her car, I finish my story. "It blows me away, Phyllis. I can't believe this girl would walk away from everything in her life—her family, her country, her friends—she'd leave *everything* behind to go to a foreign country with a complete stranger, without any guarantees of ever coming back."

Phyllis's matter-of-fact expression surprises me. She shrugs her shoulders, unphased by the girl's request. "Her chances with you, Karen, are much better than they are here."

Her response does nothing to relieve my angst. My only choice is to quash my feelings.

» » »   « « «

"Do you have take out, here?" I ask. In charge of dinner for the boys tonight, I feel too drained to cook.

"Take out?" Thulani looks puzzled. He looks up from the living room floor where he and Siphelele lie, surrounded by piles of school books.

"You know. You call the restaurant, order food, and they bring it to the house?"

The boys' eyes widen. They look at each other as if they've just won the lottery.

"Yes, Ma'am!" Siphelele says. "There are several places in Maritzburg that will bring food to this area. Our favorite is the Pizza Man."

"Awesome! You guys make the call, and I'll buy the pizza."

Neither of them have ever ordered takeout before. They call Siphelele's friend to find someone who has a phone book, call that friend to get the number and, finally, thirty minutes later, place our order with the Pizza Man—all the while bickering over who has the most available cell phone minutes and how they'll reimburse each other at the end of the week when Mhambi gives them their allowance.

The Pizza Man delivery guy tilts the box sideways to slip it through the iron gate. No matter that the sauce and cheese have slid across the crust. Stretched out on the sofa with a can of Coke and a pepperoni pizza, watching the African version of *Survivor* on television while the boys do homework on the floor, provides me a sense of normalcy—something I desperately need.

» » »   « « «

Kitty Baby, my nickname for the household cat, slips into my room with me at the end of the evening. I turn off the light and crawl between the damp, cool sheets with her curled against my belly. I'm grateful she's taken to sleeping with me, especially tonight.

Sleep comes hard after such an intense day. My mind drifts to remembering how I used to lull Kevin to sleep with stories when he was little.

"Once upon a time," I whisper, stroking Kitty Baby's long, soft fur, "there was a young girl who wanted desperately to be rescued from her life." Tears flow as I realize I'm telling my own story. "She wished she could be as brave as the girl she met today."

DAY 22
THURSDAY, FEBRUARY 21, 2008

"Tonight I will be home at eight o'clock," Mhambi says, downing his morning cup of tea at the kitchen counter. "We will leave then to go to Ntwana."

"Sounds good," I say. "I'll be ready. Do I need to pack anything special?" My bedroll, sleep sack, snake bite kit, and water purifier come to mind.

"Your cameras. I am very pleased that you will take photographs of this special day."

I smile, grateful for Mhambi's confirmation that it's okay to record this once-in-a-lifetime event.

In the driveway, waiting for Phyllis to pick me up for school, I watch Mhambi and the boys leave. Siphelele stuffs his backpack under his legs in the front seat of Mhambi's tiny red pickup truck. Thulani unsnaps the corner of the tarp that covers the truck bed, shakes off the puddles from last night's rain, steps on the rear tire, and climbs in. It's the same ritual every morning, rain or shine. I don't understand why Mhambi doesn't take the Lexus so they can all stay dry.

» » »   « « «

Through the living room window I watch Thulani and Siphelele plod up the street. Thulani is accustomed to the after-school walk from the coombie stop; Siphelele looks miserable. With wide parcels balanced on their heads, school blazers in one hand, five-gallon blue plastic buckets in the other, they're both drenched with sweat from the intense afternoon heat and humidity.

I rush to open the kitchen door. "What do you guys have there?" I ask.

"Ah, Miss Karen," Thulani says. "We have a special treat for you."

223

They tilt their heads to allow the enormous red and brown plastic bags to fall into their arms, then stack them on the counter. The label, printed in large block letters, reads MNANTI BEER POWDER. SMOOTH AND CREAMY HOME BREW. NO COOKING. MAKE TODAY DRINK TOMORROW.

"Beer? You're going to make beer?" I ask. Not on my watch. I know how Mhambi feels about alcohol in his home.

"It is our tradition," Siphelele says. "This is what the men will drink at Granny's funeral on Saturday."

"But you can taste it here, before we go to Ntwana," Thulani says. "No one will know." He rips open one of the bags and steadies himself to pour the mealy brown powder into one of the filthy buckets.

"Wait! Don't you want to wash the bucket first?" I ask. It looks like it's been used for hauling fertilizer.

Thulani peers into the empty bucket. "Aye, no, Karen. This is good."

Siphelele reaches for the other bag.

"Hey," I say. "Before you do that, can I try carrying it on my head like you do. The kids at school carry my backpack that way. The women in town carry their packages like that, too. I want to see if I can."

Thulani stands with one hand on his hip, the other on the counter, as Siphelele lowers the weighty sack onto my head. No wonder Ruby's had problems with compressed vertebrae! And this is nothing compared to a pail of water.

Siphelele and Thulani grin with anticipation as I take my first step. The slick plastic wrapper slides on my baby-fine hair. I throw my hands to my head to prevent the bag from crashing to the floor. I readjust the bag, stick my tongue between my teeth to aid with balance, and stiffen my neck in a way that would no doubt give me spasms if I kept it up for long. Then, in a poor imitation of Michael Jackson's moon walk, I slide my feet across the floor, inch by inch.

The boys slap their hands on the counter in fits of laughter. "Haybo, Karen," Thulani says. "At this rate it would take you all day to walk home from the coombie stop."

I tilt my head forward, allowing the bag to drop into Siphelele's outstretched arms.

"It's no use," I laugh. "I'll never be a Zulu woman!"

"I am not sure of that," Thulani says. "You are the most Zulu white person I will ever meet."

I watch as the boys fill the buckets with water, stirring the mixture with giant wooden spoons until the brown powder dissolves, creating a layer of frothy flotsam—the color of vomit—across the surface.

"Are you sure it'll be ready by Saturday?" I can't imagine anyone actually drinking it, much less enjoying it.

"For sure," Siphelele says. "It will be ready by dinner tonight!"

Thulani retrieves two pieces of plywood from the garage and lays them over the tops of the buckets.

"What's that for?" Aside from hiding it from view, I can't see a purpose.

"The beer is better when it has been covered," Thulani says.

Because it keeps out the flies?

"And how will you transport this to Ntwana?" I ask. Since it brews so fast, maybe we should have waited until tomorrow to make it.

"In the back of my father's truck," Siphelele says, as if I should have known.

» » »   « « «

Packed for Ntwana, I sit in my room with the door open, enjoying the breeze, writing letters. Eight o'clock. Nine o'clock. Ten o'clock.

I peek my head through the patio door. The boys sit in front of the television, giggling like little kids watching cartoons.

"Hey guys," I say. "I'm heading off to bed. Will you come and get me when it's time to leave for Ntwana?"

"No problem," Thulani says without turning his head away from *The Simpsons*. "Yo, Karen. You should see this. This Bart man is funny."

DAY 23
FRIDAY, FEBRUARY 22, 2008

At dawn, still dressed from last night, I cross the patio with my towel and toiletries only to find that the gate across the back door is locked. I knock at Thulani's bedroom window to let me in. No answer. Maybe he's in the bathroom. I knock again. Still no answer. I poke my head around the corner of the house. Mhambi's truck is gone. Has he taken the boys to school? To Ntwana?

"Shit!" I mumble under my breath, shuffling back across the patio to my room. Don't I rate enough to be informed when plans change? Am I going to school? I don't even have keys to get out the front gate if Phyllis shows up. Maybe Rolina will let me out. I'm not her favorite person, though. She might not let me back in. I resort to a bird bath in my bedroom sink, just in case I actually leave the compound.

"Hallow," a man says.

I spin around and through my partially open door see a Zulu man crossing the patio toward my room. My heart pounds. Stay calm, Karen. Stay calm. I close the door, slide the chain in place, and slip my T-shirt back over my head.

He raps on my door.

"Can I help you?" I ask, through the closed door.

"I hear you knock."

His English is rough, different from what I've grown accustomed to, difficult to understand.

"I was sleep. You come in house now."

I open my door as far as the chain allows. He looks to be in his mid-twenties, tall, rail thin, with a wide grin. Who is this guy? Where did he come from? My fear begins to subside as I realize that if he intended to hurt me, it would have already happened.

"You come to house now," he says.

"Where are the Ndlelas?"

227

He thumps his palm to his chest, juts out his chin. "I Ndlela!" he shouts.

Shit. I've offended him. Not good.

"I Mhambi Ndlela brother. I am protect you." He smiles again.

At least he's a brother who doesn't hold a grudge. "Where are Mhambi and the boys?"

"They go Ntwana."

So Mhambi took the boys to Ntwana last night, after I went to bed, and left his relative here to guard me? That's kind of him—I suppose. But a total stranger? Without telling me? I finish my birdbath, stuff my cameras into my backpack and head for the house. My security guard has boiled water for tea and discovered the leftover putu in the fridge. He eats in front of the television; I eat in the kitchen. I take the keys from the kitchen window sill and dangle them in front of him to make it clear I'm taking them with me.

"Will you be here when I come home?" I don't need another heart-thumping surprise.

"I go coombie Ntwana today."

» » »   « « «

Phyllis, apparently up on current events, slows her car to a stop in front of the house. "Good morning, Karen. How are you today?"

It's become easy to skip the ritual Zulu greeting that we share when Ruby's with us. "I'm good," I say. "I'm confused, though. I guess Mhambi decided not to take me to Ntwana?"

"I spoke with Ruby last night. You will go with me and Pamela tomorrow morning."

"Okay." I pause. "There's a guy in the house who says he's Mhambi's brother. Says he's protecting me. Do you think it's okay to leave him here until Rolina arrives?"

"It is fine, Karen. This is Mhambi's cousin. You are safe

with him. It would not be proper for Ruby's husband to leave you alone without someone to watch over you."

» » »   « « «

Samke's Grade Four kids drag their chairs next door to Nelly's classroom. I've devised a way to work music into their week without giving up academic time. The double-sized class exhibits stellar behavior for forty minutes of math. Their reward: twenty minutes of song and dance.

The kids bubble with enthusiasm as we form a line around the classroom. Each with their hands on the hips of the kid in front, with me in the lead, we snake through the room once before we head for the door. One, two, three, kick! One, two, three, kick! They giggle as I show them how to wiggle their hips. Our conga line moves along the upper footpath, past the other Grade Four classrooms. The kids grin at each other through the windows—they know their turn is coming.

Phyllis has asked me to take a group of students to the rural music competition after the school holiday. Amazed that the children are so eager to show off their musical prowess, she's offered me the assembly hall for rehearsals, confident that Zinti will be this year's winner.

» » »   « « «

Rolina calls to me as she crosses the patio toward my room. "Karen, come now!"

I don't want to get up. I like having an afternoon off, relaxing the day away, waiting to go to the funeral in the morning. Besides, I enjoy losing myself in my book, even if it is my third time through. "What do you need?" I shout back.

"Come now."

Her insistence piques my curiosity. As I enter the house, through the living room window I see a string of four or five unfamiliar cars pull up out front, the last—a black hearse. Another change of plans? We're having the funeral here?

Ruby steps through the front door wearing her traditional Catholic woman's uniform, wrapped in a thick, pink wool blanket. Sweat drips from the tip of her nose. I didn't expect to see her before tomorrow. She seems to be in a trance, oblivious to me and Rolina. Without a word Ruby takes up her spot on the floor against the sofa. Rolina curls her legs under herself, on the floor next to the dining room table. She tugs on the hem of my skirt, pulling me out of my confusion. Her scowl reminds me that I should also be on the floor. I wedge myself between the table and the wall, at the entrance to the hallway. The three of us sit in silence.

Within minutes, four hefty men unload the casket from the hearse and labor to carry it up the driveway to the front door. Stymied by its size, their size, and the narrow doorway, they set it on the front lawn to wipe their brows and discuss options. One of them races to the hearse, returning with a metal trolley. Granny's casket, a beautiful light wood with exquisite grain varnished to a flawless sheen and adorned with brass hardware—along with her hefty corpse—must weigh a ton. The trolley's accordion sides nearly collapse as the men lower the massive casket onto the narrow platform. With one man in the living room and another on the front walk, they jostle the top heavy trolley up the step, into the house. Only the narrow margin of clearance prevents a disaster.

I lean over to whisper in Rolina's ear. "Now what?"

"We wait for the priest to arrive," she whispers back.

Before long, Mhambi and Father Mnganga, the tiny Zulu priest I met on my one trip to church, step through the door. He sprinkles holy water everywhere as the men maneuver the trolley through the living room, inches from my face, and down the hall. I can't imagine what this is all about. I turn to Rolina, my eyebrows raised, begging an explanation.

"Granny must see her final home before she is buried," she whispers.

I nod, pretending to understand, grateful for Rolina's unusually generous attitude. The men grumble in the hall, roll the trolley back to the living room, spin it around, and maneuver it into the hallway again, following Father Mnganga.

"Now what?" I ask. I steal a glance at Ruby who sits motionless, head bowed to the floor.

"Granny must see into her room," Rolina whispers. "See now? Her face is at the door rather than her feet."

I peek around the corner just in time to see Mhambi slip one of his white T-shirts into the casket as Father Mnganga recites his final prayer in Zulu. Rolina sings softly while the men wobble the trolley back to the living room. Wiping their brows again, they slap each other on the back for a job well-done before Mhambi and Father Mnganga lead the procession back to the hearse. Head still bowed, Ruby follows.

"Ah," Rolina sighs, rising to shut the front door. "Mr. Ndlela gives his last gift to his mother. It is good now."

Through the window I watch the cars pull away. I presume they're headed to Ntwana.

DAY 24
SATURDAY, FEBRUARY 23, 2008

My back against the cool fence rails, both cameras slung over my neck, I wait for Phyllis. Eight o'clock, eight-thirty, nine. The intensity of the sun builds, beating on my skin. My loose, light-weight blouse and cotton skirt feel smothering; I appreciate that Ruby doesn't expect me to heed the traditional layers of clothing and headscarves today. I rush back to my room to lather up with sunscreen and grab my hat. Finally, at nine-fifteen, Phyllis and Pamela pull up to the house, all smiles. The funeral starts at ten. It's a two-hour drive.

"It is a beautiful day for Mr. Ndlela to bury his mother, is it not?" Phyllis asks, rounding the traffic circle. Her lack of concern about our late start annoys me.

"Beautiful as usual, and no rain." I roll my window down to create a breeze. "I thought Paula was coming."

"Yes. Her husband, Phumlani is also coming. We will pick them up now."

"And Patrick and Amahle?"

Phyllis's wall of silence doesn't surprise me anymore. I take it as a sign that I've asked a difficult question.

"Ruby called this morning," she says "She wants us to go to her sister's house to collect something she forgot."

It'll take an hour to do all this. I'll be so pissed off if I miss this funeral, this once-in-a-lifetime opportunity. I console myself by hoping I'll have a chance to see Zodwa at JoJo's. It would be good to know she's doing well since her surgery. But this is just a dream. Phyllis carefully picks her steps down the front yard to JoJo's house, where Zodwa's father opens the screen door just far enough to hand off the all-important item: a black apron.

At ten we arrive at Paula's subdivision on the fringe of Pietermaritzburg. Through the web of electric wires that criss-cross the neighborhood, I survey the vast rolling hills of KwaZulu-Natal, stretched out as far as I can see to the south. The bustle of city life ends at Paula's street. An array of unique, intricate iron work covers every window on her street. It seems an odd way to personalize a home.

Two new compact cars sit behind the cyclone fence, where two toddlers ride tricycles across the concrete yard. Paula bends to kiss each of them on the forehead before she hands the infant in her arms to the babysitter. Patrick and Amahle are nowhere to be seen.

Despite Phyllis's argument, it makes sense for me to ride in the back seat—for once in my life, I'm the smallest passenger. I trade seats with Phumlani, an easy-spoken, polite man in a three-piece suit. The five of us exchange light-hearted conversation as we head west on the Edendale Highway for Ntwana. We might be late, and we might be wilted, but we'll be in good spirits when we arrive.

We pass the turnoff to Zinti and I have my first taste of the remote region of KwaZulu-Natal. The foothills of the Drakensburg Mountains rise higher and higher as we near Lesotho. The sky, a surreal shade of blue tinged with yellow at the edges, frames the emerald green hills. The sway of the tall grass, shimmering with the fresh morning mist, gives the impression that the earth itself pulsates with life. The vibrant red dirt along the edge of the road captures my heart. I vow that when I return to Ntwana on the school break, I'll bring my empty peanut butter jar to scoop some dirt to take home. Smuggling it through customs will be worth the risk. I'd never plant anything in it, only take a tiny bit on my finger each morning and rub it into my skin to remember the magic. I sense the truth of Africa as the "womb" of mankind. I could lie in the tall grass, let my body be held and nurtured by the earth, and I wouldn't mind at all if my life ceased to exist in this union. It's no mystery why GuGu chose to be laid to rest here, why Ruby refers to Ntwana as a place of God's beauty, why Mhambi cries when he speaks of his ancestors' homeland.

As we leave the main road in Ntwana, we pass an impressive, spanking-new library. It feels out of place wedged between an abandoned gas station and a one-room market whose hefty wooden doors are held upright between stacks of bricks.

"The government is working hard to bring literacy to the rural communities," Phyllis says.

I'd love to explore the library on the way home, but it's closed on Saturdays.

We travel on, down a one-lane road through fields of cows, goats, sheep, and the occasional ramshackle barn or rondavel. Phyllis slows to make a sharp, uphill turn to the right. As we climb the deeply rutted dirt drive, two large rondavels come into view, then a pale yellow stucco house and an enormous blue and gold tent—a traditional Zulu funeral tent. We've arrived at the Ndlela family compound, surrounded by a cattle fence lined with hydrangea bushes that drip lavender and white blossoms the size of volleyballs.

As we cross the lawn, I'm relieved to see that we haven't missed the burial. A half-dozen shovels are wedged into an enormous mound of red dirt next to Granny's open grave. Under the sparse shade trees, the grave diggers, dressed like American horse racing jockeys, enjoy their white bread sandwiches and dip their mugs into the bucket of finely-aged Zulu beer.

At the far side of the compound, under a smaller white tent, Mhambi's family, two Catholic priests, a black-cassocked altar boy, and the emcee sit with Granny's casket. Hundreds of guests fill the plastic lawn chairs under the massive blue and gold tent, spilling out onto the lawn. Teenagers sit on concrete blocks, their backs against the stucco house, while young kids race back and forth across the compound chasing dogs and chickens.

I'm separated from Phyllis and the others when an usher greets us at the rear of the guest's tent and directs us to the few empty seats that remain. Feeling awkward about my late arrival and my status as the solitary white guest, I keep my

head down—attempting to be as inconspicuous as possible—
as I climb over the knees of the other guests in my row. It's
all for naught, though, as I hear my name come through the
loudspeakers. When I look up, Mhambi smiles at me, his
arm stretched in my direction. It warms my heart that he is
so welcoming.

Perhaps Phyllis's tardiness was purposeful. For hours we
sit shoulder-to-shoulder, alternating between hymns and
what I assume to be prayers and eulogies. By early afternoon, trapped in the stifling air under the tent, I feel faint.
Weighing my options, I choose the lesser spectacle.

"Excuse me. Excuse me," I say. Pressing my cameras
against my chest so they don't dangle in their faces, I climb
one more time over the guests in my row, headed for an open
spot in the shade alongside the house. My bum on the dirt,
my back against the cool stucco wall, I close my eyes and
take a deep breath.

"Karen," Thulani whispers, tapping my leg.

I open my eyes to his worried expression.

"You do not look well."

"I'll be okay. I'm just a little overheated."

"Would you like a glass of water, Karen?"

I nod.

He rounds the corner at the back of the house and within minutes returns with a glass of cool water. I down it without coming up for air.

"Would you like another?" he asks.

This time he sits next to me on the ground. "You must not
allow yourself to become so hot before you ask for water."

"You're right," I say. "I didn't mean to scare you. I feel
better already."

Before long, the crowd stirs. Refreshed and back on my
feet, I take up a spot in the corner of the yard to capture the
forming procession on video. The cassocked attendant, carrying a gold chalice, leads the way, followed by the two
priests. Behind them, I'm shocked to see that the church
ladies carry Granny's casket. Mhambi, Siphelele, Ruby, and

others I presume to be close relatives, come next. Thulani falls into line at the rear of the group.

Ruby, dressed in her Catholic woman's uniform, sits at the edge of the grave under a small blue canopy. Wrapped from shoulders to toes in the wool blanket she's worn for three days now, she keeps her head bowed as other Ndlela women crowd under the canopy. She looks like a mourning noble, perched on her throne, surrounded by humble servants. The church ladies lay the casket at her feet before the priests present communion to the immediate family.

» » »   « « «

Mhambi stands proudly at the foot of the grave as the diggers, five on each side, carefully lower Granny into the ground. Suspended on ropes tied to poles they carry on their shoulders, the casket swings from side to side over the hole. Despite my best efforts to remain solemn, I imagine Granny's casket slipping off the ropes, sliding across the sloped lawn, landing in the hydrangeas at the edge of the property. I look away, hoping to collect myself, and spot Uncle Leonard standing alone on a rise at the far side of the lawn.

"It is good to see you again, Karen," Leonard welcomes me with a broad smile. "What do you think of our funeral traditions thus far?"

"It's like nothing I've ever seen before." I pause. "Is this a good time for me to ask questions?"

"It would be my pleasure to help you understand our customs," he says.

I've never heard Nelson Mandela speak, but I imagine he would sound like Leonard: slow, measured, without a hint of judgment toward anyone—including me. I feel safe. "Who are all these people?" I ask. "Where have they all come from? There aren't enough cars parked on the road to have brought this many people."

"Nearly everyone here is a Ndlela by either blood or marriage," Leonard says, in his perfect British accent. "In the

Zulu tradition you are considered to be brother or sister when you share a surname. Everyone with the Ndlela name is obligated to attend if it is even remotely possible. Some of them walked all day yesterday to be here to show their respect. Their respect is not only for Granny GuGu, but also for Mr. Ndlela and Ruby."

We stand side-by-side, watching the grave diggers lower themselves into the hole alongside Granny's casket.

"Everything that is done today has a specific purpose," Leonard says. "Not only have Mr. Ndlela's relatives come to show respect, they have also come to assure that the body is buried properly to protect it from the witch doctors."

I turn to look at him, my eyes wide, mouth agape. He speaks with the perspective of someone who has lived both inside and outside the Zulu culture. If only I could be as non-judgmental as he is. I'd give anything for a week alone with him and Rose in Durban.

"Do you see there, what they are doing now?" Leonard asks.

I jostle from side to side to see through the crowd. Mhambi unrolls a cowhide and hands it to the men in the hole. Then, one-by-one, each man standing at the edge of the grave lowers a thick, stripped tree branch into the grave.

"The hide will protect the casket from being damaged by the poles. It is also evidence that Mhambi provided a proper feast for his guests."

"And the poles?"

"They are laid across each other, in layers, making it difficult for the witch doctors to remove the body from the ground. Some families even take the precaution of pouring concrete over the casket before they replace the dirt. As you can see," he points to the grave next to Granny's, "Mr. Ndlela has placed a concrete slab over his father's grave to prevent this type of invasion."

"Why would the witch doctors want to dig up a dead body?" I ask, embarrassed by my raw question.

"There are many ways that our people are trapped in old

beliefs. The witch doctors still wield great power. They use the bones and innards of the deceased for their black medicine. A respectable family would not want the bones of a deceased relative to be used by a witch doctor to cause harm on another."

Leonard must have been a wonderful minister—he still is. Today, I am his congregation of one. I marvel at his patience as he explains the conflicts between traditional and modern Zulus, and the bridges that must be built for them to co-exist peacefully.

"In fact," Leonard says, his posture erect, almost regal, "one month from now there will be a cleansing ritual here in Ntwana. When someone dies, it is possible that 'black energy' is left behind that needs to be cleansed away. Everything that Ruby has worn since Granny's death, all of the shovels that were used to dig her grave, will all be burned. Everyone who lived with Granny GuGu, or had a hand in her burial, will attend. I am quite sure you will be included in this ritual since you live at Mr. Ndlela's home."

"What will that ritual be like?"

"It will be much smaller than the funeral. There will be a great fire and afterward everyone will cleanse their bodies with the ashes. Then there will be a meal prepared from a roasted goat, and finally Ruby will be released from her mourning."

"There seems to be more focus on Ruby than on Mhambi," I say. "I'm surprised since GuGu was his mother. And from the little I've seen, Ruby didn't appear to be that close to Granny."

"Ah," Leonard says. He takes a long, pensive pause before he begins. "As you must know by now, it is not easy for Ruby being the wife of a traditional man. She comes from Durban, raised in a family that did not always follow the traditional ways. She chose to leave her modern life behind when she married."

I turn to look at Leonard; his warm smile tells me he loves his niece. An unexpected breeze cools the sweat on my back.

Staring straight ahead, Leonard mops his forehead with a white handkerchief.

"And because Mhambi is the eldest son, Ruby's life has just become very complicated. When Granny died, Ruby became the matriarch of the entire Ndlela family. And a very large family it is, as you can see. As the matriarch, it is her responsibility to set the example of a traditional wife for the entire family. Her movements will be more restricted. She will have even less freedom than she has now."

"So I see why she's been a bit grumpy," I say.

"Ruby has always known that this time would come," Leonard sighs. "However, I am sure she wished for Granny to live a very long time. She is not happy about her new responsibilities. Most of Ruby's grief is actually for herself."

We stand in silence as the priest says a final prayer and sprinkles his holy water into the grave.

"Come," Leonard says, as he takes me by the arm. "You are a deeply prayerful woman, Karen. You must participate in our ritual and add your prayer to Granny's grave."

Slowly, we make our way across the lawn toward the mound of red dirt. Leonard guides me into line, along with every man, woman and child. He steps away for a moment to speak with Mhambi. I feel awkward without him and step out of the line to take photos. The elderly woman behind me wraps her arm around my waist and reins me back into line. My tears flow as I scoop the powdery soft red dirt into my hands. To the soft hum of the women, I stand over Granny's grave, say my silent good-bye and toss the dirt through the poles, onto her casket. I didn't know her well, but I liked her—and I think she liked me. I wish her soul a peaceful journey.

After every guest has taken their turn, the grave diggers fill the grave in earnest. Under Mhambi's watchful eye, while Ruby remains seated under the canopy, her body bent under the weight of the blanket, eyes to the ground, the diggers alternate between adding layers of dirt and compacting it with their heavy work boots while the women chant. At last the grave is filled and Mhambi plants a wooden cross, bearing a mangled metal plaque, in the fresh dirt. Written in black magic marker pen, the plaque reads:

Mrs. M.D. Ndlela
Born: 1920-08-03
Died: 2008-02-15
Rest in Peace

Ruby stands, removing her blanket and black velvet hat. The men shake hands and pat each other on the back. Everyone heads for the shade of the blue and gold funeral tent—except for the church ladies.

Dressed in their black skirts, white blouses, and colorful headscarves, the women scatter white daisies over the fresh dirt. With their closed umbrellas tapping the ground next to their feet and their free hands pointed skyward, they raise their voices in song. Forming a circle around Granny's grave, the women stomp out the rhythm of their final good-bye, waving proudly as they pass my video camera. The men may be in charge of earthly business, but it seems the women are responsible for safeguarding Granny's journey to the other side.

I'm in no hurry to leave the gravesite. Uncle Leonard comes to stand with me. His dignified posture adds to my sense of awe at being included in such an ancient ritual.

"How are you doing, Karen?" he asks.

I know he sees the tear tracks on my cheeks. "I like your tradition that everyone throws a handful of dirt into the grave," I say, admiring the red stains on my palms. "In my country, sometimes the families don't stay for the actual burial. It's too painful." In my own life I've walked away from many caskets sitting atop the ground, waiting to be lowered into the earth, out of site, avoiding the finality of death. I struggle to hold back my emotion as I turn to face Leonard.

"There is a purpose for our custom," he says. "It would never be accepted your way here in our country. Everyone must look into the grave and put their portion of dirt over the casket. This way they can be assured that the burial has been done properly."

» » »   « « «

From atop a small knoll on the property I survey the guests milling about the Ndlela family compound, jealous that I am still an outsider. What I wouldn't give to know this kind of deep, cultural bond. I wipe my face on my bare, sticky arm as one of Mhambi's friends approaches.

"Follow me," he says, turning on his heels.

My stomach flutters. I hope I'm not in trouble for taking so many photos. I feel like a child, struggling to keep up with this tall, wide man who takes giant strides across the lawn. He stops in front of the yellow stucco house and turns to face me as he opens the door. Inside, my eyes struggle to adapt to the low light. A long narrow table, covered with a white linen cloth and zebra printed runner, fills the entire length of the single room. Red plastic lawn chairs line each side of the table, with spares along the walls.

Mhambi's friend pulls out the chair at the head of the table. "You will sit here," he says. "You will be our honored guest."

I want to tell him that isn't necessary, but he has already nudged me into the chair and pushed me up to the table. I force a smile as I glance up and down the table, through the bottles of Sprite and Coca-Cola, at the other guests. About a dozen men and women, all in expensive suits and dresses, smile back at me. A pitcher of water, with ice, sits in front of my place. I drain it before the meal is served.

Women bring enormous platters of food, stopping first to serve me before they set the platters in the center of the table. While the others talk among themselves, I feast on beef, putu, fruit salad, roasted yams, red beans and stewed carrots. Just when I think I can't possibly take another bite, a woman sets a plate of something I don't recognize in front of me.

"This is the finest meat from the cow," she says. "You must have some."

"What is it?" I ask, trying not to sound as suspicious as I feel.

She points to her own belly.

The entrails! "Oh," I say, puffing out my cheeks. "I'm so full. I can't eat another bite."

"But you must," she says. "It is the most tender meat."

"Really, I can't. I'm too full now. Maybe I can come back later?"

"Ah," she smiles. "It will not last long. You should take it now while you can."

I smile, too. I'll take my chances.

» » » « « «

Outside, the men sprawl across the lawn with their plates piled high and kids race back and forth between the house and rondavels chasing chickens and dogs.

But it's the women who capture my attention. They sit on plastic lawn chairs under the main tent with plates of food on their laps, eating in silence. Their soft pinafore aprons— traditional mourning attire—float on the afternoon breeze. Layers of bright, silky scarves drape diagonally across their bodies, under one arm, knotted over the other shoulder. Yards of gauzy fabric, wrapped tightly around their heads, frame their solemn expressions. When I raise my camera and say please, they pose willingly; some with smiles, most with stoic eyes that give nothing away.

I follow the children around the back of the house and nearly collide with Thulani, engrossed in conversation with a woman different from all the others. Her clothing is ordinary. It's her face that sets her apart—she radiates joy.

"Haybo! Karen," Thulani says. "I have been looking for you. This is my auntie, the traditional healer. The two of you will have much to talk about."

"It's so good to meet you," I say, offering my hand.

She smiles at me with every inch of her being.

"Thulani, come quick," someone yells from around back.

"Stay here. I will not be long," he says as he runs off.

Auntie the Healer and I stand face-to-face, smiling at each other, lost without Thulani to translate. I raise my camera to take her photo. She obliges, one hand on her hip, her head tilted, with the most engaging smile I've seen in all of South Africa. When I nod that I'm finished, she bows and bounces off across the compound. Afraid of missing my chance to finally speak with a traditional healer, I head in Thulani's direction.

The scene behind the house stops me cold. There, in a thirty-by-thirty waist high enclosure made of corrugated sheet metal, sit two enormous, black cast iron pots perched on wood fires. Steam rises from each pot—along with cow legs: skin, hooves and all. Elderly men, wearing thick leather gloves, haul enormous chunks of steamed meat from the pots, throw them onto halved tree trunks lying on the ground, and swing their machetes through the swarm of hovering flies to hack the meat into platter size portions.

I turn my back on the spectacle and take a deep breath. It takes every ounce of self-control I have not to barf. I take another breath and tell myself this is not the beef I just ate. On my next breath I congratulate myself for not eating the intestines. As my stomach settles, I know I'll never see anything like this again. I can't allow this opportunity pass. I spin around to snap photos before returning to the lawn.

» » »   « « «

Settled into my room at Ruby's, ready for bed, I melt into my memories of the day: the music, red dirt, women's faces, even the toothless church ladies hold a special place in my heart. I feel as much a part of the Ndlela tribe as is possible for a white woman from the other side of the world.

My heart jumps when I hear the chain rattle on the driveway gate. I listen for the sound of monkey chatter. It rattles again, this time accompanied by a man's voice. He shakes the gate so hard it sounds like it will rip from its hinges. My heart pounds as I realize he isn't going away. I slip on my clothes, stuff the keys in my pocket, grab my flashlight, and tippy toe up to the edge of the house. A tall, lanky man—wobbling from liquor—stands on the other side of the gate, grasping the bars to hold himself upright. I hold my flashlight out to the side of my body, turn it on, and shine it into his face. He squints against the bright halogen beam.

"Who are you?" I shout from behind the wall.

"I Mhambi brother. He send me to stay night with you."

Oh shit. I shouldn't be surprised, though. My bare feet pad across the driveway, my flashlight trained on his face as I unlock the gate. This is not the same brother who "protected" me last night. He slides the chain off the gate and bumps against the bars as he staggers onto the property. I back away. A twinge of guilt hits me for feeling so suspicious. But not too much.

I cross the lawn and unlock the kitchen door for him before retreating around the side of the house, back to my room, with the keys in hand—my insurance, my small measure of control. I lay awake most of the night, poised to protect myself against my newest guard.

DAY 26

My stomach wakes me with a grumble in the middle of the night. Granny's funeral food has caught up with me. Unable to sleep, I spend hours deciphering the sounds outside my open window. Wild dogs, monkeys, roosters, birds—and something new off in the distance. A hyena? The wild screeches remind me of the wails of the grieving mother who lost her little boy on the side of the road.

» » » « « «

"Sawubona, Karen," Phyllis says, as I slide into the front seat of her car. "How are you, today?"

My stomach distress doesn't faze her. "The food was very rich," she says, with a smile. "Everyone ate very well. Mr. Ndlela prepared an excellent feast for his guests."

She sees it differently than I do. Mhambi bought the cow, but the women did all the work.

"So, Karen, what do you think of our funeral traditions?" she asks. "Do you have any questions?"

"Uncle Leonard did a great job of explaining everything to me. I loved the part where we all took a handful of dirt and threw it into the grave. I've never done that before."

Phyllis nods as she negotiates traffic, headed to Pamela's house. "America sounds like a very strange country. You speak of many things that are different, things that surprise me."

I don't know how to respond. Even in our differences, life here is still so similar. It confuses me to attempt to sort out what is odd, what seems normal, how we are really different.

Phyllis interrupts my thoughts. "Do you have questions now that you have had time to think about it?" she asks.

"Well, I do have one question. But it's not about the funeral."

"Yes, Karen?"

"It's true that Patrick and Amahle are Paula's children, but they live with you. Right?"

"That is correct."

"I assumed that they lived with you because Paula wasn't able to care for them. Like maybe she didn't have a big enough house, or couldn't afford to feed them. So I was surprised to see her home on Saturday. See how big it is. And she and Phumlani seem to have plenty of money. They each have a new car, good clothes, and their kids have nice toys. I don't understand."

"Patrick and Amahle live with me because Phumlani will not permit them to live under his roof." Phyllis glances across the front seat at me, as if that explains everything.

"I still don't understand."

"Phumlani is not their father. He permits only his *own* children to live in his home."

No emotion. No apologies. Nothing to suggest that this is unusual, or unfair, or hurtful to the teenagers who must miss their mother.

» » »   « « «

Missy rushes across the library to greet me at the door. She grabs my backpack and with her massive, strong hand on my arm, leads me across the room. I feel like a child, tugged along behind her. She pulls my chair away from the table, pushes me down into place, slides my tea toward me, and motions for me to pay attention. Pamela and Phyllis watch with wide smiles as Missy unties the handles on two plastic grocery sacks. She extracts bundles wrapped in layers of wrinkled butcher paper, softened from repeated use, all the while chattering as if I understand. I raise my eyebrows at Phyllis to translate.

"Missy is very excited to show you what she has made," Phyllis says.

With great care, Missy unwraps an impeccably pleated, black wrap-around skirt and ties the wide band around her waist. Like delicate strings of cascading light, tiny colorful seed beads are sewn down the crease of each pleat, meeting rows of perfectly spaced ribbon sewn around the hem of the skirt.

"This is beautiful!" I gush, standing to touch the fabric.

Pamela giggles as Missy smacks my hand and stretches my arms out from my sides, parallel with the floor. She unties the skirt from her own waist and circles it around mine.

I have never felt more elegant. I run my fingers along the rows of tiny beads. "This is amazing!" I glance at Pamela to translate. She and Missy exchange words.

"Missy wants you to know that she made it with her own hands, without a machine," Pamela says. "She is pleased that you like her work."

"Like it? It's gorgeous! I have never seen anything so exquisite."

As Missy unwraps the other parcels, I tap her on the shoulder to snag her attention. She turns to see me with my fingers at the corners of my mouth, stretching my smile as far as my lips will allow. I hold the skirt out with my hands and turn in a circle like Cinderella trying on her ball gown. Missy pulls me into a bear hug before releasing me to fasten a wide, beaded belt at my waist and a traditional beaded rope around my neck. She stands back with her hands on her hips. The look on her face begs my response.

"It's beautiful, Missy," I say, running my fingers over the beads at my neck.

"There is more," Phyllis says. "Missy has saved her best piece for last."

Missy turns me by my shoulders, my back to her and the others, and shoves a tight headpiece down over my forehead. I reach my hands to my head and feel the bowl-shaped hat with a flat top. I recognize it from the Johannesburg airport—the traditional Zulu Isicholo. Missy cinches the hat tie in place and spins me around to face the table. All three women inhale in unison, sucking the air from the room.

"What?" I ask, shocked at their reaction. "What's wrong?"

Phyllis and Pamela cover their gaping mouths with their hands. Missy, eyes wide, whispers under her breath.

"You're scaring me," I say. "Tell me what's wrong."

Their expressions begin to soften. Pamela is the first to speak. "Nothing is wrong, Karen. It is just that we are all surprised."

"Surprised at what?"

"We are surprised at how you resemble a traditional healer," Phyllis says.

"We did not expect this," Pamela says. "That is all."

Disarmed by their strong reaction, I pull the hat off my head and tuck it under my arm like a football. Missy grabs it, jams it back on my head, and pats the top with her hand as if to dare me to take it off again.

"You must not be embarrassed, Karen," Phyllis says. "It is just that we have never seen a white woman who could be one of our own."

Dressed in full Zulu ritual regalia, I sit in silence eating my peanut butter and jelly sandwich. The many ways I feel like I *do* fit in tumble through my mind, mixed with the many ways I clearly don't belong. I feel both so strongly, but struggle to reconcile them peacefully. I bounce back and forth in my heart, hitting the wall of each extreme with a thud.

In a flash, I have a stroke of inspiration. "Phyllis," I say. "These things Missy has made are fantastic. People at home would pay a lot of money to have something so authentic from Africa. Maybe we can start a cottage industry here in the village."

"Cottage industry?"

"Yeah. A cottage industry is when women make things in their home and sell them. Missy could send skirts and hats and necklaces home with me. I can sell them in shops near my home and send the money back to Missy."

Pamela's eyes light up.

"It takes Missy a very long time to make these skirts and hats," Phyllis says in a serious tone. "I do not know that it is possible for her to complete one before you go home."

"Well, she doesn't need to do it all right now. And she doesn't need to do it alone. Maybe other women in the village could work with her."

"How much do you think this skirt would sell for in America?" Phyllis asks.

I stop to really consider what I've seen in the ethnic shops in Berkeley, Oakland, and San Francisco. "This is so well done. Authentic ritual items, hand-made in South Africa, could easily sell for one-hundred dollars. That's seven-hundred rand."

A whistle escapes on Pamela's breath. She whispers to Missy as Phyllis and I carry on with our conversation.

"And how much of that money would Missy receive?" Phyllis asks.

"I don't know for sure. Maybe half. I don't need to keep any of it. The only expense I'd need to cover is the shipment of the merchandise from South Africa to California."

"And how much does that cost?"

"I don't know. But I can find out the next time I go to town. I do know that it would be most cost efficient if the women send a lot of skirts and hats at once, instead of one or two at a time."

"And how would you send the money to Missy?"

"By international money order. A check that can be cashed at any bank."

"And how would Missy do that without a bank account?"

"I don't think you need a bank account to cash a money order. At least not in America. I can check on that in town, too."

"And where would you send this money order? Missy does not have a postal box in Maritzburg."

Shit! I'm offering Missy and the other village women a

chance to earn maybe two-hundred rand for each skirt. That's Missy's entire monthly salary for mopping Zinti's sidewalks and making Phyllis's margarine sandwich and tea every day. Can't Phyllis have at least *one* positive response?

"Maybe I could send it to Zinti's address, and you could deliver it to Missy."

"Humph. We shall see, Karen. What you say sounds like a lot of work." Phyllis crosses the library, our conversation over. The siren in her office wails, sending the children back to their classrooms.

I feel deflated. Again. Lost in hopelessness. Not mine. Phyllis's. I shake my head at Missy and Pamela.

"What you offer is very generous," Pamela says. "I have heard of this 'cottage industry' that you speak of. I believe I can get my sister to listen to you."

"I hope so. I really think it's possible."

"And Missy says that she knows several women in the village who will help her sew."

I smile across the table at Missy.

"You stay here, Karen," Pamela says, rising from her chair. "Missy wants to teach you her dance, but I have told her not to begin until I return. Cook must see this as well."

Pamela hurries from the room. She returns with Cook in tow, drying her hands on her apron, her ever-present wide smile radiating from under her straw hat. I'm surprised that Pamela opts to stay in the library instead of returning to her classroom.

Missy leads me by the hand to the rear of the library where she motions for me to watch her. She takes three lumbering steps—left, right, left—then swings her right leg into the air, far above her head. The next time she keeps her elbows bent, tight at her waist, her hands closed in fists until she kicks. Then she straightens her arms and flings her hands toward the floor, letting out a deep grunt as her foot flies toward the ceiling. She steps back, hands on her hips, and nods her head for me to take my turn.

I position myself with lots of space in front of me, march

my three steps in rhythm across the concrete floor, grunt my best grunt and kick my right foot over my head.

Pamela and Cook nearly fall out of their seats with laughter.

"Hey!" I say, in mock indignation. "That was a good kick. Especially for a white lady."

Missy grabs me in a bear hug, laughing into my neck, before she stands in front of me inches from my face and, with her hands on my shoulders, says what I assume to be, "I love you for trying." Then she positions my arms, coiled at my side, and nods for me to go again.

Cook hurries across the room to join in. Soon she, Missy and I dance together, stomping, kicking and grunting our way across the room. When we turn to head back the other way, dozens of little faces peer into the room, their noses pressed against the windows, giggling as they whisper in each other's ears.

With undisguised pleasure, Pamela opens the library door and ushers the children to the floor under the windows. They take in the scene with silent amazement: the white lady from America kicks her legs high into the air; Missy and Cook chant in their mother tongue; Pamela, their teacher, wipes her tears of laughter with a lace handkerchief.

» » » « « «

On the way home from school, Phyllis stops in an unfamiliar area of town—a modern, urban section that could easily be mistaken for my home town. She and Pamela have found a bank that may lend them money for their B&B.

"There is a grocery store around the corner that you might like," Phyllis says. "We will find you there when we are finished with our meeting."

I round the corner and pause in awe in front of a *real* grocery store. Inside, enjoying the relief of frosty air-conditioning, I'm tempted by beautiful displays of non-essential foods: deli meats, cheeses, fruits, nuts, figs, and elegant soaps and candles, products that rival the best natural food markets in California. Young, urban couples—whites and Zulus—push wire carts, their babies strapped in car seats, unhurried as they stroll the aisles.

Not in need of anything when I walked through the door, I fill my cart with every luxury I've been missing: Oreo cookies, a fresh washcloth, a bar of lavender scented soap, almonds, dried apricots, sliced ham and a jar of instant coffee. But my favorite is the vanilla ice cream bar, dipped in chocolate, that I devour on my way to the checkout. I smile sheepishly as I hand the empty wrapper, licked clean, to the clerk.

DAY 27
TUESDAY, FEBRUARY 26, 2008

Yesterday's tummy trauma continues. Intimately acquainted with the pit toilets at school again today, I'm running low on hand sanitizer. The books, toothbrushes, pencils, and plastic recorders that I brought for the kids are all well and good—but soap would be great, too.

One of my friends at home has devised a plan to earn money for Zinti. A talented quilter, she can transfer the children's artwork onto fabric. Baby quilts made from the art panels would sell well at arts and crafts fairs; surely well enough to send crates of basic hygiene supplies to Zinti. We can even send some of the quilts for the orphaned kids.

Phyllis is quick to prepare and sign a release to use the children's art in return for the proceeds—free money without any effort on her part. I try not to have judgments, but fail. For this Friday's art class I'll have the children draw pictures of their homes and favorite animals for me to take home.

As I wait for the after-school session, I listen to the Grade Two kids in Pamela's classroom next door. Slowly and clearly, they recite their numbers in English. I tippy toe up to Pamela's door and peek my head around the corner. Oblivious to my presence, the children sit in rows on the floor, almost still, engrossed in their numbers. Pamela glances my way, with pure joy on her face.

» » »   « « «

Ruby's car sits in the driveway when Phyllis pulls up after school. I race across the front lawn, like a child with exciting news to share. Ruby meets me at the kitchen door.

"Haybo!" she says, flinging her arms around my shoulders, kissing my cheek. "It is good to see you, Karen. I did not think that I would miss you so much. You feel like my sister who was torn from me at birth."

"I know. Me, too, Ruby. It feels like you've been gone forever."

She smiles her most mischievous grin. "Although we must have a different father."

We fall into each others arms in hysterics. At the dining room table we catch up on the week's events over tea. I share my awe for the Zinti Rock and Tathum Gallery, my news about selling Missy's skirts and hats in California, and my shopping adventure with Paula. Ruby shares her joy that the boy she stole from Zinti thrives at her home in Ntwana.

"He smiles all the time," she says. "It is very good to see him be strong and healthy. I asked him many times if he is happy at Ntwana. He says he wants to stay. I love him now like he is my own son."

DAY 28

As the new Ndlela matriarch, Ruby dresses for traditional mourning: a long sleeved black shirt, a black pinafore apron, black headscarf, and another scarf draped around her neck. Her mood, a stark reversal from yesterday, matches her clothing.

"I wish that I would be permitted to remain in my home for the next month," she says. "I do not like that I must wear these clothes every day. That I am not permitted to have fun with my friends. I cannot even smile in public!"

Even though Ruby eats in her classroom today, her pallor of despondence with underlying subtle aggression, spreads throughout the school. No more dancing. No more laughing. No more fun. Phyllis, Pamela, Missy, and I eat in silence.

Phyllis exhales a long sigh of frustration. "I am not eager for my afternoon meeting."

"Are you going to Pietermaritzburg again?" I ask.

"No. One of our Grade Two learners is not progressing and his mother will come to school to speak about it."

"It's great that she's taken an interest in his school work."

Her exasperated expression suggests I'm way off base. "We have spoken about this many times. She does not wish to accept his condition and she becomes very angry with me." Phyllis shrugs her shoulders. "But if she wants to speak again, what am I to do?"

"What do you mean?" I ask.

"Perhaps you have seen the boy, Karen. He is quite tall, and even for his age he has never learned to speak properly. He is never in his classroom. He creates a distraction for the other learners. I have told his mother that it is no use for him to be at Zinti. But she refuses to accept that he is not right in the head."

Is she talking about the deaf boy? The tall, skinny boy

who follows me around all day, eager to help, smiles all the time, sits alone in the library looking at the books? "Are you talking about the boy who always wears the red T-shirt?"

"That is him!"

"He's deaf, Phyllis. He's not 'off' in his head. He's deaf. His speech is odd because he can't hear well, so he can't mimic language."

Phyllis's eyes widen. Her chin drops before she quickly recomposes herself. "You sound very much like his mother," she says.

I pause for a moment, choosing my words with care. "His mom could be right, Phyllis. Is there any chance we can take him to the hospital to have his hearing tested? It's free."

"He is twelve years old and remains in Grade Two," Phyllis says. "I do not see that what you suggest will make any difference."

Her resistance bowls me over. "What will happen to him if things go on like this?" I ask.

"Eventually he will quit coming to school. That is how it happens. Our government will not allow me to refuse him. Truly, Karen, I am quite surprised that he has continued this long."

A lazy, uninterested twelve-year old doesn't sit in the library thumbing through books every day. Maybe I should take a different approach. "It might still be worth a try," I say. "He seems eager to read. I bet if he had a hearing aid he'd catch up pretty fast. It would make his mom happy, and you wouldn't have to worry about him being a disruption." I wait for a glimmer of encouragement.

Phyllis dismisses me with a stone-faced empty stare—the unfailing method she and Ruby use to close the door on every uncomfortable conversation. I glance to Pamela for support; after all, the boy's in her class. Her head tilted downward, she eats her margarine sandwich in silence. Missy looks torn. She doesn't understand what's been said, but she feels the tension.

» » »   « « «

Ruby and I drive across town in silence. She's lost in her thoughts; I'm lost in worry about her silence. Something shifted overnight. If I had another place to stay, I'd move in a heartbeat. I asked Phyllis about it at lunch. Apparently Ruby is the only one who has space to house me.

At the end of Church Street we take the cloverleaf onto the freeway, heading north in her search for new shoes for Siphelele's sixteenth birthday. Ruby says now that he's a man, he wants slip-on leather shoes like his father, instead of the ordinary white tennis shoes she could buy anywhere in town. We round a curve, past a jungle forest, into a wide clearing where rows of car dealerships line the freeway in front of the Liberty Midlands Mall.

Except for the unusual store names—Biltong Boys, Ghela Outfitters, John Dory's Fish and Grill, Mugg & Bean, Truworths—Liberty Midlands could be easily mistaken for any California mall: elevator music emanates from the ceiling; shoppers wander aimlessly, dangling packages at their sides; diners enjoy bistro meals in the neon-lit food court.

We could bond over shopping, but Ruby appears anxious to leave me behind. We agree to meet in the courtyard in an hour. I'd love to sit and linger over a coffee, but "to-go" is almost as good. I can't wait to explore the shops. The dresses and shoes look just like home, but the tourist gift shops draw me in. Here, the Africa I thought I'd experience can be purchased a million different ways. Wooden placemats etched with images of the big five—lion, elephant, water buffalo, rhinoceros, and leopard—are beautiful. Even though I'll never see these magnificent animals, they seem like perfect souvenirs. But I don't want to be hasty. I explore shop after shop. The beads are gorgeous, but ten times the price of the old lady on Church Street, and so perfect they lack the feeling of being hand-crafted by nimble, aging fingers.

"Karen, we must go now," Ruby says, dragging me out of a fabric shop.

"Have you found Siphelele's shoes already?" I glance at my watch. It's only been thirty minutes. I'm not finished. I want to go back and get my placemats.

She heads for the exit without a word, stopping only to greet a friend. I stand idly by as Ruby keeps her head bowed, careful not to smile, extra careful not to introduce me.

» » »   « « «

Mhambi and I sit next to each other on the organ bench for his first music lesson. I pen the scales on the staff paper he's brought home, and explain the concept of sharps and flats. I admire his willingness to be vulnerable with a woman—a foreign woman.

"You must give me a song to learn before our next lesson," he says, smiling like an eager school boy.

Mhambi plunks out the piece I played for him two weeks ago, nearly perfect on the first try. I pen the notes, asking him to repeat some sections so I can get it right. He doesn't need my roughly written notes to play this song, but he's proud to own his first piece of written music.

"Aye, Karen," he says. "This is a great deal of work."

"Compared to how easily you play by ear, it sure is."

"But it is very exciting to learn a new way."

DAY 29

I'm jolted from a deep sleep by the sound of splashing water outside my door. Startled, I listen for clues. It's not rain, more like a mop bucket being emptied over and over onto the concrete. Someone's cleaning in the middle of the night?

» » »   « « «

"Ruby," I say, stepping around her in the kitchen in the morning, "I swear I heard the sound of water pouring onto the patio in the middle of the night. Did you hear it?"

"It was me, Karen. I did not mean to alarm you."

"You didn't alarm me," I lie. My relief that it was only Ruby gives way to curiosity. "Couldn't you sleep last night?"

"I have no problem sleeping. It is only that I must perform this foolish tradition to satisfy my dead mother-in-law." Ruby spits the words through her lips.

I tip my head to the side in question. "What do you mean?"

"There are things I must do as the wife of her eldest son. One is to wear this apron every single day for the next month." She tugs on the black, ruffled apron that covers her from neck to knees, its heavily gathered skirt tied at the small of her back. "And this black scarf on my head all day makes me drip sweat into my tea. It is too hot for such things. Still, I must show respect for my husband's family."

"And the water?"

"I cannot put my apron in the washing machine with the family clothes. Every night I must wash it in cold water and hang it to dry under the moon. Then I must make myself naked and pour the water over my body."

"Why?"

259

"It is necessary to wash away the evil spirits that linger after Granny's death. If I put my apron in the washing machine, the spirits will be on my husband's and my son's clothing. That is not good."

I'd like to ask why the evil spirits linger around Ruby and no one else.

"I will be very happy when the cleansing ritual is here," Ruby says. "Then I will burn this hot apron and scarf and return to my regular clothes. Then I will be allowed to laugh again." She pauses, looks at me through pleading eyes. "That is the hardest part, Karen. I like to laugh. Now I am afraid that if one of my friends sees me laugh in town, it will come back to my husband and he will know that I have disgraced his family."

» » »   « « «

Several Grade Four girls take me by the hand and skirt. We stroll along the dirt path from the assembly hall to class. My head tilted back in laughter as they sing for me, I nearly bump into Nelly leaving her classroom. We pause for a moment, staring at each other in silence: she at my mouth hanging open; me at the shimmering white head scarf, trimmed in lace and pearl beads, that frames her swollen, bruised eye. I want to give her a hug; ask what has happened. But I already know. Her husband makes a habit of this. She drops her chin to her chest and walks past me. I will forever regret not reaching out to her.

» » »   « « «

Curious why Ruby doesn't come to the library for lunch, I pack mine up and head up the hill to look for her. She sits alone in her classroom, downtrodden, as though she's lost her last friend.

"Can I eat with you?" I ask, stepping through the doorway.

"Aye, Karen. If you like."

"Are you okay, Ruby? I'm concerned. You haven't been yourself lately."

"I am tired, Karen. Tired all the time. There is never a day that is easy." She pauses, picking at last night's dinner leftovers in her bowl. "Today my car is leaking oil. This afternoon I must go to Maritzburg to find the correct part so that my sister's husband can repair it for me. Can you imagine walking up and down Longmarket Street in this heat? Wearing this hot, black apron?"

I shake my head. "I can't, Ruby." Mhambi, Thulani and Siphelele wear tiny squares of black fabric pinned to their shirt sleeves. Ruby makes all the sacrifices. You would think her husband or son could at least look at her car for her. It's a wonder JoJo's husband will. I don't understand that man, he refuses medical care for his daughter, but he'll repair Ruby's car.

"I can help you," I say. "If we each walk down one side of the street we'll find the part faster."

"It is not your responsibility, Karen."

I vow to have a cup of tea ready for her when she gets home.

Missy and Cook bounce through the doorway of Ruby's classroom, all smiles. Missy plops her ritual hat on my head. Cook stands, hands on her hips, ready to dance. Ruby snarls her face at Missy, raising her chin in angry Zulu words. I'm stunned that Missy argues back and Cook's smile remains as wide as ever.

"If you are going to dance with them," Ruby barks at me, "I will not be part of it."

"It's fun, Ruby. We had a great time the other day. You can dance with us. It might make you feel better. No one here will care if you laugh."

"Humph!" Ruby says. "This is not a dance for Christian women." She storms from the room, lunch in hand.

Tired of Ruby's irritable mood, I laugh and dance with Cook and Missy.

DAY 31
SATURDAY, MARCH 1, 2008

I feel protective of Ruby as she prepares to head off for another funeral. Why, as the mourning matriarch, can't she just *attend* the funeral? Why does she have to cook all day? Only seven o'clock, already stifling hot and humid, I can't imagine her standing over an open flame in her black mourning apron and head scarf. I'd like to offer her excuses to stay home, but she hasn't asked. Besides, this is her girlfriend who died of AIDS at the hospital while her husband paid off the witch doctor for the magic cure that never happened.

"Are you sure you don't want me to come help with the cooking?" I ask.

"That is not necessary, Karen. It is very hot today, and you do not do well with such heat."

She's right. And it's bound to be easier for her without the white woman from America in tow.

"Phyllis is going to Durban for her aunt's funeral today," Ruby says. "She will pick you up at ten to take you to Maritzburg on her way. I will fetch you at the corner near the coombie station at four. You must wait for me there on the grand steps."

Together we carry loads of giant cooking pots and dishes to the trunk of her car. I hug her good-bye, silently wishing her an easier life. As she pulls out of the driveway, I notice a puddle of oil. Apparently Zodwa's father isn't quite the mechanic he believes himself to be.

» » »   « « «

I meander through Woolworth's to buy a bottle of ice-cold water. On the street out front, I visit the old bead lady again, this time choosing a traditional rope bracelet with matching earrings. Then on to the Internet café to check my emails. They barely hold my interest anymore. Where my friends are eating out and the battle between Obama and Clinton seem irrelevant.

I pass a row of modern shops, one with unboxed shoes piled in heaps on the floor, paired together with plastic zip ties. The next sells washers and dryers with bulbous edges that remind me of my grandma's. Another displays bright bangle jewelry. I presume this is where the young teachers from the AIDS conference shop. I almost miss the tiny book store, no more than ten feet wide, next in line on the street. Excited, I browse the half-empty shelves for something new to read. It takes a few minutes to absorb why none of them appeal to me. The two basic categories are coffee table picture books and novels with adult content written at sixth-grade reading level. I settle on a book of word puzzles, imported from Australia, and vow to find a library.

On the balcony of the Tathum Art Gallery I enjoy my lunch of cucumber and cream cheese sandwiches, black tea, and a rich chocolate brownie. I feel so cosmopolitan basking in the oasis of calm, two stories above the chaos of the park across the street where smoke rises from the vendors roasting impala kabobs. Under makeshift tents of blue tarps, blankets spread on the ground display impala hide garments, earthen pottery, buckets of spices, and Ziploc baggies filled with loose beads. I want desperately to explore the acres of treasures, but I'm afraid to walk through the line of derelict loiterers on the curb. Young men pass cigarettes down the row, followed by bottles of booze hidden in brown paper sacks, followed by hypodermic needles. A tiny voice in my head warns that I might enter the park—and never come out.

"Can you tell me if there's a library nearby?" I ask my waiter.

"Yes, Ma'am," the young Indian man replies. "Stay on Langalibalele Street until you arrive at Timber. Then turn right and go to Church Street. From there you cannot miss it."

Only three blocks away! All this time and I had no idea.

Rounding the corner onto Timber, a sign taped to a light pole catches my eye: the ever present red circle with a diagonal slash—this time with a new-born infant in the center. As I read the language under the picture, my stomach turns, ready to expel my fine lunch. I've seen lots of abortion advertisements, but this is the first for full-term abortions. Only a desperate woman—a desperate girl—would believe "full-term, same day, safe and painless" is possible.

I cut through the narrow brick-cobbled alley to shorten my walk in the mid-day heat. On both sides of the alley, women sit on bright wooden folding chairs outside beauty parlors painted in traditional Pan-African colors: green, yellow, and red. I exchange smiles with the women who chatter back and forth across the alley in Zulu, laughing easily as they have their hair braided in corn rows. Their little girls sit on stoops polishing each others' nails. I long to slide into a chair, gossip about the week's events, and feel like one of the girls.

The Msunduzi Municipal Library feels misplaced among Pietermaritzburg's centuries-old brick government buildings. The children's collection is housed in a round glass structure topped with a silver dome that resembles a space ship. I enjoy browsing the expansive library, but without Ruby's driver's license, I have no hope of checking out a book.

» » »   « « «

Perched on the massive steps of a government building, I wait for Ruby. Across the street, coombies—Volkswagen and Toyota vans refitted with padded bench seats—peel in and out of the depot. Shoulder-to-shoulder passengers stuff each coombie. The drivers honk their horns incessantly to draw attention to the one remaining empty seat, because, well, fifteen people crammed into one non-air-conditioned vehicle just isn't enough!

Young men, still immortal, avoid the crowd inside the coombies by balancing their rear ends on the open window ledges, their backs to traffic. Braced with their hands on the roof, they lean out to catch a breeze, bouncing as the coombie flies over each speed bump. It appears that their unofficial job is to spot a potential passenger in the hoards of walkers. When they spot one, they wave one arm wildly— careful to keep the other on the roof for balance—to warn the other drivers that the coombie is about to make an illegal maneuver: run a red light, make a sudden turn across two lanes of traffic, swerve to miss a stray goat, slam to a stop to pick up their new passenger.

My most sincere prayer is that I never have to ride in a coombie while I'm here.

DAY 32
SUNDAY, MARCH 2, 2008

The atmosphere in the house feels stagnant, thick with oppressive, muggy heat. Ruby sits slumped at the dining room table mindlessly stirring her tea. Dressed in her night-gown and faded cotton housecoat, her short hair slicked back with oil, her eyes betray a sleepless night. She looks old—ready to give up on life.

"Good morning, Ruby, how are you today?"

"Aye, Karen, I am very tired. I feel like I cannot even move from this chair. Do you mind to make your own tea this morning?"

"Of course not. You stay put. I'll make you another cup, too."

As we sit with fresh red bush tea, Ruby pulls a yellowed handkerchief from her sleeve to wipe her brow. Then, in her nervous habit, she twists it through her fingers.

"What's wrong Ruby? I can see you're worried about something."

"My husband says I must go to church this morning and I told him I do not believe I can." She pauses. "He says I must allow myself to be seen as I mourn."

"You look tired, Ruby." She needs to take care of herself. "You were worn out before you went to the funeral yesterday. It seems reasonable that you need to rest today."

"Honestly, Karen, I do not even want to go. Yesterday wore me to my last bone, but that is not the reason. If I go to church as a grieving woman I must sit alone in the back. I am tired of all the things I must do because my mother-in-law has died and I am married to her eldest son. I miss laughing with my friends. I cannot even smile."

"That's hard, Ruby. Laughing is such good medicine, and you're so good at it. What can I do to help?"

She breaks the rules and smiles at me with the mischievous grin I've grown to love. I know I'm about to be her partner in crime.

"You can help me decide a reason to stay home that will satisfy my husband."

I marvel that after the tragic events of the past two weeks, cooking all day yesterday in horrendous heat, and the pressure of being the new matriarch, she *still* needs an excuse to stay home from church. The need to justify her own care does nothing to lighten her burden.

But, I'm game. Together we concoct a litany of "female ailments" likely to satisfy Mhambi. Before heading down the hall to present her case, she practices with an I'm-about-to-die expression. I listen intently for clues, but hear nothing from behind their closed bedroom door. On her return, she flashes a toothy grin. Mhambi and Thulani, dressed in their Sunday suits, pass through the dining room on their way to the front door. Ruby reinforces her story by collapsing into a chair, her face contorted with pain, gripping her belly in a show of excruciating menstrual cramps. Meryl Streep has nothing on Ruby.

Within minutes she looks ten years younger, happily preparing birthday breakfast for Siphelele: fried eggs, creamy putu, fresh tomatoes, and toast with jam.

Just as she's about to set our plates on the table, inspiration strikes. "Ruby, do you have any of those little candles left over from Ntwana?"

She looks puzzled. "Candles, Karen?"

"Yes. It's a surprise for Siphelele. Where are they?"

"In the closet in Granny's room."

I race to the closet and grab the stub of a partially burned candle. Despite being much thicker than a typical birthday candle, it'll do. When Siphelele has cleaned his plate, I plant the candle in the left-over egg yolk goo, strike a match to it, and begin my rousing round of *Happy Birthday*. Siphelele— despite being sixteen and entirely too cool for his britches— and Ruby can't conceal their pleasure.

"Thank you, Miss Karen," Siphelele enthuses. "That was just as I have seen on television many times."

Siphelele's eyes well up as he pulls his new slip-ons from the shoe box. Ruby watches with pride as he examines the stitching and runs his fingers across the smooth auburn-colored leather. He and his mother exchange a hug, and she kisses him on the cheek—the only time I will ever see them express affection for each other.

I slink out to my room as they settle next to each other on the sofa to admire his new shoes.

DAY 33

"Sawubona!" I say, slipping into the front seat next to Phyllis.

Ruby's somber mood carries on. She's taken to riding in the back seat with Pamela, making it possible for me to discreetly turn on the windshield defroster. Phyllis doesn't seem to notice, and it makes the ride into the foothills less stressful for me.

"You must be excited, Karen," Phyllis says. "There is only this week and next before the school holiday. You will enjoy being at Ntwana with Ruby."

"I'm looking forward to that. Are you and Pamela coming out for the cleansing ritual?"

She shakes her head. Her expression says once is enough. "You have only two more Fridays to practice with the Grade Four learners. The music competition will take place the first week we return to school. Do you think they will be prepared?"

"They will. I'm sure of it. They love to sing and they've caught on fast to the dance. Zinti has it in the bag!"

"In the bag?" Phyllis asks.

"In the bag. That means we're sure to win."

"You are probably right, Karen. I am quite certain that none of the other rural schools will do this thing you call the Hokey Pokey."

Pamela taps me on the shoulder from the back seat. "You must teach me this dance," she says. "The Grade Four learners talk about what fun is this Hokey Pokey. Now the young ones want to learn."

My belly laugh feels good.

» » » « « «

They neglected to tell me that the Grade Four kids are taking proficiency tests this week. The morning drags on as I cool my heels in the library. Bored, I need a project.

I pop my head into Phyllis's office. "Is it okay if I look through the boxes in the library for art supplies?" I ask.

I scrounge through the pile of boxes that contain colored pencils, rulers, crayons, pens, workbooks, and reams of copy paper. The copy machine has no ink; I can put the paper to use. I fold a piece down the center and cut out half of a butterfly. I open it up to confirm that it actually looks like a butterfly. Not bad. I make a heart with another piece. Then, with nothing else to do, I fold and cut an entire ream's worth of hearts and butterflies. I know better than to trust the kids with scissors.

Missy arrives with the lunch tea tray and reaches for one of the hearts. She holds it against her chest and smiles, as she stirs two teaspoons of sugar into my cup.

"Thank you, Missy," I say. "I love you, too."

"This is quite clever, Karen," Pamela says. "What will you do with these?"

"I'll give them to the kids to decorate for art class. Then we can tape them up in the classroom. You know, like a gallery wall."

Pamela smiles. "May I have one of each of them to do the same with my learners?"

I scoot my things to one end of the table when Ruby and Phyllis arrive for lunch.

"Ruby," Pamela says, "look what Karen has made for your learners' next art lesson." She holds one of the butterflies aloft, floating it over the table.

"I have seen such things before," Ruby snarls.

I try to let it roll off. Nothing makes her happy these days.

"Karen!" Ruby snaps. "While I was away at Ntwana, why did you not stamp the library books with the Zinti School ownership stamp.

It's news to me that this was supposed to happen. I've been here over a month and none of the teachers have even *looked* at the books yet. I glance across the lunch table at Phyllis for help. She appears to have not heard the question.

"I didn't know I was supposed to, Ruby. But I'll be happy to do it if you give me the stamp. Do you want it to go inside the front or the back cover?"

She grunts with disgust. "You did not do anything while I was away. Ma'am says you did not even take my class for me. After I give you a home, you do not even take my learners for one week."

Why this? Why now? She must have known about this all along. "I had your class for two days, Ruby. I can't teach them because I don't know Zulu, and they don't know English. It was impossible to communicate with them. Ma'am must have told you what happened in the classroom."

"Yes, she told me you do not know how to manage the children. And perhaps they would be able to speak English if you did not ignore them."

I look across to Phyllis. She packs her leftover bread and margarine in the plastic bread sack and hands it to Missy before she leaves the room, her chin jutted into the air. There is no point in arguing with Ruby. Something I don't understand is under her skin. I taught the Grade Three kids the first week, and *she's* the one who put an end to it.

"I'll be happy to teach them, Ruby. How about right after lunch every day? I don't do anything but sit here and wait for the little kids, anyway."

"Very well. You shall begin tomorrow. Even though your books are not new, they should not go to waste."

» » » « « «

The little kids slip out of their shoes on the door stoop and slide across the library floor. They elbow each other for position, wrestling for the two available spots on my lap. Today's lesson: how to wait in line without pushing and shoving.

I set two chairs facing each other in the middle of the room, and line the kids up in single file. My arms stiff at my side, I smile. They jump to mimic my pose.

"Very good," I say.

"Very good," they scream in unison.

I motion for the girl at the front of the line to sit in the chair opposite me. The kids rush to grab chairs.

"No," I shout. I stand in my stiff position again and point to them to do the same.

I lead the girl at the front of the line by the hand to the chair opposite mine. "Pay attention," I say, pointing my finger up and down the line.

"Pay attention," they shout back.

It's been years since I last played patty-cake. I smack my hands on the top of my thighs and nod for her to do the same. Then I clap. She mimics my clap. I hold my hands, palms facing hers, and wait for her to do the same. We laugh together as she scrambles to learn the new game while a row of tiny eyes watch intently. Gradually, we pick up speed, until she makes the inevitable mistake. I throw my arms in the air, roll my eyes, hug her, and motion for her to go to the end of the line.

Next up is a little boy. Again we start slow and pick up speed. By the fourth child's turn, the kids in line have paired themselves up. They chant and stomp their feet to the rhythm of their tiny clapping hands, as if they've been doing this all their lives.

I look up to see Phyllis and Pamela peeking through the open door. Pamela wipes tears from her face with her lacy handkerchief. Phyllis smiles, nods to me that it's time to go home. The kids giggle as I go faster and faster, until finally the boy opposite me collapses in a fit of laughter.

"No more," I say, herding them with my arms to shoo them out the door. "See you tomorrow."

"See you tomorrow," they shout.

"See you tomorrow, *Miss Karen*," Phyllis corrects them.

"See you tomorrow, Mees Karreen."

Bent over, packing up my backpack, one of the girls nearly knocks me off my feet as she slides up to me in her socks and throws her arms around my legs. I drop to my knees and grab her into my arms for a tight squeeze. When I let go, she kisses me on my cheek, turns and races from the room.

My heart melts. These are the moments I dreamed of.

DAY 34

Ruby and I swing by Pamela's to pick her up for school; Phyllis has a meeting in town today. We drive through the hills in silence. The tall grass, weighted with thick morning mist that hovers close to the ground, refuses to bend on the air currents.

I've become adept at parceling my load into small bundles—backpack, purse, lunch sack, water bottle—dividing them up between different kids each morning so everyone has a turn to carry my things up the hill.

As always, Pamela leads the songs at assembly, but today she surprises me by including *Twinkle, Twinkle, Little Star*. The young ones at the front of the room study my mouth intently, mumbling through, while the Grade Four students at the back, well-practiced now, hold their heads high and sing at great volume. Pride overwhelms me. I can barely sing along through my emotion. Pamela smiles at me as she taps out the beat on the front wall with her piece of rebar.

With only two weeks left in the term, the Grade Four students are occupied with assessment exams. I wander through the office, reading the posters on the walls. Phyllis must be a fan of Ralph Waldo Emerson. His quotes, printed in flowery hand writing, cover the wall over the copy machine:

LIFE IS A SUCCESSION OF LESSONS
WHICH MUST BE LIVED TO BE UNDERSTOOD.
NEVER FORGET WHERE YOU WERE,
WHERE YOU ARE, AND WHERE YOU WANT TO GO.
WRITE IT ON YOUR HEART THAT EVERY DAY
IS THE BEST DAY OF THE YEAR.

DAY 35

Phyllis sounds the lunch siren. Every Zinti teacher, including me, files into the library. We gather around the two long tables shoved together and share the available food among ourselves. Across the table, a thirty-something Zulu man in a three-piece suit with a silk handkerchief tucked in his breast pocket, smiles at us with perfect teeth. School officials have decided that teachers who cope effectively with stress have better health, miss less school, present better lessons, and set a positive example for the learners. Stress Management 101 is underway.

"Good morning, ladies," he says in immaculate English. "How are you today?"

Fourteen pairs of absent eyes stare back.

"Come on, how are you?" he asks again.

His unnaturally perky voice annoys me. The others don't look excited, either.

"How many of you feel like you have stress in your lives?" he continues.

The women's stares shift from empty to "you must be joking."

"I'm here today to talk about stress," our presenter says. "How it affects our bodies. How we can make changes in our lives that will reduce stress. Does that sound like something of value to you?"

A few women nod. That would be hard to deny.

"Excellent. Medical research shows that when we suffer repeated incidents of stress in our lives, eventually it takes a toll on both our physical and emotional health. Stress produces a chemical reaction in the brain." He pulls a color photo of a human brain from his black leather portfolio. "Here, in the center of the brain, is a tiny organ called the hypothalamus gland. This organ plays an important role in the cycle of stress."

He pulls out another diagram. "When something of concern or danger takes place around us—for instance not having enough money, arguments with husbands, even the death of a loved one—the hypothalamus gland senses the problem and sends a message to the pituitary gland. The pituitary gland distributes the message throughout the rest of the body by releasing a hormone into the blood stream. This hormone has the specific responsibility of activating the adrenal gland which produces glucose. In the time of our ancestors, glucose was required so that one could either fight or flee."

So far it's an interesting lesson in body chemistry. I can't wait to hear the part about how to avoid stress. That's where he'll have his work cut out for him.

"Glucose makes your legs tremble and your heart beat faster," he says. "It also makes it difficult to sleep. It takes time for the adrenal gland to recognize that the problem has passed. If you experience another incident of stress before this happens, the cycle will repeat itself and you will continually be processing excess glucose. This weakens your immune system. It affects your ability to perceive life accurately. It causes stubborn behavior. And it creates a false sense of knowing everything. Does this sound like anything that you have experienced in your own life?"

Some of the teachers nod. Two excuse themselves to go use the outhouse.

"Very well. So now we will talk about the causes of stress in a modern life." He pauses for effect. "Ninety percent of stress is attitude!"

Attitude? Does he even have a clue what these women's lives are like?

"It is true," he continues. "Research has proven beyond any doubt that the attitude you assume toward the events in your life has a tremendous consequence to your health."

This may be true. But it's hard to maintain a positive attitude while your husband beats you, when you can't open a bank account, when you're dying in the hospital and your husband won't come to visit you, when you know your children will be orphans next month.

"It is not the situations in your life that are the cause of stress," he says. "It is your *attitude* about the situations that creates the stress."

Not only are these women beaten down by their culture, now they're being made to feel guilty about how they respond. He needs to shut up. Now! There I go, breaking the first law of stress management—I have a bad attitude about his presentation.

"Many times we involve ourselves in the problems of our neighbors. We allow ourselves to feel stress about problems that do not even belong to us!" he says.

If these women don't stick together, they're sunk.

"Other times we look at our neighbor's success, and feel envy."

How can you not envy the family that has food?

"Do you understand what I am saying, ladies?"

Dead air fills the room.

"When you feel that your neighbor receives more love than you do, it is not for you to try to steal their loving husband away from them."

The women giggle.

"It is for you to decide that it is necessary to love yourself better."

Easier said than done, under their circumstances.

"There has been much research done that indicates that specific physical ailments are associated with specific emotional stresses. Would you like to hear about that?"

The teachers who remain, nod.

He mops his brow with a handkerchief. At ninety-five degrees and ninety percent humidity, he must be miserable in that suit; losing water weight by the minute.

"I have a list of common ailments that women like yourselves experience. The causes of the ailments will show you how you can better take care of yourself to reduce your suffering." He produces yet another handout and slides it across the table for the women read.

CAUSES OF STRESS
Painful Shoulders – I am not receiving emotional support
Middle Back Pain – feeling guilty when I am not truly guilty
Waist Pain – stress about money
Sinus Problems – irritation to one particular person very close to me
Asthma – over protection by fearful parents
Headaches – don't like to be pushed around; need more freedom of expression
Fibroids – ego as a woman has been belittled
Ulcers – low self-esteem

WAYS TO RELIEVE STRESS
Self-love
Mind your own business
Manage finances without competition, greed or accepting another's criticism

"So, ladies," the smiling stress expert asks, "do you suffer from any of these ailments?"

A wall of horrified faces stare back at him.

"It is a lot to take in," he says, in a well-practiced sympathetic tone. "It will take time to adjust the way you look at your lives." He pauses before he pulls a half-dozen brown, pint-sized glass bottles from his briefcase and sets them in the middle of the table. "Science has also discovered that there are certain chemicals which decrease stress. One spoonful of this chemical with your morning tea will help to lower your stress level."

Everyone buys a bottle of the magic chemical. Including me.

DAY 36
THURSDAY, MARCH 6, 2008

At the wail of the lunch siren I step from Nandi's class-room into a frenzy of kids rushing into the field with their tin plates. In the clearing, Cook stands over an enormous black iron pot wedged into the burning logs of an open fire. The hem of her apron floats on the breeze, flirting with the flames. A wave of dizziness rolls through me—the déjà vu of having already experienced this scene. I lay my hand against the wall to steady myself as I reel backward through my memories, all the way to my childhood.

Then it hits me: the Castle Shannon Library in Pittsburgh. Endless days spent with my nose buried in books, escaping my life. Fantasies of a romantic adventure. A favorite book—*Little Black Sambo*. My dizziness gives way to nausea as I absorb the shame that it's taken almost fifty years for the reality of little black Sambo's life to register with me. Cook waves to me across the field. Her wide, toothy grin glows against her black skin. My legs wobble as I traverse the hill to the lunch room.

"Phyllis," I ask, "why is Cook making lunch over a wood fire?"

"There is no more money for the gas stove," she says.

I had imagined Cook was making the kids something exotic for lunch. Delusions of romance will have to be pounded out of me.

"The children's parents are required to send seven rand every month to pay for their food and school supplies," Phyllis says. "They have not done so since the term began. I have been purchasing gas for the stove from my own purse!" She ends on an indignant note.

Phyllis shouldn't have to pay. One more reason to solicit funds from friends back home—less than one dollar to feed a child for a month. Should I offer? Or should I let it be what it is? Cook doesn't seem to mind the open fire.

» » » « « «

I follow Ruby to her classroom, ready to teach her kids to read. She hands every child in her room a copy—made where?—of several pages of *Five Silly Fishermen*, the first time a teacher has used one of the books I brought. I struggle with the chalk and the slick blackboard, efforting to write the simple words: ONE CLIMBED UP A TREE. ONE LAY IN THE GRASS. Ruby sits at her desk, thumbing ahead in the book to read the entire story.

"Okay, learners," I say. "Look at the board and read the words with me."

The kids heads stay buried in the stapled papers. Ruby shouts at them in Zulu.

I lay my finger against the chalkboard, under the first word. "One," I say.

The girls are first to catch on. "One," a few repeat.

A boy in the back of the room snickers. Ruby jumps from her desk, grabs her ruler and storms through the rows of desks, banging chairs with her hips. She grabs him under his arm, yanks him from his chair, and smacks the ruler across his head as she drags him to the front of the room.

My heart breaks. Maybe he was just silly excited about having something to read. He might be one of last week's problem boys, but her rough treatment of him feels out of line. He spends the remainder of class cowered on the floor at my feet, reading along from the crumpled papers Ruby threw at him when she finished humiliating him. Every time she leaves her desk, expecting to be hit again, he recoils.

Ruby's ruined the joy of learning to read. I struggle to hold back my tears as she patrols the classroom, striking any child who dares to show feelings—good or bad. I can't wait for class to be over. When the bell rings, she saunters from the room. After the last child leaves, I turn back to the chalkboard, eraser in hand. Tears flow as I wipe away the horrible experience.

"Ma'am?" a tiny voice calls from the open door.

I turn away, raising my shoulder to dry my face. "Yes, sweetheart?"

Wendy stands outside on the stoop, her face peeking around the edge of the doorway. "May I come in, Ma'am?"

I set the eraser on the ledge and wave her in. She bounces across the front of the room, wraps her arms around my legs and buries her face in my skirt. "I love you, Mees Karreen." She turns and races from the room.

"I love you, too!" I shout after her. I drop into a chair at the front of the room, fold my arms on the desk, lower my head to my arms, and let loose my grief.

» » »   « « «

"Ruby, please tell me what's happened," I beg, as we pull away from the gas station. "Ever since you've come home from Ntwana it feels like you're angry with me. Please tell me what I've done to make you so mad. I'd like to apologize, but I don't know what I've done."

"It is not you, Karen." Her voice carries the same irritation I've sensed all week.

"Then what is it?"

"It is not your problem."

"But it is. Whatever's going on makes me feel like I've done something wrong, like I'm in the way. Please tell me. Maybe I can help."

Her reply is swift and sharp. "You cannot help."

I hold my tongue as we round the traffic circle into Oribi Village. Maybe she'll say more.

Her shoulders drop. "I am very tired, Karen. Tired of answering questions from everyone in town about why I have a white woman in my car."

Relief washes over me. I knew something was up. My momentary relaxation is quickly followed by empathy for

Ruby's struggle, and a new concern for myself. She's right. I can't help. I can't change the color of my skin.

"I'm sorry it's hard for you, Ruby."

She sighs. When she speaks I still feel the edge in her voice. "I did not know that my friends would be angry at me for having a whitie in my home."

Whitie? Whitie! A knot forms in my gut where this word lands.

"At first they did not mind. But now they ask all the time why you are still here. Why you think I should take you in my car every day."

So this is why she leaves me at home when she goes to town, visits Simangele, runs errands. I thought it was my probing questions, my curiosity in every shop that slows her down. It's much worse to know it's who I am, not what I've done. I could change my behavior. I can't change my race.

» » »   « « «

I sit on the sofa, my feet propped on the coffee table, watching the BBC news from India in a three-bedroom brick house with a gardener out back mowing the lawn around a swimming pool. And Ruby's taking grief for housing a white woman from America? There is no place in myself to reconcile this swirling mass of contradictions.

Rolina has gone home for the day. Ruby is out running errands. Siphelele is at basketball practice. Thulani isn't home from school yet. The house feels empty, devoid of life. Not just people. Life. With the sound turned down on the television—I know even less Punjabi than Zulu—I listen to the radio.

"... my wife promised we would have only two children," the caller says.

"And so what is the problem?" asks the female host, the Zulu version of Ann Landers.

"We already have our two children, and now she is pregnant again. I do not know how to punish her for disobeying our agreement."

His comment startles me. I feel my hackles rise.

"Aye, man," the male host says. "You are in a tough spot. For sure you cannot punish her now. You would not want to harm the baby she carries."

Sympathy that it's not a good time for this man to beat his wife? I can't believe this. Where is the female host? Maybe she's beating the crap out of her co-host for sympathizing with the caller. Or maybe she's walked out of the studio, refusing to be party to this obscenity. Who's going to defend this pregnant woman?

"Perhaps you can accept this child as a gift from God and be happy about the pregnancy."

Ah, there she is! The voice of reason. Can't she at least make the bold statement that punishment is out of the question?

"Of course I will accept the child," the caller says. "But still, she must know that it is wrong for her to reverse her promise."

Maybe it was an accident! Is anyone going suggest that?

"I know it is too late this time," the male host says. "But if you wear a condom, man, she cannot deceive you again."

"You can take charge of the number of children you bring into the world," the female host suggests.

Yes! Let the man have some responsibility. Coming from her it sounds more like placating him, but she's on the right track.

"I will need to do that, for sure," the caller says. "My wife cannot be trusted to keep her word." He pauses. "There is still the issue of how to punish her. She must not be allowed to believe it is okay for her to do this."

"Aye, man," the male host says. "You must wait until after the baby is born, though. Promise me you will not raise your hand to your wife while she is pregnant."

Only its hefty size, and the bars on the window, prevent me from thrashing the radio.

DAY 37

Phyllis stands in front of the assembly and unleashes fury on the kids. Her milk chocolate "colored" skin flushes with anger as she shouts and shakes the steel rod at them. Her behavior seems out of character. Like puppy dogs beaten on a leash without escape, the children cringe every time Phyllis waves the rod over her head. She marches down the side aisle, grabbing boys at random, shaking them by the collar before she shoves them back into line. Spittle flies from her mouth, along with my name.

Don't you dare include me in your rage! They're kids. Little kids. They've done nothing to deserve this.

After assembly the children sulk away in silence, their shoulders drooped forward, heads held low in shame. There is no frivolity on the way to class. No running. No pushing. No little kid energy. Even the teachers appear burdened by Principal Zondi's scolding—a scolding I don't understand and no one seems eager to explain. I can't bring myself to ask.

The kids usually bubble with enthusiasm on our art and music Fridays. Today though, I have a classroom of fifty solemn children staring at their desks. I decide to perk them up by skipping the English lesson altogether, assigning it for homework instead. They aren't accustomed to having work to do away from school and seem proud of the new responsibility. Their assignment is to write a list of ten nouns and ten verbs, using each in a sentence. They nod in agreement. I distribute the folded paper butterflies. Heads bent over their desks, they color in silence.

At lunchtime, on my way down the hill, I notice that Cook's serving table isn't out yet. The kids wander the hillside with their empty tin plates in hand. Only Pamela, Missy and I come to the library to eat. Silent and gloomy, neither of them smile when I sit down at the table. Missy stirs sugar into my tea without our ritual acknowledgment.

"Where are Ruby and Phyllis?" I ask.

Pamela seems reluctant to answer. I persist with a questioning expression.

"Ruby is taking her lunch in her classroom," Pamela says. "Ma'am has left already for her principals' meeting in Maritzburg."

Several of the older girls wander into the library and curtsey at Pamela before speaking. Their conversation, in Zulu, is hushed. Pamela speaks with gentle resignation. Missy keeps her head down, her gaze fixed on the table. Expression drains from the girls' faces. They curtsey again and leave in silence.

I presume the girls are wondering about lunch. "Is Cook ill today?"

"No. She is not needed at school today," Pamela says, her eyes locked on her teacup.

"Why not?"

"The children will have no lunch today."

A knot forms in my stomach. "What do you mean?"

"Ma'am is punishing the children."

My gut clenches. They haven't done anything to justify being starved. Frantic energy rises from my groin to my chest. You can't just refuse to feed kids. "Why?"

"This is why Ma'am was so angry with the children this morning," Pamela says, her voice low, her demeanor flat. "Ma'am says their parents are being lazy. They have not sent their money to school this month."

"I thought the government provides the lunch food."

"You are correct. They give us bags of beans and rice. But we must cook them, and Ma'am has no more money to purchase gas for the stove."

Hundreds of pairs of empty eyes and long faces stream through my mind; little kids who realize they aren't important enough to be fed. My heart breaks for Nomusa. How can they punish such an innocent little girl? She doesn't deserve this. None of them deserve this.

The reality of starvation as punishment hits my heart. I lean into the table. My voice rises as I struggle to keep my rage in check. "What about the big pot Cook used yesterday, with the wood fire? Can't she make lunch in that pot again?"

"Ma'am has told the men to put the pot away in her office." Pamela's chin hangs against her chest. "It is no use to keep feeding the children. This is the only way the parents will understand that they must pay their seven rand every month."

My anxiety grows to panic. This needs to be stopped! Seven rand. That's less than one dollar. "It's not a lot," I say, trying to control my voice, "but maybe it's more than they have. Maybe they can't pay."

Pamela shrugs. "Ma'am says they keep it for themselves. They must be more responsible with their money and send what is required to school."

I slump in my chair. Defeated. Disgusted. Dozens of little faces press against the library windows to watch us eat. Tears well up in my eyes. Missy drags her feet across the room to close the door and shoo the kids away from the windows. Oppressive energy hangs in the air. I can barely breathe. Is Ruby appalled by this decision? Is that why she's not here? Or is she too ashamed to face us because she agrees with Phyllis? Pamela and Missy devour their white bread and margarine sandwiches. It doesn't matter that my ramen noodles and tea have gone cold. I've lost my appetite.

"You must eat, Karen," Pamela says. "The children will be fine."

"I can't." I don't even try to hide my tears dripping onto the table. I push my bowl of noodles across to Missy and raise my eyebrows to ask if she'd like my food. It shouldn't go to waste. What I'd really like to do is take it outside to the kids. But how would I ever choose which one of them gets to eat? Missy holds my spoon out toward me, gesturing that I should eat my own food. I shake my head. She's thrilled to have such a treat.

Most of the kids haven't eaten since yesterday's lunch. Chances are they won't eat over the weekend. This is way too long for these tiny bodies to go without food. They'll be weak by Monday.

» » » « « «

On the way home from school, Ruby and I make our weekly stop at the Spar Market where she shops for her family. I shop for my own breakfast and lunch food and give her one-hundred rand for my evening meals. In addition to my usual bread, bologna, ramen noodles, yogurt, granola, and raisins—I include a bag of eight small green apples. On Monday I'll give an apple to a boy and girl in each Grade Four class; a reward for the best homework papers. If the other teachers can give bananas as rewards, I can give apples. Besides, I need to do *something* to let the kids know that I'm not part of the decision to starve them.

DAY 38

The gauzy fabric of my new printed skirt clings to my belly and hips, flaring into ruffles at my knees. The thin coffee colored shirt stretches across my breasts. I feel exposed.

Ruby stops cold when I enter the kitchen. "Haybo! Look at you!" She lays her spatula on the stove, wipes her hands on her apron, and spins me around by my shoulders.

"Do you like it?" I ask.

Her smile feels like the approval of a good friend. "Why have I not seen this before? You must dress like this more often."

"I bought it when I was with Paula. It's so different from what I usually wear."

"You should not feel bad," Ruby says. "Simangele will be proud of you at her party today. You must eat your breakfast now. She has called to say she is on her way."

» » » « « «

I don't know what to expect of a coffin party; a funeral I would understand. But today is all about the Bekwa's success in the coffin business, a celebration of their new showroom in the most prestigious district of Pietermaritzburg. The AIDS crisis isn't their fault, but it's done wonders for their business.

Death is everywhere. Today, Ruby and Mhambi are off to his nephew's funeral in Durban, the young man who was shot in the head while driving his coombie. The boys left last night for a cousin's funeral in Ntwana. He was in a car accident three months ago and died of his injuries on Monday. It's like this every weekend. Ruby squeezes in as many funerals as she can manage; Mhambi attends only for relatives.

At nine-thirty Simangele pulls up in her sleek gray Lexus

and jumps out to hug me. Until now I've only seen her at the factory in her blue gingham uniform. Today—wearing a bright skirt, crisp white blouse, and gold hoop earrings—she looks like a different woman.

"Good morning, Karen. Are you ready for our party?" she asks, with her usual warm smile. "My friend Ruby says you are eager to have ice cubes in your drinks today."

We hurry across town to the Catholic church, serenaded by Simangele's four-year-old daughter, Awonke. A wide grin spread across her face, she bounces with energy in the back seat belting out *Jesus Loves Me This I Know*.

The church parking lot teems with families huddled together in the sparse shade of a few withering trees. The women, dressed in colorful revealing outfits, hold babies in their arms—stacked high with bangles—and cool themselves with the wood fans they carry in their purses.

"Come," Simangele says. "I will introduce you to the men from Durban who will film our celebration today. You will have much to share with them while I help my husband inside."

We cross the parking lot toward two very tall, middle-aged white men who are busy assembling a tripod under a tree. Both are thin, clean shaven, and wear black company logo T-shirts tucked into their pressed blue jeans. We have so much to share because we're the only white people in the crowd.

"This is my friend, Karen," Simangele says. "Karen, this is Will and Theo, from Durban."

In turn, they shake my hand and welcome me to South Africa. Their British-tinged English feels comforting. Semi-embarrassed by my elation, I enjoy listening without effort. The past few weeks have been more isolating than I realized. I want to lean in, ask how things are in the "outside" world.

"So, where are you from?" Will asks. "Are you enjoying your stay in South Africa?"

"I'm from California and yes, I am enjoying your country. It's beautiful. I've been mostly in this area, but I did see a little bit of Durban a few weeks ago. Have you ever been to the US?"

"No. I'd like to go one day, though," Will says. "So what brings you here?"

"I'm here with Simangele."

Will glances at Theo, then back to me. "I mean, who are you here with, in South Africa?"

"How did you meet Mrs. Bekwa?" Theo clarifies.

"Oh. She's a friend of the woman I'm living with, Ruby Ndlela."

"And who is she?" asks Will.

I feel like I'm being drilled. "She's one of the teachers at the school where I work."

They both sigh, like finally we're getting somewhere with this conversation. "So you're here with a relief organization."

"No." I shake my head. "I'm just here teaching at their school."

Eyes wide, they look at me as though I've just run naked around the parking lot. "Do you mean to say that you are here by yourself?"

Their interrogation perturbs me. Attitude creeps into my voice. "Yes. I came to teach at one of the rural schools. I live with Ruby, in Pietermaritzburg. She and Simangele have been friends since childhood."

Their mouths hang open.

I don't see why it's such a big deal.

Theo, movie camera still in his hands, steps around the tripod to stand next to me. They tilt their heads down toward my face. They look grim. Will raises his eyebrows and lowers his voice. "Where is the school you're teaching at?"

"It's west of Pietermaritzburg, about forty minutes from town, in Ezimolo Village."

"And how do you get yourself there every day?"

"I ride with the principal and some of the teachers."

"How do they treat you?"

Their tone makes me nervous. "They treat me fine. Why all these questions?"

Theo returns to the business of setting up the camera. Will pulls a handkerchief from his hip pocket and wipes the perspiration from the back of his neck. He turns so that we now stand shoulder-to-shoulder, folds his arms across his chest, and looks out over the parking lot. "You are not safe there alone," he whispers.

Now *my* mouth hangs open. My heart pounds.

"They take good care of me." I try to keep my voice from wavering. I feel defensive of Phyllis and Ruby despite yesterday's events. I attempt an objective mental review of exactly how I've been treated. My senses feel skewed—even peeing in the sink feels normal now. I can't fight my way through the fog of what is right and appropriate to expect. What constitutes good care? Should I compare here to home? I take a deep breath.

"Do you know why there are two of us here today?" Will asks. He doesn't mean for me to guess. "We always travel in pairs. You will never see a white person alone in Zulu territory."

Old enough to be affected by years of Apartheid indoctrination, he sounds paranoid. Nonetheless, I feel the strength draining from my legs. "I haven't had any problems."

"All the same," he says, looking straight into my eyes, "be careful. Watch your back. If you make them angry they will just as soon kill you as look at you."

His words land in my gut.

» » » « « «

Church is packed. The elderly woman across the aisle from me wears traditional dress. Her head scarf matches the checked fabric of her dress. Her eyes narrow each time she looks at me. My smile does nothing to soften her glare.

Will's words have rattled me. I feel awkward now, even here in the front pew with Simangele's family. The organist begins. Simangele and her husband lead the processional walk down the aisle in front of Father Mnganga. Mr. Bekwa holds a large gold cross at arm's length in front of his chest. Simangele carries a gilded bible over her head. After the procession, she sits next to me and wraps her arm around my shoulder. Mr. Bekwa sits at the other end of the pew.

Will and Theo, their equipment set up in the center aisle several rows back, capture the priest's welcome of the honored guest from California, his prayer for the Bekwa's continued success, and a prayer for the health of the factory workers. I appreciate that Mass is in English. As we file out, Theo busies himself packing the camera away. Will refuses to make eye contact with me. Maybe he's just being professional; careful not to fraternize with the guests. But it feels like he's distancing himself from me. I need to talk with him about what he said.

» » »   « « «

Our next stop is the new funeral showroom, wedged between the tire dealer and McDonald's in downtown Pietermaritzburg. Simangele takes me by the arm and leads me inside, past the guests who linger on the street, leaning against sign posts and parked cars.

A framed poster-size photo of the factory workers hangs on one wall. The showroom displays vary from simple pine coffins with a cross carved into the lid, to ornate caskets made from exotic woods varnished to a glossy sheen, lined with white satin ruffles, and adorned with shiny brass hardware. Some caskets are even painted: salmon pink, pistachio green, and pale blue. Father Mnganga sprinkles his holy water over the displays. I hope the water spots don't damage the wood.

The children, anxious to have their photos taken, jump up and down in front of me until I oblige. Their favorite place to pose? Kneeling next to the tiny white infant's casket. Holding the paradox that one family's grief is another fami-

ly's gold—without naming either as right or wrong—challenges me.

» » » « « «

Well past noon now—hot, thirsty, and hungry—I'm eager
for the ice I've been promised. While guests linger at the
showroom to socialize, Simangele and I travel across town to
the factory, where steel stakes have been driven into the
asphalt parking lot to anchor the elegant white canvas tent
that shades the caterer's tables.

Simangele makes a dive for the ice chest and comes up
with two wine coolers and a handful of ice chips. She drops
a few chips into my hand before she rubs the rest over her
face. Smiling, she drops another handful down the front of
her blouse. "Here," she says, handing me a peach cooler.
"Drink this. You will feel better."

Enjoying the shade of the tent, I take in the party scene: a
goat and pig roast on spits over large coal bins in the corner
of the lot; rows of white plastic lawn chairs wait for guests;
stacks of commercial amplifiers line one side of the tent; a
female singer runs a sound check with her crew; and the fan-
ciest, most opulent caskets are on display under the tent with
a sign that reads: PLAN FOR THE FUTURE—ORDER TODAY AND
SAVE 10%.

Others begin to arrive. Mr. Bekwa, a few close relatives,
and the school Inspector park inside the fence. The rest park
outside and drift in on foot. Will and Theo negotiate with
the sound crew for the best filming location.

Simangele pulls the ropes that raise the corrugated industrial doors of the main factory room, revealing stacks of
coffins under construction. Everyone crowds around to
watch as the carpenters form a semi-circle around Father
Mnganga. One-by-one he anoints each of their hands with
oil, blessing them in their work.

After the ceremony, Simangele tracks me down, another
wine cooler in hand.

"Oh, Simangele, I can't. The first one went straight to my head. I need to eat before I drink more."

"I wish the men would do the same," she says. "The cook says the meat will not be ready for at least another hour. The men will be drunk by then." She shakes her head. "I do not want problems today. I have sent my sons to guard the gate."

"Why?"

"The smell of roasting meat will draw hungry men from the surrounding area. My sons will do their best to keep them out. To keep peace today."

Her serious tone intensifies the sense of dread created by Will and Theo. I decide to stay close to the factory door so I can slip into the sewing room if things get out of hand.

My concern must show. Simangele slides her arm around my waist. "It will be okay," she says. "You should relax and enjoy yourself today. Let me introduce you to some of our guests."

The small group of women, segregated from the men, are polite. We talk about the stifling heat, the fantastic food, the many different kinds of bottled beer the Bekwa's have provided—followed by an awkward silence. I smile. I don't have it in me today to struggle with conversation.

Only the Inspector's wife continues. "And how do you enjoy teaching at Zinti?" she asks.

"I love it. The kids are amazing. They're so sweet, so eager to learn."

"They are very lucky to have you, Karen. The Inspector says he wishes all of his schools could be so fortunate. The children learn fast when they have an English speaking teacher."

"I hope that's true. There's so much I want to show them. It feels like there isn't enough time for everything."

"You must not trouble yourself with that thinking. They learn well from you. The Principal has told me so herself." She waves her arm to dismiss my concerns. "Now, have you had something cold to drink, yet?"

"I have. But I'll have another. Do you know where the non-alcoholic drinks are?"

She leads me to the children's cooler where bottles of Coke and orange pop sit buried in ice chips. The kids squat around the red cooler, plunging their hands into the ice, up to their elbows, before they pull them out and wrap them around themselves.

"You can put your hands in the ice, Ma'am," one little girl grins. "It feels very good."

Stooping next to the cooler, I shove my hands to the bottom of the ice. It does feel good. The children giggle, one hand over their mouths, the other pointing at me as they whisper to each other in Zulu. They must think I'm a silly adult for playing with children.

Our Zulu singer oozes sex appeal as she shakes her generous body to the thundering beat of the Zulu music. Dressed from head to toe in skin-tight white shirt and pants, beaded ropes adorn her forehead and wrists. The bright colors pop against her dark skin. Her hair is braided in cornrows with stubby tufts, and when she throws her head back on long, high notes, her gold teeth glint in the sunlight.

One little boy, no older than four or five, dances like nothing I've ever seen. He glances over his shoulder at Will's camera, smiles, then turns back to the crowd and wows everyone again before he plops to the ground for a rest.

I feel content, sitting alone, watching the fun until our feast begins. The long food table overflows with chafing dishes of green salad, scalloped potatoes, stewed cabbage, carrots, fresh fruit salad, rolls, and succulent meat. A feast without grease!

As the sun dips under the edge of the tent, I drag a lawn chair into the shade of the factory, to eat with the group of women. I feel timid about my first bite of goat meat—a bit gamey, but not too much to enjoy. Kids race back and forth with dessert plates for the adults: carrot cake, brownies, and poached pears. I'm in heaven. Ice *and* great food.

One of the teenage girls pulls her chair close to me. She

sits with her back straight, her legs crossed at the ankle, her hands folded in her lap. She has a nervous smile. I know what's coming.

"How are you today, Ma'am?" she asks.

"I'm doing well, thank you. And you?"

"I am well, Ma'am." She hesitates. "You are from America?"

"Yes. Have you heard of California?"

"No, Ma'am. But I know of America."

I smile.

She looks down at her lap for courage, then at me. Her eyes beg. "Can you take me there with you?" she asks. "I will work very hard for you in America."

I have to say no, but I'm slow to answer. I want to tell her that her family would miss her, that she would miss them. I want to tell her that if she works hard she can make a good life for herself here. I want to believe all these things are true. I think of the eight-year-old girl in Ruby's class who's being raped by her cousin on the way home from school every day. Phyllis, Pamela and Ruby all know about it. Everyone would like to put a stop to it, but the girl's uncle feeds the family. I don't know what to tell this sweet-faced young girl of twelve or thirteen. Her eyes plead with hope. She deserves a chance. Telling her "no" might kill me.

"I'm so sorry, sweetheart. I wish I could help you." I hold my hand out. She grabs it with both of hers. "I can't take you home with me. Everyone who comes to America must have a passport." I sound pathetic. She doesn't care about legalities. Her tense smile fades. I feel like I have personally destroyed her hope for a better future. "There are laws that prevent me from bringing children from other countries into America. But if I was allowed to, I would certainly want to take you." If I could import kids who need a home, parents, food, love—I'd have a houseful.

She tries to smile.

"Do you know how to use a computer? Or write letters?"

She nods.

"I'll give you my address and my email." I dig through my purse for a piece of paper and a pen. "I would love for you to send me letters. And I'll write back to you. I promise. Maybe one day we'll see each other again." I print my addresses and hand her the paper.

She holds it in front of her, reading the words out loud.

"Your English is very good. Keep doing your lessons. You can practice by writing me letters." My weak smile is a sorry substitute for real help. This is excruciating. There has to be more I can do. "May I give you a hug?"

"Yes, Ma'am!"

She throws her arms around my shoulders and squeezes hard. I rub my hand over her back and kiss the top of her head. She curtsies as she turns to leave. I thought it would be easier this time, knowing what was coming. I was wrong.

» » » « « «

At five, Will and Theo pack up their equipment. I hurry to catch them on their way out. "It was nice to meet you," I say. "I'd love to have a copy of the DVD from today. Is that possible?"

Will pulls a business card from his T-shirt pocket as Simangele steps up beside me. "The DVD will be ready in a few weeks," he says. "You can contact us through our website to order a copy. If you'll pay for the postage, we can mail it to you in the US."

"When you send my copies," Simangele says, "you can include an extra one for my friend. I will see her again before she returns home and give it to her myself."

"Thank you, Simangele," I say." I can't wait to see it."

"We wish you well in your teaching," Will says. His tone is cool and distant. He shakes my hand before they leave.

"So, Karen," Simangele says, steering me back to the tent, "have you had a good day?"

"I have. The music was fabulous and your food was yummy."

"That makes me very happy." She gives me a warm hug. "It pleases me that you are here today. I must say good-bye to our guests. Then I will drive you to Ruby's home."

» » » « « «

Dusk settles over the factory grounds as the party winds down. Without the loud music and dancing as distractions, I notice the condition of the lot—and the men. Paper plates and napkins are ground into the asphalt with beer and scraps of food. Broken beer bottles lie scattered from one fence to the other. The men stagger with drunken steps.

Most of the women have already left. Only Simangele, her sons' wives, the Inspector's wife and teenaged daughter, and little Awonke, remain. Mr. Bekwa and a half-dozen men stand around the Inspector's white pick-up truck parked in the center of the lot. Their conversation, all in Zulu, gradually shifts from light-hearted laughter to an argument.

Mr. Bekwa raises his voice and waves a beer bottle over his head as he leans into the Inspector's sober face. The Inspector, a good foot shorter than Mr. Bekwa, appears unaffected by the tirade. The other men become silent. Spit flies from Mr. Bekwa's mouth as he unleashes more angry words in the Inspector's face. My name is the only word I understand.

I feel sick. It suddenly occurs to me that it wasn't Mr. Bekwa's idea to invite me. He hasn't said one word to me all day. The Inspector's wife walks the twenty feet to where I stand, stepping over the broken bottles without breaking her stride. "Come with me," she says. "My husband and I will take you home now." She places her hand in the small of my back and directs me to their truck.

My legs feel rubbery. I can barely walk. I slide into the sweltering heat of the rear seat next to their daughter.

"Lock the door," the Inspector's wife says, as she climbs into the front passenger seat.

The Inspector backs Mr. Bekwa away from the truck.

More angry with every backward step, Mr. Bekwa waves his arms wildly through the air. Fifteen feet from the truck, Simangele steps between the two men, speaking to her husband in a low voice. He brushes her aside with his arm, spilling beer down the front of her blouse. She and the Inspector stand their ground, their voices calm. I feel terror. Adrenaline pumps through my body. I want the floodlights at the corner of the lot to come on. I want a clearer view of the situation.

"What's happening?" I ask.

"My husband says he will take you home," the Inspector's wife answers. "It makes sense since we live very near to Ruby. Mr. Bekwa says you are his guest, and therefore you are his responsibility."

This isn't the time to mince words. "He's drunk. I don't want him driving me around."

"You must not worry. It will not happen. Mr. Bekwa is just angry with my husband that he is leaving the party so early. He says that my husband is rude, that if he were a true friend he would stay and drink with the men."

She sounds too calm. Does this happen often? The girl also seems to take it in stride. Am I the only one with panic thumping in my chest? I close my eyes to think. Ruby's is too far to walk. I don't even know the way. I remember what I taught Kevin when he was little—just run to a neighbor's door and ask for help. Not here. I don't even have a phone. Breathe, Karen.

Simangele comes around to my side of the truck and knocks for me to unlock the door. She leans into the truck. I grab her wrist.

"I am very sorry," she says. "My husband behaves poorly. Come with me."

"I don't want to get out, Simangele. I want to go home."

"My husband will not allow the Inspector to take you home. Even though it is a reasonable request the Inspector makes, my husband will not hear of it."

"Simangele, I want to go home. Now." I sound like a terrified child. "You promised that you would take me home whenever I said I was ready. I'm ready now."

"You are safe, Karen" she says. "Come with me."

I slide out of the seat. She holds my hand as we walk across the lot, away from the fray, toward her car. She opens the back door. I crawl in. "Do not look at them," she says. "My husband behaves like a fool in front of his guests. Wait here. I will find someone to take you home."

Someone? Not Simangele? The constriction in my chest hurts. Oh, dear God, help me stay calm. Help me think. Just get me back to Ruby's house. Safe. Please.

I slink down in my seat until my head is hidden behind the triangle between the door and rear window. I peek out the side window with one eye. Simangele stands in front of her husband with one hand on her waist. She shakes her other hand in his face before she turns, grabs her eldest son's arm, and heads for the car. Awonke runs to catch up, grabs her mother's free hand, and skips along beside her.

Simangele opens the back door. "My son will take you home," she smiles as her daughter climbs over my lap into the seat.

"No, Simangele. I want *you* to take me home. Please," I beg.

"My husband will not permit me to leave the party while we still have guests. My son will drive you to Ruby's house. You will be safe, Karen. He is not drunk and he is a very good driver."

Her son takes the keys and walks around to the driver's side. It's not going to happen the way I want.

"Does he know how to get to Ruby's? I can't give him directions."

"You will be fine, Karen," Simangele says. "I will come to visit you tomorrow at Ruby's." She hugs me and closes the door.

Simangele's son puts the car in gear and drives through the gate. Breathe, Karen. This twenty-something young man was friendly at church this morning. He feels safer than his angry drunken father who somehow believes I belong to him. But I still feel guarded. Dear God, please don't let this be the last ride I take in South Africa.

» » »   « « «

The young man looks at me in the rearview mirror. He has a pleasant, warm smile. "You are safe. My father does not mean you any harm. He is just drunk and angry at the Inspector because he does not respect my father's responsibilities."

Unconvinced, I try to smile. We pull onto the freeway. It's dark now.

"This is not the route Ruby takes when we come to visit Simangele," I say. "Do you know where Ruby lives?" He must hear the fear in my voice.

"Yes. My mother has given me excellent directions. We are not far away."

Awonke snuggles against my shoulder. "I like you," she says. Her voice is so little. Sweet. Innocent.

I take her hand in mine. "I like you, too, sweetheart."

We exit the freeway and the surface streets begin to look familiar. I could walk from here. I grow more calm with every block. The dashboard clock reads 6:08 when we pull up to Ruby's. Not a single light is on in the house. Simangele's son honks the horn to rouse someone to unlock the chain around the driveway gate. No response.

"Do you have a key?" he asks.

"No."

"Do you have Ruby's phone number?"

"Yes." I scramble through my purse for the slip of paper with Phyllis's and Ruby's numbers.

He dials the number and waits. "There is no answer."

"Try again. Please."

He dials again. "There is still no answer."

My calm evaporates. "Please call your mother and see if she knows where Ruby is."

"Yes. Very good." He dials again. Thank God Simangele carries her phone in her bra—and answers it. Their conversation is short.

"My mother will try to speak with Ruby. Then she will call me."

We sit in silence, except for Awonke's version of *Jesus Loves Me This I Know*. I watch the minutes tick away on the clock.

His phone rings. "Yebo." He listens. "Haybo!" Another pause. He hangs up.

"My mother says that Ruby and her husband are driving home from Durban. It will be at least one hour longer before they arrive."

Oh, my God. I can't sit on the curb that long. There's no place to hide on this side of the fence except in the forest across the road. With who knows what kind of creatures.

"Did she say what to do?"

"My father will be very upset that I have been away for such a long time. She says I must bring you back to the factory."

No!

» » »   « « «

The floodlights at the corners of the factory property cast an eerie orange glow over the rolls of razor wire along the top of the fence. Would people really break into the factory to steal coffins? How do families who are barely eating manage to bury their dead? Do they build their own coffins? I haven't seen anyone with tools. Come to think of it, other than the pygmy palms, I haven't seen many trees.

Simangele's son leaves the keys in the ignition and the headlights on to illuminate his path across the lot. He uprights the toppled chairs on his way to his mother. The Inspector's truck is gone. The men are still drinking. Their voices are loud.

Simangele greets her son, then turns to her husband, her back to the car. He grabs her arm. She shakes herself loose, turns and walks toward me. Thank God he doesn't follow. She slides into the car behind the steering wheel.

"Karen, I will take you home. Come sit in the front seat with me."

I finally feel safe. Ruby has told me that Simangele and her husband have problems in their marriage. I hope she won't pay later for helping me now. I take deep breaths for the first few blocks.

"Simangele, what happened?"

"It is okay now, Karen. You must not worry."

"Simangele, I need to know what's going on. It's scary when I don't know the language and people fight around me."

"My husband is very unhappy with the Inspector for offering to take you home."

"But it makes so much sense. He lives right around the corner from Ruby."

"We have traditions that must be followed. Because it is my husband's party, it is his responsibility to provide trans-portation for his guests. My husband and the Inspector have very old arguments with each other that continue to cause unhappiness between them. They always argue. You are what they have chosen to argue about *this* time."

She feels calm and honest, convincing. But Will the cam-eraman's warning this morning still rings in my mind. I want to believe Simangele, but I don't want to be stupid.

We drive through the countryside around Pietermar-itzburg, killing what's left of the hour before Ruby arrives home. "I look forward to the day that Ruby brings you to Durban to visit my home," Simangele says. "We can have tea and I will invite more of Ruby's friends for you to meet. We will have fun together."

Fun feels impossible. "I'd like that. Maybe we can go to the outdoor market that Ruby's told me about." I know it will never happen. Ruby will never assert her independence with Mhambi.

The kitchen light is on when we arrive home. The gate is open. Ruby hurries out to the driveway to talk with Simangele. I stand idly by, like a child. I don't even care that they speak in Zulu. This day has been too long. Too strange. Too scary.

Simangele hugs me. "I am very happy that you came to our celebration today, Karen. I will come to visit you tomorrow."

Weak from the repeated surges of adrenaline, I drag my feet along the walk, following Ruby into the house.

"I am making tea for myself and my husband. Would you like some?" Ruby asks. Her voice lacks any trace of vitality. Her empty expression says burying her nephew has taken a toll.

"No thank you. I'm exhausted. I need to go lie down. I'll see you in the morning."

We share a silent hug.

In the living room, Mhambi sits slumped in his usual chair. Still dressed in his black suit, a faraway look on his face, he takes a drag on his cigarette. I stand next to the sofa, too tired to sit and rise again.

"Hi, Mhambi. How are you doing?"

He begins to answer, then pauses. "As you have discovered, Karen, our lives are often very difficult."

"I see that. You look exhausted."

He nods. "I hope your dream of having ice was satisfied today."

His sincerity touches me. I smile. "Yes, I did have ice. It was wonderful."

"We must take pleasure in small rewards," Mhambi says. "Sometimes that is all there is."

DAY 39
SUNDAY, MARCH 9, 2008

I feel the premature ventricular contractions in my chest; the thud of my heart as it struggles to maintain a normal rhythm. Yesterday's stress has taken its toll. I place a nitroglycerin tablet under my tongue, close my eyes, and wait for the pain to subside.

» » »   « « «

Ruby sits at the dining room table in her nightgown. With her elbows propped on the table, she holds her head in her hands.

"Ruby! I thought you'd be at church. Are you okay?"

"I do not feel well. My husband has gone to church without me today."

"Can I do anything to help? Have you had breakfast yet?"

"No. My stomach is not well."

"Can I fix you a poached egg and some toast? You like my poached eggs," I smile. "Maybe a little food will help."

"Yes please, Karen." She lifts her head to look at me. Her eyes sag, heavy with emptiness. "You are very kind."

When I return with our plates, she hasn't moved. I've never seen her be so still.

"Here you go," I say. "Just eat really slow and maybe this will help you feel better."

Ruby pushes her eggs around on her plate. "Simangele has called me. She says she is very sorry that she cannot come to visit you today. She must return to Durban with her husband."

A sense of horror prevents me from asking if Simangele's husband has beaten her. "Maybe I'll see her another time?"

Ruby nods. We finish breakfast in silence.

"Ruby, you stay here while I do the dishes. Then I'm going to my room to rest. If you need anything, please come and knock on my door."

She stares at her half-empty plate. Ten minutes later, on my way to the back door, she still hasn't budged. I stop, lay my hand on her back. "Ruby, I'm worried about you. Promise you'll come get me if you need something?"

"Yes, Karen. I promise."

» » »   « « «

Mhambi sits in his arm chair watching the evening's soccer match. Ruby sits on the floor, polishing his shoes. I watch from my usual place on the sofa, wondering if anyone else feels the tension in the room, or if it belongs solely to me. Far too uncomfortable to engage in my usual conversation with Mhambi, we all sit in silence.

Ruby sets Mhambi's shoes by the front door and moves on to his briefcase. Emptying the contents onto the floor, she wipes the inside with a damp rag. Then, with a sharp buffing motion, she uses the same black shoe polish to restore the outer leather to a soft sheen. When she finishes, Ruby crawls across the floor and holds the briefcase up for Mhambi's inspection.

He nods.

"Shall I put it your car?" she asks, reloading the contents.

"No. I must add my papers after I have finished reading tonight. You may take it to my car in the morning."

Ruby sits with her legs stretched out across the floor, her head tilted downward, as though she's being punished. I try to conceal my cringe.

"So, Karen," Mhambi says. "When I return next Saturday from my conference in Ramsgate, I will take you and Ruby and the boys to Ntwana for the school holiday. You will have an opportunity to enjoy our home there while you rest from your work at Zinti. I will join you there on the weekends."

"I look forward to that." But only if Ruby lets me help with the chores. Otherwise it will be torture watching her carry water from the creek, milk the goats, collect eggs, and who knows what else. It might be fun, but only if we share the work.

"Where is Ramsgate?" I ask.

"Ruby," Mhambi commands, "fetch the map for Karen."

Damn! This is not what I had in mind.

Ruby jumps from the floor and hurries to Mhambi's office. When she returns, he spreads the map across the coffee table.

"See here," he points. "Ramsgate is a lovely city on the ocean, just south of Durban. The next time Ruby takes you to Durban you must see our ocean. It is beautiful."

"It is," Ruby says. "Whenever I am there it reminds me..."

"Woman!" Mhambi shouts. "Do you not have work to do?"

I recoil from his fierceness. This is the first time I've ever heard him raise his voice. Ruby's head drops as she hurries toward the back of the house, presumably to iron.

A wave of humiliation overcomes me. I want to rush after Ruby. Hug her. Console her. Offer help. But I don't. I sit in silence, pretending like nothing has happened.

DAY 40

Cook never fails to meet me at the water spigot in the morning. I glance up the hill and see the padlock on the kitchen door. My heart sinks. Phyllis controls her rage at assembly this morning. A half-dozen kids come forward to deposit coins into her outstretched hand.

Classes are subdued. Of course. They're hungry. Less than half of the kids have done their homework assignment. It will take time for them to understand the concept of homework. But the ones who have written their words and sentences are eager to share. I'm so proud of them as they stand to read their work out loud: "Chair. I sit on my chair. Car. My uncle drives a car. Play. Today I will play."

One boy and one girl in each class come forward, their shoulders back, heads held high, to collect their well-deserved apples. I remind them that they can't eat in class; they have to wait until lunchtime. Manners are manners. Plus, I can't bear to see twenty-eight hungry kids watch two eat. I feel guilty that I don't have an apple for every child, but that would be an obvious defiance of Phyllis's edict.

We're all together in the lunchroom today: me, Phyllis, Ruby, Pamela, and Missy. No one says a word about the kids not eating. A few girls skip by the open library door. Sindiswa lingers with a smile spread across her beautiful face, hoping someone will notice the apple she polishes on her dress.

Ruby spots her. "Wozala!" She commands Sindiswa to enter the room.

Sindiswa bounces across the library and curtsies in front of Ruby.

"Where did you get that apple?" Ruby asks.

"From Mees Karreen. She gave it to me because I did my homework."

"Can I see it?" Ruby asks.

Sindiswa glows as she hands her shiny green apple to Ruby.

Ruby takes the apple. From across the table she locks her eyes on mine. Her maleficent grin terrifies me. In a slow deliberate movement, she brings the apple to her mouth—and bites. Sindiswa's face registers horror. Ruby glares at me. She chews in slow motion. Juice runs down her chin. She takes another bite. Without removing her eyes from mine, she extends her arm to the side and hands the half-eaten apple to Sindiswa. She flips her empty hand, motioning for the girl to leave. Sindiswa curtsies before she backs out of the room. Ruby's stone cold glare is unrelenting. She juts her chin forward, punctuating her disgust.

She hates me.

Ruby's face breaks into a smile as she digs into her left-overs from last night's dinner. She strikes up an animated conversation with Phyllis, in Zulu, laughing as though none of this ugliness has happened. Pamela, Missy and I sit in silence. Lunch break lasts too long. Ruby packs up her dirty dishes. She saunters from the library, headed back to her classroom.

I've been intimidated in the cruelest way I can imagine: by hurting a child. Ruby's implied threat feels ominous. How will I manage to live with her for another six weeks when I can't even pretend to respect her for another minute.

One bite of an apple has changed everything.

» » » « « «

At the end of a long silent drive, Ruby drops me off at home. I'm barely out of the car before she backs out of the driveway to go run her errands, alone, just as she has for the past couple weeks. After today, she'll probably never take me to town again. I'll have to get Thulani to teach me the coombie system. Maybe Phyllis will take me. *She* doesn't seem angry with me, just perpetually tired and worn out. All the teachers drag themselves around like it's their last day on earth.

Making nice for the white lady from America is over. No more showing me off. No more big smiles. No more pretending. Nothing left but ordinary life with me as a witness.

I fall into bed without supper. My stomach hurts. Skipped heartbeats create constriction in my chest. I could blame it on the heat. That would be a lie. Stress. Fear. Anxiety. They all have a grip on my heart. I lie still to focus on my breathing. I try slow deep breaths. Breathe in. Breathe out. Slower. I resort to my nitroglycerin, praying for my heart to pump a steady rhythm. I need every beat.

Outside my window, monkeys chatter in the neighbor's tree. Roosters crow. Wild dogs howl. The hadidas circle in a gray halo overhead. Their loud caw-caws invade my thoughts as they speak their message of death.

DAY 41

The Grade Four teachers announce that I should begin the comprehension curriculum today. This hardly seems like a good time to start something new. The kids are four days now without food.

They take turns reading the workbook story out loud. Their pronunciation is beautiful. I write three simple questions on the chalkboard. The answers are available, verbatim, in their workbooks. A sea of blank faces stares at me. Only one or two children in each classroom can answer the questions. I feel devastated; unable to decide if I've failed to teach them well, or they're just too hungry to think. To make matters worse, each of the Grade Four teachers is present in their classroom today. This hasn't happened since my first week. They're short-tempered with the kids and scold them for not answering my questions.

I nearly choke on my anger. How can they learn without food? I confess to the teachers that we may need to work more on vocabulary before comprehension improves. My thoughts race with fear. Have the kids been learning by rote, without truly understanding their lessons? I should have figured this out sooner. The kindergarten workbook I brought, the one with simple pictures and words, would be helpful—if only the copy machine in the office worked.

At lunch break, Phyllis, worried about an approaching storm, dismisses school for the day. I worry about the kids staying warm as autumn approaches. The afternoons are still comfortable, even hot at times, but the mist lingers further into each day. Cool damp air blows through the broken windows all morning. They still leave their shoes outside the classrooms. Only their thin socks insulate them from the cold concrete floor. A few of them have zip-up sweatshirts. Sindiswa, one of the fortunate girls, has a fleece scarf.

» » » « « «

Thunderous rain on the car roof makes conversation impossible on the way home. Roadside ditches between Zinti and Pietermaritzburg overflow with red, muddy water. In town, adults walk calf-deep in the gushing streams along the curbs. Older children hold the little ones' hands to help pull them through the current.

Ruby drops me at home and offers Rolina a ride home. As they leave the house, Ruby turns to me, with a smirk. "I am going to visit my friend, Simangele." She looks pleased that she hurts my feelings by leaving me behind.

With the electricity out, and the sky so black, the house is unusually dark. Deafening claps of thunder rock the house. I see brilliant white flashes of lightning, even with my eyes closed. I wonder how many of the children at Zinti live in rondavels with watertight roofs.

At three o'clock Thulani bursts through the kitchen door. His blue wool blazer sags with the weight of the water it holds.

"Thulani! You're soaked. I'm just getting ready to make tea. Would you like some?"

"Haybo! It rains hard out there, Miss Karen. Tea would be very good now."

"Can I fix you a bologna sandwich, too?"

"Ah, yes. Thank you, Karen."

Changed into dry clothes, Thulani joins me in the dining room. He stands at the table, staring at the places I've set for us.

"Come on," I say. "Sit down. Let's eat."

"Haybo, Karen. This is quite unusual for me."

"What's unusual?" He has a bologna sandwich every day after school.

"This." He spreads his hands in a wide gesture. "All of this. I do not eat at the table."

"I've noticed that. It seems like you and Siphelele never eat at the table."

"You are different on the other side. This is not how we do it here."

"Other side?"

"How shall I say it? You know, the other side. America."

"Do you mind sitting with me? We can visit while we eat."

He pulls out his chair and smiles. I'm happy to be the first to invite him to eat at the table.

"Tell me, Karen, what is it like on the other side? I mean, how is your life different from here, in South Africa?"

"We have different customs than you do. For instance, at dinner many families sit at the table together and talk about what happened for each of them during the day. We often invite our friends to have dinner with us. At home, meals are about a lot more than just eating."

"Haybo! That would never happen here. What else is different on your side?"

"Well, when my son lived at home, his friends came over to watch TV together."

"Haybo! Sometimes I see my mates in Maritzburg for time together. When I have money, we go to the cinema."

"Yeah? That sounds good, too. So tell me, how do you earn money?"

"My uncle gives me an allowance every week. But he is not happy with me in recent weeks. I'm broke!" he laughs.

"I'm sorry to hear that, Thulani. Do kids here ever have after-school jobs?"

"Aye. Some of my mates work in the shops in Maritzburg. They are quite fortunate. My uncle will not allow me to work."

"Really?"

"Aye. He forbids me to take time away from my studies." Thulani hangs his head. "My marks are not very good this term."

"Is that why he's not happy with you?"

He nods. "There are other reasons as well. Last week my teacher took my cell phone from me because I used it during school hours. The teacher told my aunt, and she told my uncle."

"Bummer. That sounds a lot like the school rules at home. When do you get it back?"

"Not before the end of the year!"

I pause. "Thulani, you seem like an intelligent young man. Why don't you get good grades?"

"I do not see that it matters. I will not go to university like Siphelele. I will work in a shop in Maritzburg. It is hard work to get good marks. I prefer to have fun with my mates rather than work hard at my lessons."

His assessment seems accurate. Sad. I don't know how to encourage him when opportunity is that bleak. "If you could go to college, what would you study?"

"Ah. Technical drawing is my favorite class." His grin belies his supposed lack of ambition. "This is where I have my best marks."

"Really! I was a drafter for many years. I liked it, too."

"Seriously, Karen? You did technical drawings?"

"Yes. Seriously. Do you have any of your drawings at home? Can I see them?" I ask.

"This is fantastic! I would like you to see my drawings."

He knocks his chair over in his rush to get up from the table. He takes our empty dishes to the kitchen on his way down the hall. When he returns, we spread his pencil drawings out on the table. They're rudimentary, but I have no idea if this is because of his skill or the lack of necessary drawing equipment.

He points to the elevation view of a wood-frame house with landscape features. "As you see, Karen, I have drawn a home with a grand yard."

"This is nice, Thulani. You have great potential. It seems to me that you would make an excellent draftsman."

"You really think so, Karen? Really?"

"Yeah. Really. You just need a chance to grow into it. And a good work attitude."

"I hear that in America, anyone can get a job. A job with lots of money."

"It's true that we have more available jobs than you do. But most people work hard to get the jobs they have. And most of the jobs don't pay nearly as well as you might think they do."

"How much money could I make in America?"

"Well, let's say that you worked in a shop like those in Pietermaritzburg. Our government says that every worker must be paid a minimum amount of money. Right now it's about six dollars for every hour. That's about forty-five rand."

"Haybo! This is amazing. My allowance is fifty rand. Do you mean to tell me that I could make that much money for every hour I sell food at the market?"

"Yes. But it's not quite as spectacular as it sounds. It's expensive to live in America."

He nods his head like he understands, but the grin on his nineteen-year-old face says he still thinks he can live like a king in America.

"Thulani, if you didn't live with you aunt and uncle, how much would it cost for you to rent a place to live."

"Rent?"

"You know, how much would you have to pay someone else to live in their house?"

"Ah." He pauses. I doubt he's considered this scenario. "If I live with a few mates, it will not be expensive. This much I know."

"That's good. In California it costs about eight-hundred dollars every month to have a place to live. That's almost six-thousand rand."

His jaw falls open as his eyes widen. "Are you serious? That is more money than I will have in my whole life!"

We sit in silence for a few minutes.

"This is not what I expected to hear about your country, Karen. Me and my mates figure if we can get to the other side, we will have an easy time of life."

"I wish that were true, Thulani. You can make more money in America, but you have to spend a lot more to have a place to live, food to eat, and a car to get around."

He looks devastated. Momentarily. "Still," he smiles, "I would like to come to your country. I think I would have a very different life on the other side than I will have here. Even if I have to work hard, it would be better."

He's right. I take a deep breath. "You know what's true, Thulani?"

He looks at me. Hopeful. Scared. Confused.

"You deserve a chance at being successful in life. And that chance might be harder to come by here than it would in America."

"Haybo! Everyone deserves a chance, Karen."

"They do. I know what it's like to need a chance, Thulani. So I'd like to make you an offer."

His eyes light up. He sits up straight in his chair.

"I don't have enough money to send you to America. But if you can get yourself there, even just as far as the East Coast, I'll come get you and bring you to California to live with me."

"Are you serious, Karen? You would do that for me?"

"I would, Thulani. I would like to help you."

"This is amazing!"

"You'd need a permit from the American government to stay in our country. I can help you with that. Once you're in America, you'd need to go to school and improve your skills. Then you'd need to get a job. If you failed to do any of this, our government would take away your permit and send you back to South Africa."

"I could do all that you say."

"I'm sure you could. You'd also need to get permission from the South African government to leave your country. I can't help you with that part."

"My uncle would help me."

"You think so?"

"Yes. I am quite sure. He would be happy for me to have a life in America."

"Good. So here's my offer. You and your uncle get the permit from your government. You work hard, save your money, and get yourself to America. I'll take care of the paperwork on the other side."

"Haybo! This is fantastic. My mother will also help me. She has the government money from my father's death. It will not be long before she dies and I receive the money for her death. She would like to know that I am well in the world before she dies."

I flinch. The last time I saw her it was obvious AIDS would take its toll. But I didn't expect him to talk about it so freely.

"So, do we have a deal, Thulani?"

"Yes, Ma'am. This is very exciting."

I extend my hand. "Let's shake on it then."

"No, Karen. We must pinky swear."

His pinky swear includes a hug. I take a sheet of paper from his binder and write every possible way for him to contact me at home. "Put this in a safe place, Thulani. Remember that I'm on the other side waiting for you."

"Thank you, Karen." He stares at what I've written. "This is my most important paper in all the world. I will protect it with my life."

"You're welcome, Thulani. I look forward to seeing you in America."

» » »   « « «

Siphelele slogs through the kitchen door at five. "Haybo!" he shouts, flinging his backpack into the middle of the living room floor. "I waited for my mother for an hour at the coombie depot. Just now I walked all the way from the nearest stop. Where is my mother?" he demands.

"I don't know, Siphelele." I can't hide my irritation. "Maybe you should go dry off."

He storms down the hall. Ordinarily, I'd offer to make dinner for them—but not after this temper tantrum. I won't condone Siphelele's sense of entitlement. And Thulani won't starve; he doesn't expect anyone to wait on him.

DAY 42

My alarm goes off at four-thirty in the middle of an intense dream.

> *... I'm home from Africa, at church, sobbing, can't say why. My friends hug me. Susan sits with me so I'm not alone. Even Jay's smile doesn't make me feel better ...*

Mhambi's absence is rough. Leaving the house forty-five minutes earlier than usual to drive the boys to school takes its toll. Ruby looks as exhausted as I feel. At least the rain has ended. Other than silt accumulated in the gutters, there's no evidence of yesterday's deluge. I can't imagine where all the water has gone in such a short time.

On the east side of town, near the hospital, Ruby pulls onto the shoulder of the highway opposite Thulani's school. He hustles to collect his backpack and blazer.

"Good-bye," he says as he climbs out of the back seat.

"Hey," says Siphelele.

"Have a good day," I say.

Ruby stares into the distance, without a word.

I turn to watch Thulani cross the highway. He may be nineteen, but still I want him to be safe. My line of sight is obscured by the rush of traffic.

We travel north, winding our way uphill through narrow tree-shaded streets, past mansions with elephant and giraffe topiaries. Fountains decorate the driveway entrances. Gardeners rake leaves behind the ornate fences. Before Monday, I didn't know Pietermaritzburg had such wealthy neighborhoods. Ruby parks at the top of a staircase that leads down a vine-covered hillside. At the bottom, a paved path crosses a lush lawn. In the distance, Siphelele's private school, a massive complex of old stone buildings, looks like a castle from rural England.

Siphelele takes his time, leaving his door open while he comes to talk to his mother through her open window. Their exchange, even in Zulu, sounds like they're annoyed with each other. Ruby digs through her overflowing purse for her change container and gathers a handful of coins for him. He mumbles and slams his knee against her door. She jumps at him with her voice, but gathers another fistful of change. Siphelele will eat lunch at school. Thulani will wait until he comes home to have a bologna sandwich.

We hurry on to meet Phyllis at the gas station. Our daily rides to Zinti have become routine. Ruby and Phyllis banter with the radio in the front seat. Pamela and I ride quietly in the back.

"Pamela," I whisper, "I'm not really using my white mats and markers with the Grade Three kids anymore. Would you like to have them?" She admired them when she first saw them, in awe of the different colored markers and how the mats were so easily erased with pieces of an old T-shirt I'd cut up.

"Haybo! Yes, I would like to have them," she whispers back. Her smile makes me feel helpful. "My learners are beginning to write their letters. They will be very excited to practice with your mats."

We turn off the paved street onto the dirt road to Zinti. Yesterday's rain has darkened the soil to a rich rust color. Dew glints on every blade of grass. As we approach Zinti, we look like a carload of explorers, each with a hand to our forehead to shield our eyes against the glare, stunned by what we see up ahead—hundreds of Zinti students block the driveway.

"What is going on?" Phyllis whispers under her breath.

"Why is the gate closed?" Ruby asks.

We park on the road behind Samke's car. She, the other teachers, and Missy huddle around the gate. Phyllis and Ruby shoo the kids out of their way as they approach. The women speak in subdued tones, as though passing a secret from one to another. Ruby turns toward me and Pamela. Her expression portends of trauma.

"The lightning has struck the gate!" she says. "The lock will not open."

Phyllis's concern about the storm was real after all. Along with the other teachers, I take my turn inspecting the lock—a mass of metal welded to the gate latch—the first time in my life I've actually seen the results of a lightning strike. It's impressive. My mind takes off on ideas for a science lesson.

The women push and pull the gate in an attempt to free the latch, while the kids chase each other up and down the road. Phyllis yells at them with a stern voice and matching scowl, waving them off with her hand. They scamper down the road, disappearing into the tall grass. One-by-one they reemerge on the other side of the fence, walking along the fence line until they stand opposite us on the other side of the gate.

I look at Pamela. "How did they do that?"

"They went around the end of the fence," she says.

"What?"

"The fence does not continue past the edge of the school grounds," she says. "Ma'am has sent them around."

What is the use of having a fence that only lines one side of the property? All this time I've erroneously assumed that the fence surrounds the entire site, hidden by the tall grass.

"Ma'am has sent several of the children into the village to fetch the men to come open the gate," Pamela continues. "We will wait here until they arrive."

I look again at the lock, searching for the perfect angle for a photo of nature's welding job. Streaks of blue fan out from the black burn spot. The glob of brass that used to be a padlock shines brighter than when it was new.

A young man arrives with enormous wire cutters. I now understand Phyllis's concern about protecting the computers with razor wire in the ceiling. It takes him only seconds to clip through the chain around the gate posts. One side of the gate falls away from its hinges. The teachers step across the chain-link gate and climb the steep drive on foot. I head back to Phyllis's car to retrieve my backpack. Missy beats me to it. She carries my bag in one hand, Phyllis's in the other. She won't hear of me taking it from her.

Everyone gathers in the clearing at the top of the hill. No one makes a move toward the classrooms, except me. I take my bag from Missy and head for the dirt steps carved into the hillside, expecting that the kids will follow.

Pamela grabs my arm as I walk past. "Not yet," she whispers. "You must stay here now."

"Okay. Why?" I whisper back, confused by the air of secrecy.

"Before we go to our classrooms we must cleanse our bodies."

"What do you mean?"

"The spirits of the lightning linger on the gate. We have all touched it so we must cleanse ourselves of the spirits. We do not want to spread them throughout the entire school."

It seems so?—so primitive. I shouldn't be surprised. But I am. On the other hand, who am I to say that there's no residual "energy" from the lightning that could be harmful? I don't know much about ions and particles. Maybe this is a remedy for a well-known ancient problem not yet confirmed by science. Who am I to judge this ritual as unnecessary?

"So how will we do this?" I whisper in Pamela's ear.

"The men will collect the necessary plants from the hill. They will add them to pails of water and we will rinse our hands and arms in the water."

Two old men arrive, each with a long machete and tin bucket. They climb the hill behind the upper tier of classrooms, grab handfuls of leafy plants, and whack them off at the ground. They lay the plants on the dirt in the clearing and make swift work of dicing them. Once the dime-sized pieces are distributed among the buckets, they fill them with water at the spigot. Everyone stands with their heads bowed, as if in prayer, as the men speak softly in Zulu. I keep my head down, but move my eyes from side to side to watch everyone's behavior. Even the children are solemn. We approach each bucket in single file, dipping our arms up to our elbows in the first, bringing handfuls of water to our shoulders and faces at the second.

» » »   « « «

The Grade Four teachers shake their heads as they watch me attempt to teach the meaning of English words without the benefit of flashcards or the Zulu language. I look to them for help. How would they do it? They shrug their shoulders. It's up to me to figure it out.

Phyllis has given me strict instructions to *always* speak to the children in English. Not that I have a choice. How can I explain "market," "summer," "winter" using other English words that are equally meaningless? I feel lost in this new English comprehension curriculum. Classes let out for lunch just as I reach frustration overload. I need to get a grip on how to do this.

Friday can't arrive too soon—our big rehearsal in the assembly hall for the regional music competition. We're sure to win. Who else in KwaZulu-Natal is doing the Hokey Pokey?

At lunch, Phyllis announces that she and Ruby are leaving early. I raise my eyebrows at Ruby in question. Nonchalant, she says, "You can take a coombie home."

"But I can't. Leslie told me not to ride in taxis."

"You will be fine."

She doesn't understand my precarious situation—not knowing the language or the lay of the land. "But I'm scared. Maybe I can leave with the two of you."

"That is not possible," Ruby says. "We are attending a meeting."

I look at Phyllis. "Can you drop me off in Pietermaritzburg while you're at your meeting?"

"That will not be necessary," Phyllis says. "I have arranged for Samke to drive you home."

"Thank you, Phyllis," I sigh with relief. "I appreciate that." Why is Ruby messing with me? Why does Phyllis let her?

Ruby's phone rings. She pulls it from her bra and answers. Her expression fades from arrogant to grim. She hands it across the table to me.

"For me?" I ask. No one calls me. "Hello?"

"Karen, it is Simangele. How are you doing?"

"Simangele! I'm good. How are you? It's so good to hear your voice."

"I want to tell you myself that I am sorry I could not visit you on Sunday. Truly I wanted to see you. It just was not possible."

"It's okay, Simangele. I mean I wish you could have, but I'm glad you called now."

"You are my friend, Karen. I would like very much for you to visit me in Durban. Ruby has promised me that you will come on the school holiday."

"I'd like that, Simangele. I look forward to seeing you." I know her offer is sincere. But I can't imagine that Ruby will take time away from Mhambi and the boys, that she'd actually drive me to Durban, that Simangele's husband knows about this invitation.

"Very well then," she says. "I will see you soon. Be well."

"Thanks for calling, Simangele. Bye for now."

» » »   « « «

As we finish lunch, two young Zulu men, maybe in their early thirties, enter the library. Dressed in black suits, white shirts, ties, carrying briefcases, and wearing sunglasses, they remind me of *Men in Black*. They ask to see the person in charge.

"I am the principal," Phyllis says. "What is your business?"

Insurance salesmen! They've come to sell life insurance to the teachers.

"My teachers are busy in their classrooms. You may not disturb them. You are welcome to speak with Missy, if you like," Phyllis says, as she exits the library.

Ruby lingers to give the men a hard time. "I have already purchased my casket," she laughs. "Besides, my husband and I receive insurance from our own private business." She puts on a good show, in both English and Zulu, before sauntering off, her chin in the air, leaving me and Missy to deal with them.

"I'm just visiting," I say, eager to squelch their sales pitch. "I don't need life insurance."

They turn to Missy with engaging smiles and typical GQ poses: one perches himself on the edge of the table, his foot on a chair, chin in his hand, elbow on his knee; the other unbuttons his suit jacket and slides his hand into his pocket. I watch in disbelief as they double team Missy. Surely they can see she doesn't have a spare dime to her name.

One salesman slides a blank piece of paper and a pen across the table to Missy. She writes her name in block letters: MSIZI MUSENGE. I know everyone's afraid of AIDS. I know Missy's single and that she loves her teenage daughter. But they're preying on her. Bullshit sounds the same in any language.

I feel protective. I widen my eyes at Missy and shake my head, silently pleading, "Please don't."

The salesmen leave without a signed contract. If they return, I hope Phyllis or Pamela will help Missy make a wise decision.

» » »   « « «

After dinner Siphelele asks his mom to take him to the Internet café to print his school report.

It's been a while since my last visit. "Hey, can I ride along?" I ask. She can't refuse me in front of the boys.

326 | KAREN BALDWIN

Ruby drops us at an outdoor shopping center about five minutes from home. I follow the boys into the glow of neon lights. A restaurant balcony, overflowing with noisy patrons, hangs over the entrance to a flashy clothing store. The cinema marquis advertises seven movies; none I recognize. I gawk through the windows as we wind our way deeper into the shopping center, past an upscale yuppie bar, a book store, and a jewelry shop.

"So boys, where are we headed?"

"The Internet café is just around the corner."

And Ruby has been taking me all the way to downtown Pietermaritzburg. Why?

My jaw drops as we turn the corner. The Internet café is well-lit, with dozens of computers lined up on folding tables. Just across the walkway—an ice cream shop! I buy soft serve cones for each of us. The cool, sweet cream tastes heavenly. I vow to come back often enough to sample every flavor.

Dozens of messages have piled up in my inbox. I only have fifteen minutes. I scan them to find the ones that seem most important.

> ... *heard about your work in Africa. Check out www.capicitar.org ... their techniques help kids in orphanages around the world relieve stress, get centered and have fun ...*

Patty-cake works, too!

> ... *the news for Natal doesn't sound good ... lots of stabbings. Be careful. They're also concerned with drought, crops and the rising cost of petrol ...*

Drought? Here?

> ... *we think of you often ... you're a hero in our eyes ... we look forward to seeing you in a couple months ... we miss you ... you're in our prayers and thoughts ...*

It's hard to remember how I felt when I left home. Did I feel like a hero? I'm embarrassed to think I did. I excel at patty-cake—feel like a failure at teaching English.

I miss my friends. This journey feels so different than when we talked about it in the comfort of our ignorance.

DAY 43
THURSDAY, MARCH 13, 2008

None of the Grade Four teachers are present in their classrooms this morning. I'm relieved to be out from under their unrelenting glare, but the kids just sit in their rooms without a teacher. I move back and forth between the classrooms assigning reading tasks and lists of spelling words.

Only Pamela, Missy, and myself come to the library for lunch. Afterward, I sit and wait for the little kids to come for their afternoon lessons. Phyllis and Ruby enter the library and close the door behind them. Something feels off. They pull up chairs across the table from me.

"May we speak with you, Karen?" Phyllis asks. She sounds serious.

"Sure. What's up?"

"Can you tell us how the learners are progressing with their English lessons?"

"I think they're doing well. Their pronunciation has really improved. And their use of proper verb tenses is much better."

"Is it not true, Karen, that they have no understanding of what you say in the classroom? What good is it for them to pronounce their words well if they do not understand the meaning of what they say?"

The teachers have shared my failures. "It's true they don't understand as well as we hoped they would. We need to find ways to improve their vocabulary so their reading comprehension is stronger."

"Karen, do you actually believe they will remember any of what you have taught them after you leave? " Ruby scoffs.

Her words sting. "Of course they will. Especially if it's reinforced. The more they practice, the better they'll do. Besides," I circle my hand around the table among the three of us, "we've talked about me coming back next year."

"Our teachers are concerned that you disrupt their curriculum," Phyllis says, her voice filled with accusation. "Where is your teaching plan? You came to teach English and now you also teach math and music."

I feel defensive. What the hell is going on? "I teach exactly what they've *asked* me to teach. How can that be disruptive? If they want me to quit teaching math or music, all they have to do is say so."

"You have been here for over a month now," Phyllis says. "We do not see that there is any improvement in our learners' English skills. It appears that your teaching methods are not effective."

She and Ruby stare at me, stone-faced. They've already judged this entire venture as a failure. Why? My stomach knots.

"It's not reasonable to expect that the kids go from barely speaking English to being proficient in a month," I say. "It takes time. Repetition. You've said yourself that school is the only place they practice their English." I pause to steady my nerves. "I'm sure at the end of my three months you'll see a huge difference. And I'm willing to meet with the teachers, to listen to their suggestions for how to improve the process."

"Are you even a certified teacher?" Phyllis asks. She rests her clasped hands on the table. "Why should our teachers spend their time teaching you how to be qualified?"

What have I done to piss them off? "No. I'm not a certified teacher. I'm a volunteer helper. You already know that. What's happened? Why are you so unhappy with me all of a sudden?"

"The children sense your frustration with them," Ruby says. "It is not good for their self-esteem. Here is a white woman from America who tells them they are not good enough."

"I have never told them they aren't good enough!" My voice quavers.

"You do not need to speak the words," Ruby sneers, her

arms folded across her chest. "They can feel your disappointment. And now you tell us that you are too good to ride in the coombie with the rest of the teachers."

My heart pounds. I can barely breathe. "What's going on? What are you trying to say? I love these kids. They're wonderful. I'm trying to help." I look at Ruby, desperate, nearly in tears. "Ruby, you and Mhambi have told me how dangerous the coombies are. I didn't say I was 'too good.' I'm just trying to stay safe. Besides, most of the teachers don't even take the coombies. They drive."

"Do you think your presence is productive?" Phyllis quips.

"I certainly hope so."

Their icy expressions persist. "Your friend Leslie promised us a library for our children."

"I brought over a hundred books with me! It's not a library, but it's a start."

"Karen," Phyllis asks, feigning innocence, "do you think it will be useful for you to return to Zinti after the school holiday?"

"Yes! I do." I clamber through the pile of volatile accusations, desperate to understand what's happening.

"When you leave the children will forget about you," Ruby says. "They will return to their old habits. I do not see that it is important for you to return after the holiday."

Ruby's haughty expression hurts. My legs tremble. I lean back in my chair, struggling to hold back my tears. "I don't understand what's happening. There's something you're not telling me."

"You have done nothing but confuse our learners!" Ruby says, her voice spiteful and angry. "They do not learn well from you."

"You don't want me here?"

"That is not what we have said." Phyllis shakes her head and sighs as though I've woefully misunderstood everything. "It is only that we are not sure your presence is helpful."

I feel deflated. Shaky. This can't be happening. I'm not

finished. "What do you want?" Their glares are unrelenting. I can barely utter my next words. I know that as soon as I say them out loud, everything will change. "It sounds like you want me to leave."

"If you think that is best," Phyllis smiles.

Shit! It's true. They *do* want me to leave. They've just been waiting for me to say it first. Cowards. "I don't think it's best at all. I want to finish what I started."

"If your decision is to leave," Ruby gloats, "I will take you to the airport right now."

They look pleased, relieved that I've finally caught on to their plan. They want me gone—now! I feel dizzy. I can't go home. Not like this. I'm not ready. Tears roll down my cheeks.

This isn't right. "What about the kids? I need to say good-bye to the kids."

"That is not necessary," Ruby says. "They will understand."

Understand what? That I abandoned them? That I didn't even care enough to say good-bye?

"Come, Karen." Ruby pushes her chair away from the table. "I will take you to the airport."

It's over. They're not even giving me another day. I feel limp, like dead weight in my chair. This is what they wanted all along and didn't even have the decency to tell me. They made me guess.

"It doesn't work like that, Ruby." My voice feels weak and distant. "My return ticket is for six weeks from now. It's a non-refundable ticket. I can't leave before then."

Ruby's nostrils flare. Her eyes fill with fury as she stands and leans over the table in my face. "Who do you think you are to tell us when you will leave?" She shouts, shaking her fist at me. "You got yourself here. You can get yourself home!"

I pull back from Ruby's rage. Tension grips my chest. The muscles in my legs tighten. "I don't have enough money to buy a new ticket."

Ruby storms to the door, then back to the table.

"There is no point to remain here if you will not teach at Zinti," Phyllis says, matter-of-factly.

Ruby paces back and forth like an angry caged animal.

"I don't know what to do. I don't have money to buy a new ticket. Maybe I can stay and just not come to Zinti every day."

Ruby leans over, pounding her fist on the table. "And where will you live?" she hisses. "Where do you think you will live?"

"Why can't I keep living with you?" My voice reveals my fear.

"Do you think I will keep you when you do not even work?"

I need help. Time to think. A compromise. I need them to be reasonable. "Maybe I can help you with your chores?"

Ruby flicks her finger under her chin at me. "I already have a maid. You are of no use to me."

I look at Phyllis. Desperate.

"I do not have a place for you at my home," she states, apparently unaffected by my predicament. "None of our teachers have room for you."

With deliberate steps, Ruby saunters back to the table, her face snarled in a menacing grin. She leans over the table, her warm breath in my face. "I know!" she sneers. "We will bring you to the village to live with Missy."

At least it's a temporary plan. Missy will be fine with it. "Okay," I say.

"Hah! You are even more foolish than I knew." Spit flies from Ruby's mouth as she speaks. "Do you really think that you will continue to live if we bring you to the village?"

A chill ripples through my body. Is she saying they'll kill me? I scramble to think. "Maybe I can talk to the airline; see if they'll change my ticket for me. It can't hurt to try."

"It makes no difference to me!" Ruby's face twists with morose pleasure. "I am happy to bring you to the village. We will count how many days you live."

"Karen," Phyllis says, her voice unnaturally calm. "When we leave school today, Ruby will take you to the airport to make arrangements. We are finished now."

She stands, smoothes her skirt, and walks to the door. Ruby swaggers behind. I sit at the table, paralyzed. Ruby stops at the doorway. With one hand on the knob she turns back to look at me. Even through my tears I see the hatred in her eyes. She flicks her finger under her chin; slams the door behind her.

It's over. I'm leaving.

What happened? What did I do wrong? My heart pounds against my ribcage. Adrenaline pumps through my body. I sit up straight. Arch my back. Struggle to take a full breath. This isn't how it's supposed to end. I should hug the kids. Kiss their heads. Tell them I love them. Ripping us apart is wrong. They'll never tell the kids they *forced* me to leave. Ruby's right. I am stupid. I didn't see this coming. I collapse onto the table, head in my arms, and sob.

The library door squeaks open. I rub my sleeve across my eyes. Missy walks cautiously across the room, her forehead furrowed. I stand and reach out to let myself rest on her shoulder. My legs buckle. Missy catches me in her arms. I take a deep breath to steady myself. Missy shakes her head, lays her finger on my cheek, and traces a tear from my eye to my chin. She shakes her head again and stomps her foot on the floor.

"Home," I cry. "They're making me go home, Missy."

She shakes her head. Stomps again. "No."

I can't tell if she understands what I've said. "Ma'am and Ruby are sending me home. They're sending me back to America. Today. Now."

Recognition crosses her face. She stomps her foot over and over on the concrete floor, shaking her head in frantic jerks. "No! No! No!"

"Yes, Missy. I'm leaving. Going home. Today. No tomorrow."

She grabs me and hugs me tight. We sob together. I'll

never see her smile again. Never watch her poke the roosters with her mop. Never drink another cup of her tea. I feel limp in her arms, desperate for this day to rewind and have a different ending.

Missy releases me and steps back. She points to her tears before she strips the thin, black rubber bracelets off her wrist—the treasures she bought herself in town last week. She takes my arm, pushing the bracelets over my hand. She holds my hand over her chest; then lays it over my heart. We stand, eyes locked, and cry.

"Yes, Missy," I say, "I love you, too. I'll miss you."

She smiles, pulls a chair out from the table, and nudges me to sit. She wipes my tears with the corner of her apron, kisses the top of my head, and motions for me to stay put as she closes the door behind her.

I wait, in a fog. My mind tumbles from one memory to another. Nomusa's smile. Children screaming "Mees Karreen." Hokey Pokey lessons. Giggles when I stick my tongue between my teeth to show them a "th" sound. Grade Four kids singing their national anthem for me. Beans and rice eaten with fingers. Little voices counting over and over, louder and louder. My backpack on a boy's head. The epileptic boy—I never saw him again. There's too much left unfinished. Shards of anger rip through my gut.

Missy returns with a cup of tea in my favorite mug and a slice of bread slathered with margarine—everything she can possibly give me. She sits next to me, lets me cry on her shoulder, pushes my tea closer, and motions for me to eat my bread. I offer her a bite. She shakes her head, making a stern face to show me how strong she is. I begin to calm. How can we understand each other so well without words? Missy takes my face in her hands and kisses my forehead. She points for me to stay in my chair. When she opens the door to leave, I hear the sound of happy kids outside.

Kids! There are still kids at school. Pull yourself together, Karen, you still have time. I wipe my face on the hem of my skirt and reach for my sunglasses. I dive through my backpack for the toothbrushes stashed away for daily homework rewards and the paper hearts for tomorrow's art lesson. I hurry from the library to stand in my usual place at the top of the rocky driveway. I hold my treasures out to their smiles and excited yelps.

"See you tomorrow, Mees Karreen," they scream, as they race down the hill.

I choke on my sadness. I can't return their greeting. I can't lie. Distracted with their new goodies, they don't notice my tears. I'll never see them again. I ache for this to be different. This is not the right way to leave.

At the bottom of the driveway, I see Missy, Pamela, Ruby and Phyllis gathered around the car. I only have a few more minutes. I slide out of my Crocs and wiggle my toes into the dusty earth, desperate to store away the details that have become so familiar: the birds' music, the deepest blue sky I've ever seen, the cool moist autumn breeze that rustles the tall grass, the sacred red dirt. I want to remember everything.

With careful, deliberate steps, I pick my way down the rocky driveway to Phyllis's car. No one speaks to me. Already, I cease to exist in their world. I no longer trust them. I slide my backpack into the back seat, instead of the trunk. Missy stands next to me. Her eyes look sad. She wants more time, too. She grabs me for one last hug.

"Bye, Missy," I whisper in her ear. "I will always remember you." It doesn't matter if she doesn't understand my words. She knows my heart.

I let go of her to get in the car. She slides one arm around my waist to hold me close. Her gaze fixed on my eyes, she fumbles to slip a plastic bag from under her apron into my hands. I look down at the bag, curious at what she could possibly give me. I slide my sunglasses to the top of my head so she can see my eyes. I try to smile. I hope she sees how deeply I care.

I struggle with the knot to get a peek inside the bag. Missy takes the bag out of my hand and knots the plastic loops again. She lays one finger over her lips, nudges me into the car and sticks the bag under my legs. She places her open hand over her heart, closes the door, and blows me a kiss as we drive off.

Phyllis and Ruby laugh and chat in the front seat. Their mother tongue is as much of a mystery as ever. I don't want to cry in front of them—I have my pride, after all. But I can't stop myself. At least I cry in silence. Pamela taps my leg. I turn toward her. One tear slips down her cheek. She slides her lace handkerchief across the seat to me.

I bump along the rocky road one last time. The tires kick up clouds of red dust. We pass one of the older boys walking along the edge of the road, headed home. He thrusts his fist high into the air and waves his new toothbrush as if it were gold.

» » »   « « «

Ruby and I pull into the Pietermaritzburg airport parking lot at four-thirty. I haul my belongings, including the bag from Missy, into the terminal. Ruby follows behind. At the ticket window I stash my plastic sack and backpack between my legs and the counter and dig through my purse, slung over my neck, for my airline tickets and passport. Thank God I carry my travel documents with me at all times.

Two South African Airways employees—a Zulu man and a white woman—sit at computer terminals on the other side of the counter. Their once-crisp denim shirts, with South African flags sewn on the breast pockets, hang in wrinkles at the end of a long humid day.

"May I help you, Ma'am," the woman asks. She pretends not to notice that I'm crying.

"I have a ticket to go to Johannesburg in April. But I need to leave now."

"Are you okay, Ma'am?" the male clerk asks. His concern sounds genuine.

I pause to think. I haven't considered what to tell them. I glance around, looking for Ruby. She's by the front door, on her phone. I decide on the truth. "No. I'm not okay. I have an uncomfortable situation. I've been teaching at a rural school up in the hills. About six weeks now. I was supposed to stay until the end of April. But today they told me I have to leave."

Both clerks raise their eyebrows, eyes widened. "Did they tell you why?" he asks.

"Not really. They made lots of excuses. But none of them make any sense. But they made it pretty clear that I'll be in danger if I stay."

The elderly Zulu woman in line at the next window moves to my side. Her head barely reaches my shoulders. "Excuse me for interrupting, Ma'am," she says. "I could not help but hear what you say. I am also a teacher from the rural schools. A retired teacher now. This is a very dangerous situation you speak of. The rural areas are not stable. If there is any kind of disturbance, they will turn against you. You are wise to leave now."

She sounds like Will the cameraman! My mouth gapes.

The male clerk nods. "It is true," he says. "I am very sorry that you have experienced this side of the Zulu people. It is not one that I am proud of. This woman is right. If they want you to go, it is best that you leave."

I take a deep breath. My grief turns to terror. Ruby's threat throbs in my head.

The female clerk fixes her gaze on her computer screen. "We will put you on the next flight to Johannesburg," she says. "That will be Saturday afternoon, at one o'clock."

"Saturday!" An invisible rope cinches my ribcage. I look again for Ruby; she's still by the front door. I lean over the counter. "They want me to leave today," I whisper.

"I'm sorry, Ma'am," the clerk says. "Saturday is the first seat we have available. Today's flight has already left, and tomorrow's flight is full. Completely full."

"Is there another airline I can take?"

"No, Ma'am. South African Airways is the only carrier in Pietermaritzburg."

The rope tightens around my ribs. I can barely breathe. I shake my head. Close my eyes to think. I hear the two clerks mumble.

"There will be no fee to reschedule your flight," the male clerk says. "This is our apology for how you have been treated."

"Thank you." My heart pounds. I will myself to take a full breath. I still need more. Saturday feels too far off. "Is it okay if I go home, pack my bags, and come back tonight to wait? Can I stay in the airport between now and Saturday?"

"I am sorry, Ma'am," he says. "That is not possible. The airport closes at five o'clock every day. Tomorrow we open at noon. Saturday we open at seven."

Crap! Now what?

The female clerk hands my new ticket across the counter. "You are welcome to come at seven on Saturday morning and wait for your flight," she says. Her expression says she wishes she could do more. "I see that from Johannesburg you are scheduled to fly to Amsterdam with KLM Airlines."

"That's right."

"I cannot speak for them, of course, but I am quite certain that if you explain to them what has happened, they will be happy to arrange a new flight for you at no extra cost."

I can't even think that far ahead. I still have thirty-six hours to survive here. Thirty-six hours to measure every movement around me.

"Be safe," she says. "Watch your back."

"Be with God," he says. "We will see you on Saturday."

» » »   « « «

Ruby drops me off at home. Without a word she backs out of the driveway.

"You do not look good!" Thulani says. "What has happened?"

I slump into a chair at the table. Exhale. "I'm going home. Saturday."

"That is not funny, Karen!"

"Do I look like I'm joking?"

He shakes his head. "What happened?"

"Phyllis told me that I can't teach at Zinti anymore."

"There must be some mistake. Ma'am likes that you teach at her school."

"No mistake, Thulani. She doesn't want me there anymore."

"But that does not mean that you have to go home."

"I'm afraid it does." I pause. I'd like to preserve Thulani's trust in me. But how much is safe to say? Once again, I decide on the truth. "Your Aunt won't let me stay here if I'm not teaching at Zinti."

He shakes his head. "That is not true!"

"It is true, Thulani. She doesn't want me around. In fact, she'd prefer that I leave today."

He looks horrified. Something has registered.

Ruby comes through the door with a deli sandwich in her hand, one bite already in her mouth. I'm on my own for dinner. I grab two hard boiled eggs from the fridge, butter a slice of bread, and head to my room to pack. Thulani follows me across the patio.

"Haybo, Karen. I cannot believe this is for real."

I sit on the edge of my bed, looking up at him. "I feel the same way, Thulani. This wasn't my choice."

"I see that my Aunt is very angry. Do you know why?"

"No. I don't." I wish I did. "Do you want to help me unload the rest of my school supplies?" I've been portioning them out, making them last. I open my suitcase across the bed and load puzzles, coloring books, and boxes of crayons into Thulani's outstretched arms. "Just start a pile in the living room," I say.

I shovel my dinner into my face before Thulani returns for three more loads: yarn for the women in the village; toothpaste, tooth brushes, hand sanitizer, latex gloves; plastic recorder flutes.

"What are these?" he asks.

I slip one of the recorders out of its case and play a quick rendition of *Twinkle, Twinkle, Little Star.*

Thulani smiles. "That is beautiful, Karen. I have never heard such a thing."

I hold it out to him. "Would you like it?"

"Aye. Yes, thank you. But you must sign it for me." He hands it back.

I pull a black marker from my bag, glance up at him, and smile. "You're the first person to ever ask for my autograph, Thulani." Down the side of the recorder, avoiding the finger holes, I write: TO THULANI—I'LL SEE YOU IN CALIFORNIA! LOVE, KAREN.

He reads it out loud. "I love you, too, Karen. I will treasure this. I am happy to see that you will keep your promise with me." He looks so sad. Lost.

"Of course I will."

Together we carry the last load of supplies to the house where Siphelele has already begun hauling the pile to Ruby's car. He grumbles at his mom as he drags his feet across the living room. His sour attitude about being overworked annoys me. It annoys Ruby, too. She smacks him on the back of the head.

In a flash Siphelele turns toward his mother, his eyes narrowed. "My father will not be pleased to hear that you have struck me," he says, rubbing the humiliation off the back of his head.

I sit at the table, numb, watching Ruby ignore me. She does it well.

"Ruby," I say. I wait. No answer. "Ruby!" I shout. "I need you to listen to me."

She looks at me. Disgusted. Chews her sandwich.

"I leave for Johannesburg on Saturday. I need to be at the airport at seven o'clock Saturday morning. Tomorrow, on your way to school, I need you to take me to Pietermaritzburg."

She offers nothing but a hateful scowl.

"I need to arrange my flight from Johannesburg to America. I need to contact my family. Tell them my new plans." They need to know what happened. In case I disappear.

» » » « « «

I lock the door to my room and collapse on my bed next to my empty suitcases. Where did it all go wrong? How did I fail so miserably? So soon? My shame and grief are peppered with anger. These are the same women who were so happy to have me, treated me like a rock star, showed me off all over town, and were so adamant about protecting me. It's surreal to imagine they'd leave me to be murdered in the village.

But I bet Will the cameraman wouldn't be surprised. Folks at the airport sure take the threats seriously. Only two more nights to keep my wits about me. I'll survive. But the kids? What about them? What will they think when I don't show up for school tomorrow? What will Phyllis and Ruby tell them? Not the truth; that's for sure. If only I could get a message to them. I need to pack. Make a plan. Think everything through.

I can't leave anything valuable behind at the house tomorrow. My three impala hides—Ruby's "welcome to our country" gift—don't fit in my backpack. They're probably unlawful imports. I unzip the lining of my large suitcase, sliding them between the frame and lining. I stuff my clothes and toiletries into my small suitcase. It nestles inside the large one now. Cameras, journals, beads from Busi—my treasures—all go in my backpack.

Missy's bag! I sit in my green plastic lawn chair, my legs propped on the bed. I take a deep breath as I untie the handles. Inside, a brown paper grocery sack. Inside that, another plastic bag. Then I see it. Missy's ritual dance hat! Her prized, beautiful, handmade hat. She sewed the tiny beads around the rim with her own hands. I clench it to my chest, bursting into tears. A small bag falls to the floor from inside the hat. There's more? My fingers tremble as I open the bag. Her beaded belt and necklace! Oh, my God, Missy! All your dance regalia. You've given me everything you have to give. How will I ever thank you? I sit, her beautiful hat squeezed on my head, her belt pressed to my lips, as tears drip into my lap.

I rearrange my backpack to hold Missy's gifts. How will I ever thank her? She always admired my sleeveless cotton dress. I pull it out of my suitcase. I don't need my jewelry from home either. I wrap each bracelet inside a piece of blank paper ripped from my journal. One for each of my favorite girls. I write their names on the outside of the paper: Sindiswa, Wendy, Nomusa. I stuff them in the dress pockets. And my white canvas sunhat with the sparkly dragonfly pin. I fill it with my leftover toiletries and roll the bundle in my dress. I stick the entire wad in the brown sack from Missy, then in the plastic bags. Double knot the handles. My gifts to the girls of Ezimolo Village.

I feel vulnerable in my concrete shack. I slide the green plastic lawn chair under the doorknob, wedge my suitcase between the chair and the bed, set my travel alarm for five, and pull the string to turn off the lightbulb.

Flashlight in hand, dressed in my street clothes—ready to what? escape?—I lay down for the night. Pray. Please, dear God, please keep me safe. Please deliver my gifts to Missy and the girls. I need them to know that I love them. That I care.

My pillow is soaked before morning.

DAY 44

Thulani opens the back door at five-thirty. I stash my backpack and the bag of gifts for Missy and the girls by the front door, ready to go at a moment's notice. My purse, slung over my neck like when I'm in town, keeps my hands free. But surely I won't have to force my way into Ruby's car.

In the kitchen, I put the tea kettle on to boil and open my food cabinet. It's empty! I open the fridge. Empty. Except for the cream. Oh, my God! Ruby has stolen my food. Shit! I stand in front of the cabinets, opening one door after the other. Nothing but tea bags. I remember Zodwa's family refusing to feed her because she had shamed them. Adrenaline pumps through my body. The veins in my neck throb.

Thulani comes back to the kitchen for his tea. "So Karen, will I see you again before we go to Ntwana this afternoon?"

I didn't know the boys were going away for the weekend. Mhambi's still in Ramsgate. Ruby and I will be alone tonight? Oh shit! My chest hurts already. I need to stay calm. Think.

"I hope I see you later," I say. "When are you guys leaving?"

"When my Aunt returns from school."

"Then I'll see you for sure. I don't leave until tomorrow morning."

He smiles. "Very good. I am not ready to say good-bye, Karen."

Ruby appears, purse in hand, ready to leave for school. I grab my bags and follow her and the boys to the car, reminding her that she's taking me to Pietermaritzburg for the day. She drives the usual route to town, then skirts around the back side through a narrow alley, pulling into a parking lot behind a rundown store. I don't recognize the area, but I'm not far from the town center. The boys are still in the back-seat. Getting rid of me for the day must be more important than getting them to school on time. Ruby's blank gaze fixes on the windshield. Not one word.

I pull the plastic bag of gifts from under my legs, holding it high enough for the boys to see before I set it on the seat next to Ruby. "I need you to give this bag to Missy today. It has my brown dress, the one I promised to give her when I left."

No response. Not even a glance.

"This afternoon I will wait right here, on this sidewalk, for you to pick me up on your way home from school."

Nothing.

"Right here. I'll expect you no later than three-thirty." My voice sounds more confident than I feel. Every muscle in my body twitches. I open my door and grab my backpack. "Bye, boys. See you this afternoon."

Ruby pulls away. I'm alone in an alley at seven o'clock. My legs tremble. It seems unlikely that they'll carry me through the day. I walk to the main street, up one block, across three, to Church Street. Nothing is open at this hour. No coffee shops. No markets. Nothing. No matter. Sending messages home is more urgent than eating right now. I sit on the window ledge of the Internet café—like one of the home-less people I've cautiously avoided.

Workers begin to arrive in town. Everyone stares at the distraught white woman. My sunglasses hide my swollen eyes; my last shred of dignity.

Ronald unlocks his doors at nine. "Miss America! What brings you here so early?"

Despite everything, he makes me smile.

"Things have gone very wrong, Ronald."

He raises his eyebrows.

"I need two hours on your Internet today."

Even this early, and the only customer in the shop, my connection is sketchy. I keep my message brief.

*... drastic change of plans ... threats ...
didn't get to say good-bye to the kids ... failed
miserably ... my heart is breaking ... tomorrow I fly from PMZ to Jo'burg ... will let you
know when I am safe ...*

I copy and send the same message to everyone. One at a
time. And wait. It's eleven on Thursday night at home.
Someone will acknowledge my message. I need to know they
haven't forgotten me. That they care.

"Miss America," Ronald says, "I am making tea. Would
you like a cup?"

Yes. But is it safe? I'm too confused to know whom to
trust. He can't possibly be part of this mess. "That would be
great. Thank you, Ronald."

He returns with a china cup and saucer. My hand trembles as I raise the cup to my lips. Tea laps over the edge of
the cup, dribbling down the front of my jacket. Ronald is
kind enough not to say anything.

I sob as messages from home begin to roll in.

*... Yikes!? Please don't think of this as a
failure. Can't wait to give you a big hug! ...
Jay*

*... Please remember that the journey is
everything ... not the results ... Betty*

*... Sending you love ... sorry about your
broken heart. Love you ... Henry*

*... We will welcome you home, hold your
breaking heart. You have not failed. Come
home and heal. xo ... Susan*

Goose bumps flood my body as I recall my dream of
Susan holding me at church, while I cry, home early.

*... You must have been making HUGE
GOOD medicine for the villagers to get that*

*wound up about your presence!!! Just because
the timeline changed doesn't mean you
weren't impactful. Stand tall. Can't wait to see
you ... Lucie*

Maybe I haven't failed. At least I haven't disappointed my friends. The ones who sent me. They aren't ashamed of me. I wait for confirmation from Kevin. Nothing.

I thank Ronald for his wonderful service over the past weeks. Even leaving him feels sad.

"Will I see you again, Ma'am?" he asks.

"I don't think so." I pause. "Tell the young woman who works here good-bye for me." He knows who I mean. The one who begged me to take her home with me.

Ronald grabs me for a quick hug. "Travel safe, Ma'am. God speed."

I close my eyes to rest for a second on his shoulder.

» » » « « «

Next door I purchase a ten-minute international phone card. I need to talk to Kevin. The clerk points across the street to a row of public phones bolted to the sidewalk in front of the post office. The fourth one works.

Ring. Ring. Ring. Kevin answers. "Hello."

I spill my story. "I love you. I'll call from Johannesburg to let you know where I go from there." Our connection goes dead.

I spend my last few hours in Pietermaritzburg at the Tathum Art Gallery. From the café balcony I watch the buzz of old and new swirl together. Coombies with blaring radios whiz into the depot. Street vendors hawk impala hide vests. Goats roast on spits in the park, waiting for the lunch crowd to spill from the modern office buildings that ban guns, swords, and grenades. Homeless teenagers line the curb outside the Kentucky Fried Chicken, passing a syringe and a bottle of booze down the row. Around the corner, the bead lady feels her way with gnarled fingers along a string of tiny sparkling beads, weaving them into webs of elegant adornment for proud women—even me.

I'm not ready to leave. There's still so much to explore. And the kids! Only forty miles away, they may as well be on the other side of the world. I'll never see them again. I close my eyes and pray that there is something good for them in this experience.

On my way back to the alley to meet Ruby, I duck into a store for snacks—I don't expect to be fed tonight. Two apples, a six-pack of peanut butter crackers, and a stick of billabong jerky will last me until I arrive in Johannesburg tomorrow afternoon.

At three-fifteen I'm on the sidewalk. Early. An hour passes. Another hour. I'm afraid to leave to find a phone; I don't want to miss Ruby. She wouldn't answer my call anyway. The shops close at six. It will be pitch black by then. Five-thirty. Has she already left to take the boys to Ntwana? Will she even come get me? Five-fifty. I don't have a plan. My stomach aches like I've been kicked.

Ruby pulls up to the curb five minutes before the shops close. Alone in the car, she stares straight ahead, silent. I slip into the front seat. I drill holes into the side of her head with my eyes. Unspoken fury—tight, hot, bitter—sticks in my throat. I want to fight. But I fight with words. I'm afraid that Ruby's capable of more. Will the cameraman's warning rings in my ears: "They will just as soon kill you as look at you."

Ruby refuses to look at me.

At home, her slow swagger to the kitchen door feels like an arrogant challenge: just try to make me move faster for you. She grumbles down the hall to Siphelele and Thulani, holding her chin in the air, her purse slung over one arm. Keys dangle in her hand. She believes she's gotten the best of me.

But she's too short-sighted to see the damage she's doing to the children. Why do I think she even cares? After all, she starves them. My stomach twists with disgust for her lack of human kindness. I would never win a battle of words with Ruby. Never convince her of anything. There is no safe outlet for this anger that feels like it will eat me alive.

Ruby saunters back to her car to wait for the boys. By the time she drives to Ntwana and back it'll be at least ten. She damned well better remember that she's taking me to the airport in the morning. I need a plan in case she doesn't come back.

Siphelele and Thulani gather their duffle bags and backpacks and head for the kitchen door. I follow. This is it. The end. It will take an act of God to bring Thulani to the States.

"Haybo! Karen," Thulani says. "I cannot believe that I am saying good-bye to you. This is not right." He drops his bags to the kitchen floor and we hug.

"Remember our promise," I whisper in his ear. "Find me when you are ready."

"I know you are good for your word, Karen. I will see you on the other side."

Siphelele huffs, impatient, annoyed by the inconvenience of waiting for me and Thulani to finish our good-byes.

"See you on the flip-side, Karen," Siphelele says. Sixteen years old. Full of himself. Arrogant. He hasn't asked one question over the past twenty-four hours.

"There is no 'flip-side,' Siphelele. This is good-bye forever."

He smiles a smart-aleck grin. "Well then, have a good life."

I want to smack him.

Thulani gathers his bags. As they close the kitchen door behind themselves I race to the living room to say good-bye one more time through the iron gate on the front door. Thulani stops at the gate. He slings one duffle bag over his shoulder to free up a hand. He holds it out to me.

"This is only good-bye for now, Karen. I am sorry to see you leave."

There is nothing to say beyond my tears.

"Give me two years," he says, his face drawn tight. He

tries to smile. Lines fan out from the corner of his eyes, aging him far beyond his nineteen years.

"I'll see you again in two years," I say.

"Pinkie swear?"

We wrap our pinky fingers together through the bars, and squeeze.

» » »   « « «

I hear the chain slide over the steel rails of the driveway gate. The padlock clicks into place. This is not possible. I feel like a caged animal. I want to rant. Throw something. Scream. I scrounge through the kitchen hoping to find food. The fridge and cabinets are barren—nothing but tea bags, sugar and cream. What has Ruby done with my food? Hers too, for that matter. Is it in the trunk of her car? Her bedroom! I don't care about her privacy anymore. I storm to the end of the hall, determined. It's my food. I won't be one of the starved, shunned exiles. I grab the knob. Turn. Yank. It's locked.

"Damn!" My foot slams against the door.

On the way to my room I check the hook by the back door for the key to the sliding gate. Ruby's taken that with her, too! Her shrewd, calculating acts make me edgy. I lock the door to my room.

» » »   « « «

At eight I hear the chain slide across the bars on the driveway gate. It can't be Ruby already! Unless she didn't really take the boys as far as Ntwana. I race across the patio, squat at the rear corner of the house, peer through the carport. Mhambi! What's he doing home? Never mind why. I exhale with relief. I run through the living room and flip on the kitchen light, putting the kettle on to boil. He can tell me what's happened.

I hear the garage door close. Mhambi walks through the kitchen door. He looks exhausted.

"Karen! I did not expect to find you at home."

"I didn't think you'd be home until tomorrow," I say, trying to sound casual.

"My conference ended early today. I did not want to spend another night away from my home."

I measure his voice for anything unusual. He just sounds tired.

"I'm making some tea, Mhambi. Would you like some?"

"Thank you. That would be very nice. It is a long drive from Ramsgate."

He retreats to the living room, drops his briefcase in the middle of the floor, flings his suit jacket over the back of the sofa, and slumps into his armchair. I place our tea tray on the coffee table. I think of all the times Ruby waited on him. I could never decide if I was more angry at her for being subservient, or him for being demanding. Somehow, this feels different. He's been kind and respectful to me. Making tea for him feels like an expression of my gratitude.

"Thank you, Karen. I appreciate your kindness." He stirs sugar into his tea. "So tell me, why did you not go to Ntwana with Ruby?"

He doesn't know what's happening?

"When I spoke with her this afternoon she did not tell me you would stay behind," he says.

I tilt my head to the side, confused. "I thought you knew, Mhambi. Ruby and Phyllis are angry with me. Yesterday after school, they told me I have to go home. Right away. I leave in the morning." My words feel rushed. I struggle to catch my breath.

His eyes widen with shock. "You must have misunderstood. My wife is not angry with you. I cannot believe that Ma'am is angry with you either."

"Do you know why they're sending me home?"

He shakes his head. "Yesterday evening I spoke with Ruby and she made a joke that you would leave soon. I did not believe she was serious. Can you tell me what has happened?"

"I don't know for sure." I measure my words, wary of how much to share. "They say I'm disruptive. Ineffective. They don't want me to teach at Zinti anymore. And Ruby says if I'm not teaching, I can't stay here."

"There is some mistake, Karen. I am sure of it," he says with his stern courtroom authority. "I will speak with my wife when she returns from Ntwana tonight. I will correct this."

"I appreciate that, Mhambi. But yesterday Ruby took me to the airport to make new travel arrangements. I have a ticket to Johannesburg tomorrow. I have to be at the airport at seven in the morning." My voice cracks. "I'm going to miss the kids. I didn't even get to say a proper good-bye to them. I hope someone tells them it wasn't my idea to leave this way."

"This is not right, Karen. The children at Zinti will miss you. You have become very important to them. Ma'am has told me so herself."

He stands to take our tray to the kitchen. Amazed, I stand. His service to me feels like an incredible honor. We face each other in a long silence. I search his face, straining to understand. He looks somber. I want to hug him. Tell him how much I've enjoyed getting to know him. How special our conversations have been. That I feel honored by the way he's respected me.

I extend my hand. "Thank you for opening your home to me, Mhambi."

He sets the tray down, takes my hand in both of his. "You are most welcome, Karen. Thank you for helping our children. For giving us the gift of your presence in our home. We are most honored."

I try to smile. "Maybe I'll see you in the morning before I leave?"

"Yes. It is certain that you will."

» » »   « « «

When I finish my inspection for snakes under the bed, I stay on my knees to pray. "Oh, dear God," I sob. "Please help me understand what's happened. If I did anything wrong, I am so sorry. I only wanted to help. Please make sure the kids know it isn't their fault. They didn't do anything wrong. Please make sure they know how much I care about them. Thank you for protecting me. Keeping me safe. Please keep me safe all the way home."

I wipe my face with the sheet. Push myself up from my knees. Lock my door. Jam the green plastic lawn chair under the doorknob. Wedge my suitcase between the chair and the edge of the bed. The windows are barred. If someone comes in I'll have no place to go.

But Ruby wouldn't dare try to hurt me now that Mhambi's home.

DAY 45

All night I listen for the sound of intruders in the yard. As the sky begins to lighten, I leave my concrete room for the last time. A soft silent rain falls on the yard. I drag my suitcase past the locked gate on the patio door, around the corner of the house, and side-step through the narrow space between Mhambi's pick-up truck and the carport wall. I prop my suitcase and backpack against Ruby's car in the driveway and cross the front lawn to the kitchen door. It's unlocked. She's awake.

I stand, arms crossed over my chest, in the middle of the living room where I have a clear view of every door. At six-fifteen Ruby comes out of her bedroom, dressed, her purse slung over her shoulder, a smug look on her face. She closes the door behind her and struts down the hall like she has all day. She stops six inches in front of me. I refuse to take a step backward.

"My husband says he is very sorry he cannot come to tell you good-bye himself. He is not feeling well. He wishes you a safe journey home."

No! He promised he'd say good-bye this morning. I want to pound on his door. Scream. I took him for a man of character. I want to spit in Ruby's face. Tell her I don't believe one word she says.

My jaw clenches. "You can take me to the airport now."

Outside, Ruby unlocks her trunk. I heave my suitcase into the back seat. Only six weeks ago I was her hero. Now this? I will not allow her to see my anguish. The thick silence between us ricochets through my head. It's torture to hold my composure for the ten-minute ride to the airport.

Ruby pulls to the curb across the street from the airport entrance, stands behind the car, and watches me unload my luggage. I keep one eye on her at every moment. We stand in the rain, my suitcase between us. Her expression gives nothing away. We have that in common.

But I'll be damned if my last act will be rudeness. I hold out my hand, forcing my voice to sound solid. "Thank you for the ride, Ruby. I'm grateful that I had a chance to be with the kids at Zinti. Meet Missy. Know you and Mhambi and the boys. I hope the rest of your life is good."

Ruby spits on the ground. Without a word she climbs back into the car and drives away.

The gloomy overcast sky reaches all the way to the ground. My cropped yellow pants and green windbreaker sag with the weight of the rain. I hurry down the long airport driveway, dragging my suitcase through the puddles. With my back against the locked door, I sit on my bag to wait the thirty minutes for the terminal to open. My legs pulled to my chest for warmth, I wrap my arms around them and rock back and forth as I give in to the grief that rips at my heart. Sobs roll through my body. It's not supposed to end this way.

There are so many ways this could backfire on the kids. Phyllis won't tell them the truth. What if she uses this as an excuse to starve them again? And their parents? They liked having a white teacher for their children. Phyllis said so herself. What if they think I left because of the boys' bad behavior. Will they beat them?

Rage tightens my neck. The heat of shame rises in my face. Maybe this wouldn't have happened if I didn't piss Ruby off by handing out apples. The kids liked me. How will they feel about white people now? Did I do more harm than good? I hate myself for being so stupid, for thinking I could really make a difference.

» » » « « «

Thunk! The glass door slams against my back. My heart races. I jump up; spin around. The Zulu janitor smiles apologetically through the glass as he steers his floor mopping machine in the other direction. He unlocks the door and pulls my suitcase inside.

"You are early, Ma'am," he says. "The airport does not open until seven o'clock. But it is very wet out there. You may wait inside." He flips on an overhead fluorescent light and leads me through the lobby to the hallway across from the ticket window, still covered by a roll-down shield. "Do you need anything, Ma'am?"

I try to smile. "No. I'll be fine. Thank you for letting me in early."

He points to a set of industrial double-doors at the far end of the airport. "If you need anything, you may find me through those doors."

Seated in one of the red plastic chairs, I flash on the stress management seminar. The waves of adrenaline over the past thirty-six hours have taken a toll. Exhausted, my arms limp and heavy, I'm still half a world away from home.

The front door opens; bangs shut. A woman's footsteps click, click, click across the concrete floor. Expecting the ticket agent, I gasp when Phyllis rounds the corner. Her chin tilted high, she struts down the narrow corridor and sits in the chair opposite me. Our knees nearly touch.

What the hell is she doing here? I fold my arms across my chest. The muscles in my cheeks twitch. Does she think an apology can change things now? She crosses her legs at her ankles, wipes the rain from her bare arms with her handkerchief, and adjusts her skirt. She lays her hands in her lap on top of her overflowing purse. I refuse to be the first to speak. Why bother? I won't trust her answer. I don't even care if she takes my silence as hatefulness.

"Have you made all of your travel arrangements, Karen?"

"No. I haven't." Why should I try to make her comfortable? "I still need to figure out how to get from Johannesburg to Amsterdam to home. You've put me in a very precarious position."

We stare at each other in prolonged silence.

"You know, Karen, now that this has happened, there are

people at school who say that maybe the old ways were better." She sounds poised. Rehearsed. "Perhaps our lives would be easier if we went back to our old government."

Is she trying to make me feel sorry for her? "What are you talking about?" The repugnance in my voice is unmistakable.

"Ah! You cannot understand because your democracy in America is different than ours."

We're going to argue politics? What does this have to do with her throwing me out?

"In your country you have great freedom and privilege. You tell your leaders what you want, and they give it to you."

I shake my head in disbelief. "You have no idea what you're talking about."

She moves on with her prepared speech. "Here, in South Africa we have to fight for every little thing we receive from our government. Our leaders are corrupt. They keep all the advantages for themselves."

"Huh. That sounds a lot like my country. Our leaders aren't exactly honest either."

She pauses for a split-second. "But your government takes care of you. Our leaders only take care of themselves."

"I don't know where you get your information, but you should know a few facts. Our government only takes care of us because we fight, and demonstrate, and lobby to make sure they do. They never just *hand* us something. And if we're not careful, if we let our guard down for a minute, they start taking things *away* from us."

She cocks her head to the side. "Humph! I am not certain about what you say."

"You don't have to be certain. It's still true."

"I have heard that your democracy is fair, that your government listens to your needs."

"Fair? You ask the poor, hungry, uneducated people in my country if they think our democracy is fair! Do you honestly believe that we just say, 'I want this,' or 'I want that,' and they hand it to us? Our government only *listens* when we get really loud about what we need."

Phyllis juts her chin forward and closes her eyes. "Humph. That is not what we are told."

"Then someone's feeding you a load of crap!"

She pauses, her prepared speech over. We both take a deep breath. I still don't know what any of this has to do with being forced out of Zinti.

Phyllis shrugs her shoulders and rolls her eyes. "Well, what can we do?"

She's said that a hundred times—her habitual response whenever it's easier to back off than assert an unconventional opinion.

"You can fight for what you want," I say, surprised by the calm in my voice.

"Our lives are hard. We do not have the energy to fight as you do."

For the first time, I glimpse her perspective: life is hard; she is exhausted.

I sigh. "Phyllis, democracy is a huge responsibility. It takes a lot of effort. It's true, our lives are easier than yours. But we've been working on our democratic system for over two-hundred years. It's hard in the beginning. American women didn't even have the right to vote for the first hundred and forty years of our democracy! We fought hard to gain our rights. Theoretically, we have equal rights with the men now, but American women still make only seventy-five cents for every dollar a man makes doing the same job."

She stares at me, her face blank, empty. This reminds me of bursting Mhambi's illusions about our legal system. I pause to consider if I should say more. "Your democracy is what? Maybe fifteen years old now? That's brand new. A baby democracy. It will be easier once your government realizes they can't run roughshod over your needs. And that will only happen with lots of hard work on your part. But even when it becomes easier, you'll still need to be diligent."

She drops her chin to her chest. "No one told us it would

be this difficult to be free."

I feel sorry for her, but I still don't know what this conversation has to do with them throwing me out of Zinti. Maybe it doesn't matter if *I* understand. In her mind they're related.

"It is hard, Phyllis. Freedom is a lot of work. There are many countries around the world who've tried to move from dictatorship to democracy, and quit; given up because it wasn't instantly successful. It takes time. And effort."

Her shoulders droop. "What you say is true. We try to make them listen to us. But it is not easy. We question if this new government is a good choice for us."

"You can't give up. If you give up, they win. You have to make them listen."

"And how do we do that?"

"With numbers. Crowds."

She tips her head to the side, squints with confusion.

"For example, if you tell the Inspector what you need and he doesn't listen, go back again. But next time, take three other principals with you. If he still doesn't listen, go back with ten people. If that doesn't work, take a hundred. If he still refuses to listen, take a thousand people with you. This is how you get what you want. You push and push and push. When you have enough people the television cameras will show up. And when the media gets involved, the politicians will do something different because they won't want to look like idiots on television. They also don't want to piss off other countries who are watching, countries who have the power to help."

"What you say is a lot of work, Karen."

"Yep. It sure is." I remember all the rallies I've marched in, the election phone banks I've worked, and the letters I've written to my representatives. "And this is how we do it in America. Obviously you only hear about our success. You don't hear about all the effort it takes."

I pause to gather the nerve to say what I *really* want to say. I have nothing to lose now. "You could start by telling the children at Zinti why I left. Tell them the truth. That it wasn't my choice." I steel myself against my tears. "If you don't tell them, I'll be the white lady who loved them and left without saying good-bye. Who knows what that will do to race relations. If you *do* tell them the truth, they'll have a head start knowing what needs to change when they grow up and have a voice."

I wait for her reaction. Nothing.

"Phyllis, you know that knowledge is power. Even unpleasant knowledge is power. The kids need to know what's real. If your freedom is going to last, their generation will make it happen." I take a deep breath as I realize that despite being hurt and angry, I still want to help.

Phyllis heaves a sigh. I don't recognize her expression. I'd like to believe she's rearranging her concepts of America. Thinking about being bold. Honest. Doing something to create change.

She stands and adjusts her skirt. "Travel well," she says.

Her heels click across the concrete floor.

» » »   « « «

The lush green hills are beautiful, even on a gray day. As my twin-engine plane rises from the runway, I feel foolish. How did I ever believe I could make a difference? My simple hope died down there. I regret that I'll never know if I helped the kids—or hurt them. I worry that this question will never let me rest.

DAY 47

I step off the gangway into the Amsterdam airport—a mess. Emotionally drained, exhausted in every conceivable way; my entire body aches. And on top of feeling betrayed by Ruby and Phyllis, I feel abandoned by God, kicked around and beat up, emptied of the sense of support and assurance I felt in the beginning. How did I misread the signs so stupidly?

I stop below the KLM monitor that hangs from the ceiling. Three hours late leaving Johannesburg, there is no chance of making my connection. I study the screen anyway, squinting at the list of flights through my bleary, swollen eyes. Looking for a miracle.

"You look lost," he says.

He must be talking to me. I feel lost.

"Can I help you?" he asks.

His American accent is heaven to my ears. It takes a few seconds to spot him—a forty-something white man about my height. A mass of curly, auburn-colored hair circles his head hiding his facial features, except for his soft smile and penetrating eyes. His faded black T-shirt tucks neatly into jeans that have seen better days. He grips his tall wooden walking stick with hands leathered from years in the sun. He plants it in front of him, between his feet. His huarache sandals complete the look—every inch the vagabond traveler. He stands ten feet away, waiting for me to come out of my fog and answer him.

"I've missed my connection." My voice betrays my agitation. Rescheduling another airline flight feels like more than I can handle right now.

"Where are you headed?"

"San Francisco."

"Let's see if we can get this sorted out," he says. He

approaches, wraps his arm around my shoulder, and steers me through the crowd to the KLM counter. His walking stick taps against the floor with every step. I am simultaneously offended that he has usurped my independence and relieved to have his help. "Where did you fly in from?" he asks.

I'm not in the mood for meaningless conversation. "Johannesburg."

"Ah," he says, "I love South Africa. What a beautiful country."

"Yeah."

"And what were you doing in Johannesburg?"

My resistance falters. "I wasn't really in Johannesburg. I was in a rural village in KwaZulu-Natal teaching English to elementary school kids." I feel compelled to continue, share my trauma. "It was all going so well. At least I thought it was. Then out of nowhere they threatened to kill me if I didn't leave. I didn't even get to say good-bye to the kids." My sobs come mingled with raw anger.

He hands me a handkerchief. "T.I.A.," he says, with the hint of a smile.

"What?" I sniff.

"T.I.A. This is Africa. Nothing personal."

"What do you mean, 'This is Africa?' Like that makes it all okay or something?"

"No. Not okay. Just Africa," he says, steady and calm.

"Well," I huff. My tears vanish as I move straight to righteous indignation. "Right now I'm having a really hard time not being bitter about the whole experience."

"Ah. Don't be bitter."

Obviously, he wasn't there.

"Bitterness," he smiles, "is just Satan trying to prevent you from doing future good works."

His words stop me cold. Who the hell does he think he is? What gives him the right to talk to me this way? I don't even believe in Satan!

"Try to forgive them," he says. "Their lives are hard.

They do the best they can. You can be angry. And you have every right to be disappointed and sad. But don't be bitter. The world needs you to keep opening your heart like you did this time."

My eyes well up. He reminds me of the feelings I had at the beginning: wanting to do something useful in the world, hoping that the little bit I have to give could make a difference. I don't want to have a crusty, bitter heart.

"When you've recovered from this experience," he says, "and you're ready to go back again, let me know. I can set you up with an orphanage in Zambia that will be truly happy to have you."

A tiny spark ignites in my heart. Maybe I was just in the wrong place. Maybe I can still do something good in the world. "I would like to work in an orphanage." My voice feels soft. "There were lots of boys in the village without parents. They ran in a pack like *Lord of the Flies*. One of the girls told me I smelled like her mother. She liked to bury her nose in my clothes and remember her mom."

His expression suggests that he knows the places I've seen. He pulls a pen and scrap of paper from his pocket and scribbles. "Here's my email address." He tucks the paper into my backpack. "When you're ready, let me know. The world needs you. Don't give up."

We step up to take our turn at the counter. The clerk, her pale blue cap perched on the side of her head, asks, "How can I help you?"

My companion squeezes my shoulder. "This woman has just arrived from Johannesburg and has missed her connecting flight."

"You must be Miss Baldwin," the clerk says. "We've been expecting you. I'm so sorry you've had such a rough time these past few days."

I'm stunned. What exactly does she know?

"We have you booked on a new flight to the United States."

I can't believe this. When I turn to look at my friend, he raises his eyebrows as if to say, "See, everything will be okay."

The clerk spreads my new tickets out on the counter. "Your flight to Minneapolis leaves in one hour. You'll have a brief layover there before you catch your connecting flight to San Francisco."

I didn't know airlines could be so efficient. I look at my companion. He nods and smiles.

"We also have vouchers for you," the clerk continues. "This international calling card will allow you to call your family and let them know you're safe. Do you think ten minutes will be long enough?"

"I think so. Thank you."

"And you must be hungry," she says. "With this voucher you can purchase a meal before you board your flight. You may use it at any of the food service stations in this terminal."

I look at the array of tickets and vouchers on the counter in front of me. "This is amazing," I say. "Thank you."

My new friend still stands at my side, his hand on my shoulder. This time when I glance at him, we both smile.

"Now, Miss Baldwin, is there anything else we can do for you?" the clerk asks.

"I don't think so. This is perfect."

I scoop my package together. I feel pampered. My heart feels open, softer than it's been in weeks. I shake the clerk's hand and turn around to thank my companion for his help.

He's gone!

Panic grips me. He can't leave me yet. I have to thank him for his kindness. He's changed everything. I step away from the counter and scan the area, jostling to see through the crowd. He can't have gone very far.

I spot him thirty feet down the terminal, walking away in a slow, relaxed gait. His stick, even with his right foot, hits the floor with each step. Seeing him from behind for the first time, I notice his ragged backpack, beat up from years of travel. Across it, hand-written in bright orange paint, it reads: JESUS LOVES YOU.

Without turning around, without even breaking his stride, he raises his left hand over his head and waves, as if to say, "Good. You know it's me."

The world slows to a silent pause as I realize what has just happened. I exhale my last breath of bitterness. The seeds of new hope are planted. I'll be okay.

EPILOGUE
FRIDAY, SEPTEMBER 23, 2011

Ruby's accusations that I damaged the children's self-esteem hurt me more than anything else. For months after my return to the States, I wallowed in shame. Untangling issues of culture, politics, and my own history was slow and humbling. Gradually, I gained perspective, healed, and began to glimpse the possibility that the children of Zinti benefited from my attention. My hope of making a *big* difference may have been naïve. Not trying would have been worse.

Some elements of my journey still haunt me. My parting conversation with Phyllis at the Pietermaritzburg Airport is one of them. I regret that I wasn't able to set aside my anger, pride and sense of betrayal to question why they threw me out. At the moment, I was certain it was pointless; that I could never trust her answers, or even worse, that she'd respond with another blank empty stare. Today, I sense she was trying to deliver an important message and I missed a valuable opportunity to really listen—and learn.

Overstepping my role as an English-as-a-first-language-teacher, I flung myself headlong into the position of champion problem solver. The Zinti computers are a perfect example. I cringe when I recall gushing offers of power cords, software, and lessons for the teachers. Unable to accept Phyllis's obvious satisfaction with simply owning the computers, I viewed her messages as resistance to moving forward, roadblocks that needed to be removed. If I could do it over, instead of being a pushy American, I'd simply ask, "What can I do to help?"

After enjoying Mhambi's respect and our evening ritual of discussing current events over a soccer match, his unexpected snub the morning I left, still stings. I'd like one more conversation with him to ask what happened. I believe he would tell me the truth. Maybe that's exactly why he avoided saying good-bye—there was some truth he didn't want to share.

I imagine it was difficult, even painful, for Ruby to watch Mhambi treat me so differently than he treated her. It was excruciating for me to witness—that much I can say with absolute certainty. I don't know what I could have done to soothe Ruby's feelings. Maybe nothing. I hope she has used her discomfort to create greater freedom for women. Ruby is strong. If anyone can do it, she can. But there I go again, blurring the line between being supportive and being pushy. I still don't know where to draw that line.

Many long conversations with friends and colleagues, sleepless nights, and countless hours of consideration have produced various theories about why I was forced out:

- I disrupted the status quo of power between children and adults, men and women, whites and Zulus.

- It's hard to watch your children love someone who represents a painful history.

- The first question *every* woman asked me was some version of, "What does your husband say about you being here alone?" I suspect that my female independence made both the men and the women very uncomfortable.

- My presence at the literacy conference in Durban sparked jealousy among the rural schools. I never knew how, or if, Ruby and Phyllis dealt with the issue. Maybe it became a problem for the Inspector.

- The lightning strike at Zinti created, or underscored, unrest about having a white presence in the village.

- The witch doctors were threatened by my lack of respect for their stronghold over the people with regards to HIV/AIDS.

- Ruby was protecting me. Zulu culture dictates that you don't tell someone something they don't want to hear.

If I was in danger, as odd as her method was, Ruby found a way to get me out.

- My desire to provide western medical care for the children made Phyllis uncomfortable.

- Ruby perceived herself as a modern, liberated woman. And in many ways, she was. But after Granny's death, as Ruby assumed the mantle of torch bearer for traditional Zulu culture, the relative freedom she enjoyed began to disappear. I was a constant reminder of the gap between her reality and her desire.

- Change is hard. We often ask for our lives to be improved and then when the positive shift arrives, we find ourselves unprepared to let go of old habits to make room for the new.

Of course these are simplified explanations, there are probably more, and it's likely my expulsion was the result of a combination of factors—including futility. Most of the Zinti children will struggle with life and never have jobs. Many will die young. Coping with the challenges of a foreigner in their midst might not have been worth the effort.

But I stand by my desire to help children read. Books provide a peek into other worlds. I believe that children who are enthusiastic readers have rich imaginations, strive hard in life, and make valuable contributions to the world around them—even in a marginal world.

Isolation in a foreign culture affected me deeply. Being surrounded by educated individuals who morphed so easily between modern urban culture and traditions steeped in superstition rattled my equilibrium. My psyche was impacted far more than I anticipated. Without familiar routines that connected me to my everyday life, I was unaware of the internal changes taking place. By the time I returned home, I was untethered from my "life before Africa."

The prayer I repeated over and over on the plane from San Francisco to Johannesburg—may this work make a difference in the lives of these children, and may it anchor me in my emerging new life—was answered. Shortly after returning home, I had to admit that I no longer fit in my old life. I immersed myself in work as a hospital chaplain, left my ten-year relationship, and eventually moved to the mountains of northern New Mexico where I had longed to live for many years. The idea of writing a book didn't cross my mind until I'd been home nearly a year. In fact, it never crossed my waking mind at all; it happened in a dream.

> *Frantic pounding on my front door wakes me from a deep sleep ... my heart pounds ... I race to look through the peep hole ... no one ... the pounding resumes as I fall back to sleep ... I sit up in bed ... a disembodied male voice echoes through the house ... "Stop talking about Africa," he says. "Just write the damn book."*

Through the process of writing this book I have come to appreciate my experience in Africa as a spectacular gift. Despite having questions that may never be answered, I give thanks every day for the rich layers of growth and opportunity that continue to unfold for me. I hope that if Ruby, Mhambi, or Phyllis reads this book, they will feel that I've done justice to their stories.

In a recent interview I was asked to name my biggest surprise, my greatest lesson, and my deepest hope. My biggest surprise was easy—I was stunned to discover that the witch doctors still wield so much power and control. It never occurred to me that computer literacy would co-exist with the opportunity to pay a witch doctor for black medicine to cripple someone with whom I might be angry. I struggle mightily to reconcile the desire for western progress against traditions that injure children and rob graves for body parts.

I learned so many great lessons, it's hard to name only one. At the top of my list is the resiliency of the human spirit. The Zinti children are strong and tenacious. Despite their hardships—many have watched their parents die, are hungry, and suffer horrible abuse at the hands of their providers—they come to school every day eager to learn and willing to love and be loved. If only their tremendous spirit was met with the *chance* for an easier life.

My deepest hope is that every person who reads this story will have one less judgment when they close the book, than when they opened it. Whether that dissolved judgment is about themselves or someone else is not important to me. I just want you, the reader, to ask more questions, listen with an open heart, and understand the reality I discovered in Africa—nothing is as simple as it appears; there are no easy fixes. I'm certainly not in favor of infant scarification or female genital mutilation. It's clear to me now, though, that these practices create many far reaching ripples in a culture we outsiders barely understand. Simply terminating these practices, or others, without considering the ripples, denigrates lives in a multitude of serious and debilitating ways.

Numerous times in my life I've encountered a gap between where I was and where I wanted to be—jobs, homes, economic status, relationship—and I've struggled to make the necessary changes to close those gaps. Along the way I complained often, and loudly. My experience in Africa rearranged my perceptions. While Ruby dowsed herself with buckets of cold water in the moonlight to rinse away the lingering evil spirits from Granny's death, and Phyllis visited the Indunas for permission to cross their land with the eagerly awaited white teacher, Thulani and Siphelele watched their favorite TV shows: *Oprah, Ellen,* and *The Simpsons.* This dramatic distinction between old and new—the chasm that separates the Zulus' past and future—redefines "gap" for me. I whine a lot less than I used to.

I've never heard from Phyllis, Ruby, or Mhambi. Thulani and I stayed in touch for about eighteen months. The last time we spoke he was living on the family compound in Ntwana with his fiancé and their two children. Through Thulani I learned that Siphelele went off to college as expected, and like many young men away from a controlling home for the first time, Siphelele likes to party.

I miss the children of Zinti. I'd give anything to have them bruise my legs again as they slide across the floor into my lap, to kiss their sweaty heads, to hear them sing. I wonder if the deaf Grade Two boy ever received a hearing aid; if Nomusa went on to secondary school; if the epileptic boy is safe and well cared for; if Sindiswa regained her smile and fun-loving attitude after the apple incident; if they still use their toothbrushes.

I'd love to have a "girls' day out" in Durban with Simangele. And I long to see Missy again. Her ritual hat, belt, and necklace—her most precious belongings—hang on my living room wall. I'd like to bask in her smile one more time, drink another cup of her tea, and tell her how much she taught me about the capacity of the human heart to love beyond all obstacles.

Most of all, I'd like to know that I left behind a positive influence, that somehow their lives were touched by me even one-tenth as much as they touched mine.

CPSIA information can be obtained at www.ICGtesting.com
Printed in the USA
BVOW042139090512

289865BV00001B/11/P